Second Edition
For PC & Mac

The **Ultimate** Guide to Adobe® Acrobat® DC

Daniel J. Siegel
Pamela A. Myers

AMERICAN**BAR**ASSOCIATION
Law Practice Division

Table of Contents

About the Authors

About Daniel J. Siegel

Many people say that attorney Daniel J. Siegel can make software do things they never thought of and have nicknamed him the "Geek Lawyer." Even in college in the late 1970s and early 1980s, Dan was using what was considered "technology." Thus, it was no surprise that he has always combined the practice of law with his passion for technology.

Among the products Dan discovered were Adobe® Acrobat® and LexisNexis® CaseMap®. Dan quickly became known as an advanced Acrobat user, with a focus on practical uses of the product for legal professionals and everyday users. Dan has written numerous articles and presented dozens of seminars about the product, as well as its importance in a paperless office, with attendees regularly commenting about how little they really knew about it.

In 2005, after being a partner at two prominent Philadelphia personal injury and mass tort firms for more than 20 years, Dan decided to be his own boss. Instead of only opening a law firm, he opened a law firm (the Law Offices of Daniel J. Siegel, LLC) and a technology consulting firm (Integrated Technology Services, LLC), with both businesses located in suburban Philadelphia.

Unlike traditional legal consulting firms, Integrated Technology Services, LLC (ITS; http://www.techlawyergy.com) provides lawyer- and paralegal-focused guidance to lawyers throughout the country, with the goal of helping clients improve their workflow by using technology. Dan, Pam, and their staff continue to train lawyers and others in how to use Acrobat and numerous other products; they also provide case-specific consulting, helping clients get even more out of the products. ITS also sells and supports Acrobat, as well as case management, document management, litigation analysis, and trial presentation products, helping firms with all aspects of practice management, ranging from becoming paperless to trying a complex case before a jury. Clients regularly compliment Dan and his staff for their ability to train them, for their jargon-free approach to technology, and for their advice about how to improve case analysis and present their cases most effectively.

Dan's law firm (http://www.danieljsiegel.com) primarily works with and represents other attorneys, assisting them with appeals and complex litigation, as well as providing ethical and techno-ethical guidance, the latter being an emerging area of law practice focusing on the intersection of law, technology, and legal ethics. The firm also represents injured workers in workers' compensation and Social Security disability claims and continues to handle a wide range of personal injury matters. Dan is the author of 13 other books, including *The Ultimate Guide to LexisNexis CaseMap* (the second edition of his book *The Lawyer's Guide to LexisNexis CaseMap*); *How to Do More in Less Time: The Complete Guide to Increasing Your Productivity and Improving Your Bottom Line*; *Checklists for Lawyers* (which he coauthored with Pam Myers); *Android Apps in One Hour for Lawyers*; *Changing Law Firms: Ethical Guidance for Pennsylvania Law Firms and Attorneys* (first and second editions); and *Pennsylvania Workers' Compensation Law: The Basics—A Primer for Lawyers, Workers, Medical Providers, Insurance Professionals & Others* (now in its third edition).

Dan is a graduate of Temple University School of Law and Franklin and Marshall College.

You can reach Dan by email at dan@techlawyergy.com.

About Pamela A. Myers

Pamela A. Myers is Office Administrator for Integrated Technology Services, LLC (ITS; http://www .techlawyergy.com) and the Office Administrator, Paralegal, and client liaison for the Law Offices of Daniel J. Siegel, LLC (http://www.danieljsiegel.com).

With more than 25 years of experience in the legal field, Pam is known for her technological acumen (Dan describes her as the most "tech savvy" person he has ever worked with), her attention to detail, her ability to anticipate an attorney's needs, and her dedication to obtaining the best results for clients.

Her genuine enjoyment of technology and what it has to offer helps her to convey to others not only how to use technology but also why they should use and embrace it. While employed as a paralegal at her former firms, Pam was often called upon to help train others because of her talent for conveying things in a simple, easy-to-understand way. Her obsessive use of checklists, and lists in general, was one of the reasons she coauthored *Checklists for Lawyers* with Dan, and her use of Acrobat contributes to her success.

Pam has worked as a paralegal since 1996 representing both plaintiffs and defendants. While employed as a paralegal at a large, nationally known firm, she also served as the paralegal coordinator for her practice group, supervising and training the group's paralegals. She received her bachelor's degree, with honors, from West Chester University. After working for five years in business management, Pam decided to pursue paralegal studies at the PJA School, where she graduated at the top of her class. Her professional activities have included serving on the Board of Directors of the Philadelphia Association of Paralegals as its Second Vice President and also as Editor-in-Chief of its newsletter.

You can reach Pam at pmyers@techlawyergy.com.

Our Story

When we began working together, Adobe Acrobat was a good program but not an essential one. Adobe had not yet introduced its legal-specific features, its ability to review and search documents was good but needed improvement, and our office was still primarily paper-driven. But handling paper was cumbersome and inefficient. Fortunately, in the mid-2000s lawyers were beginning to embrace paperless technology. We quickly jumped on the bandwagon.

Our decision was an excellent one, because our practice, primarily class actions and mass torts, was also changing. Virtually all discovery was electronic. In addition, we began obtaining our clients' medical records electronically, and reading static images made no sense. When we learned about using optical character recognition (OCR), the process by which Acrobat transforms the scanned electronic images into searchable (and therefore highly usable) text, we could search for keywords and find relevant information quickly. From there, we learned how to create indices and search across multiple documents, and then how to use them to prepare for depositions, motions, and other events, all with Adobe Acrobat.

In addition, discovery was entirely electronic, primarily in image format. Although we used e-discovery software for the millions of pages of images we reviewed, when we culled the documents into what we called "hot docs," we discovered the importance of being able to annotate them using keywords and to highlight information in the documents. Then we began using LexisNexis CaseMap and discovered how other programs (beyond Word and Outlook) could dramatically improve our preparation, particularly in conjunction with Acrobat.

But in 2005, Dan left the firm, and Pam remained as the paralegal overseeing e-discovery. Dan opened a solo firm focusing on workers' compensation, personal injury, and appellate practice, often assisting other attorneys. Dan's practice was virtually paperless, allowing him to remain a solo. He also opened a technology consulting firm, which helped lawyers and their firms improve their workflow with technology. Against that backdrop, Dan honed his tech skills and used Acrobat extensively. When combined with his case management software, the use of Acrobat allowed him to accomplish more work in less time.

From 2005 until 2012, Dan knew that something, actually someone, was missing from his workflow—Pam—and she joined the firm (and the consulting firm), filling in the workflow blank. Pam also assisted Dan with continuing legal education programs, particularly programs about the paperless office and Adobe Acrobat. The programs were consistently highly rated, with attendees often commenting that they learned more in the Acrobat course than in any other, albeit without learning any substantive law. From there, Pam and Dan collaborated on the book *Checklists for Lawyers*, but Dan's passion was to write this book. The result, with Pam as coauthor, is before you.

This book also demonstrates the importance of learning Acrobat (and virtually all software) by discussing it with others. We work together, learning from each other by discussing new features and new approaches as we use the software.

We hope you will learn as much as we have. We also welcome suggestions for how to improve the book, and we look forward to your feedback. Now, it's time to jump in and learn, or learn more, about Adobe Acrobat.

Acknowledgments

When we decided to write a new edition of the "Acrobat book," we wondered how we would find the time during a pandemic, when our business and professional lives were in upheaval. Who knew a global pandemic would suddenly give us the time? Writing a book, regardless of the circumstances, requires time and effort, but we would gladly have traded the free hours we gained while "staying at home" for a different 2020. We are grateful, however, that we had this project to do together to keep us connected as friends and colleagues, and we hope that this book helps our readers manage their work lives a bit better whether at home or in the office.

In particular, Pam thanks her husband, Mark Myers, for being the constant support he has always been no matter where life takes us. Pam also thanks her daughter, Samantha Myers, for sharing my at-home workspace during her "virtual school" without too much interruption. And a huge thank-you to both of them for being enthusiastic as always about my writing a book.

Dan would like to thank his wife, Eileen Watts Siegel, and his sons, Brad and Doug Siegel. While Dan has always dreamed of writing novels, a la John Grisham, seeing the many positive reviews on Amazon has at least given him some comfort while he still awaits his arrival on the *New York Times* bestseller list. Regardless of the subject, Dan's family has always shown unwavering support.

We would like to offer special thanks to Brad Siegel, an intense Acrobat user whose suggestions for improvements to the manuscript were enormously helpful. Plus, Brad again designed the book cover.

Finally, we would like to thank the many individuals who offered suggestions for ways to make the second edition better, as well as those who contributed so much time helping to make sure the second edition was even more helpful to the readers. Of course, thanks to the ABA Publications Board, and especially to Dave Ries and JoAnn Hathaway, two great friends who also served as peer reviewers.

Let's hope that if there is a third edition, we won't have to wear masks and get vaccines and can thank everyone in person.

Pam Myers and Dan Siegel

Getting the Most Out of This Book

Welcome to *The Ultimate Guide to Adobe Acrobat DC*, your guide to getting the most out of Adobe Acrobat DC, an essential software program for most law offices and all other types of businesses. Unlike other books about Acrobat (we focus only on Adobe Acrobat Standard and Professional, *not* the free Reader), *The Ultimate Guide to Adobe Acrobat DC* discusses the features that law offices and businesses use and explains what the features are, why they are important, and how to use them.

The book includes step-by-step instructions and screenshots, showing how to use Acrobat. As a result, there are many ways to use this book. You can read it from cover to cover and learn just about everything you will need in your day-to-day office practice. Or, you can use the book as a handy reference, looking up features as you need them. We suggest that, as a start, you use a hybrid approach.

First, we suggest reviewing the Table of Contents and the Index to get an overview of all topics covered in the book. Second, look at the sections that most interest you so you can put the information to immediate use. Finally, you can go back to the other sections as you need them, to increase your knowledge of Acrobat incrementally.

By using this approach, you will reinforce your knowledge of the program by using it.

Conventions in This Book

In order to help you get the most from Acrobat, we use certain conventions throughout the book:

- We are using Adobe Acrobat DC Professional Edition for Windows: All of the screenshots and directions in this book use the latest version of Adobe Acrobat DC Professional Edition. While most of the features are available in both the Standard and Professional versions of the software, we will specify any features available only in the Professional edition. We recognize that some lawyers use Macs in their practices and have included Mac screenshots where we believe the differences between the Windows and Mac versions merit it.
- Most of the commands we demonstrate are available in earlier versions: Although we use Acrobat DC, virtually every feature we demonstrate exists in earlier versions of Acrobat, with most of the legal-specific features available in the Professional editions since version 8. The features are often in

different locations because of the dramatic change in the interface between Acrobat XI and Acrobat DC.

■ Toolbar commands are displayed with the ">" symbol: Commands are shown based on the menu and then submenu. For example, to access your preferences, the command will display as Edit>Preferences; the Save As command will display as File>Save As.

■ Keystroke commands are displayed with a "+" sign: For example, to access your preferences, the command will display as Ctrl+K; the Save As command will display as Ctrl+Shift+S.

Chapter 1

The Advantages of Using PDFs and Adobe Acrobat DC

Introduction

When lawyers and their staff were forced to work at home because of the global pandemic, those who had previously resisted loosening their dependence on paper learned the value of annotating and editing tools such as Adobe Acrobat. They quickly learned the answer to the most common questions we are asked when we teach courses on Adobe Acrobat: "Why do we need Acrobat?" and "Why do we need Acrobat Professional?" Our answer, prefaced by the disclaimer that we don't work for and are not compensated by Adobe, is that as lawyers and paralegals, we should use products that enable us to accomplish more and to do so efficiently. While many products have some or most of the features in Acrobat Professional, none has all of the features, and none works as well with as wide a range of products, including Microsoft Office, many case and document management products, and numerous other programs. As a result, law firms that need to use Bates numbers need Acrobat Professional, firms electronically filing court documents need Acrobat Professional, and so do most firms, merely because of the program's ability to create indexes and to automate so many tasks. Acrobat has other benefits:

- **Improved Workflow:** By using Acrobat, you can standardize many processes. For example, by using an "action," Acrobat can OCR (make readable and searchable) multiple documents at one time and then create a searchable index so that all users can search a virtually unlimited number of documents at one time and view the results quickly and with just a mouse click.
- **Increased Productivity:** By using Acrobat, you can save time and be more effective with many tasks. For example, numbering an appellate court record, which used to take considerable time, can be done in seconds using either Bates numbering or adding headers/footers. Similarly, the index

feature allows lawyers to locate critical information during depositions, trials, and other proceedings without the distraction of having to page through countless paper records with the hope of finding information that Acrobat can display in a split second.

- **Reduced Use of Paper:** Acrobat is one of the essential products needed to be a paperless or "less paper" office. Lawyers and staff can review documents without the need to print them, can annotate the documents to highlight critical information, and then print only the necessary pages rather than every page. Similarly, by storing all documents electronically, law firms can produce documents electronically, saving the time, the paper, the copier or printer toner, and the postage it would require to produce hundreds or thousands of pages of paper documents.

- **Better Client Results:** Using Acrobat's features, such as its indexing and search capabilities, produces better results, and quicker results, than having to review paper files and search for highlighting or "sticky notes" or other more traditional annotations. Acrobat's ability to store comments allows your entire staff to share the information in an easy-to-read and universally accessible way.

- **Fewer Ethical Dilemmas:** By utilizing Acrobat's various features, law firms should improve productivity and can reduce the possibility of errors that could lead to malpractice claims or ethical transgressions. Acrobat helps avoid ethical issues in many ways:

  - ❖ **Metadata:** Metadata is information about a document that is not visible as part of the document but can be reviewed easily with either metadata analysis software or, in many cases, the software used to create a document. Metadata may be relatively innocuous information such as the author or title of a document, but it may also reveal comments, tracked changes, and other information that could assist an opposing party. The ABA and many state bar associations have opined that the disclosure of metadata may be an ethical violation.

    Converting documents, spreadsheets, and other items from their native format to PDF format allows lawyers to retain control of the documents' content and eliminates the probability of transmitting the files' metadata. (Removal of PDF metadata is discussed in Chapter 15.)

- **Loss of Documents/Comprehensive Retrieval of Information:** Traditional paper documents can be lost, damaged, or misfiled. As a result, attorneys can lose the documents or mistakenly fail to include such documents during discovery. By converting all documents to PDF format and storing them in a central location, law firms will avoid this problem.

- **Preservation of Email:** Lawyers have always saved copies of all correspondence in a client file, but many do not treat email with the same importance. Because a client file is the property of a client, lawyers should preserve all case- or matter-related email and attachments so that (1) they may be produced should a client request a copy of the file, and (2) they have a record of all communications should a dispute arise between the lawyer and client.

- **Collaboration by Email:** Users can email a document in PDF format and take advantage of Acrobat's collaboration tools such as comments and marked changes.
- **Compatibility:** Many companies create add-ins that allow Acrobat to perform additional functions. For example, there are add-ins (some users call them plug-ins) that work with Microsoft Office, LexisNexis CaseMap, and other products. Many of the most helpful add-ins work only with Acrobat and not with other PDF creation software. Thus, if you purchase another product, you may not be able to use add-ins that are of particular value to you.

What Are PDFs?

The portable document format (PDF) is a computer/electronic file format that can preserve all of the fonts, formatting, colors, and graphics of any source document, that is, the document or other electronic item from which the PDF is created (for example, by scanning the document or converting the document from Word or a web page), regardless of the application and platform used to create the original document. Anyone using any PDF reader is then able to view, navigate, comment on, and print a PDF file using any PDF reader product, of which there are many. In many cases, users can fill in and sign PDF documents electronically.

When printed, PDF documents look the same as the source from which they were created and have appropriate margins and page breaks. PDF files can also be password-protected or have other security features to prevent unauthorized changes or printing or to limit access to the documents.

There are two types of PDFs: text-based PDFs and image-based PDFs. Whether a PDF is text- or image-based depends upon (1) how it was created and (2) whether (in the case of image-based PDFs) the PDF was converted to a text-based (or searchable) format. Text-based PDFs are created by programs such as Microsoft Word and Excel, and, during the conversion process, the text or content of the original file is used to create the PDF version. An image-based PDF is created from scanning (or even from a photo taken on a phone), that is, from a product that makes a picture of the original. A user may convert an image-based PDF into a text-based PDF by using text recognition/optical character recognition (OCR). When possible, legal professionals should always use text-based PDFs because the increase in productivity is dramatic. Users must still be mindful, however, that photographs and poor-quality original sources do not lend themselves to being used as text-based PDFs.

What Is Adobe Acrobat?

Adobe Acrobat is a computer software program that works in virtually every operating system (including Windows and Mac/iOS). Acrobat allows users to do many things, including create, edit, manage, and search PDF documents. It can also create forms, redact information, number pages, compile complex documents, and perform numerous other functions. In addition, Acrobat permits attorneys and others to add security to their PDFs, and it provides alternative methods of preserving email (rather than either printing the email or creating additional folders in Outlook).

Acrobat works/integrates with most other programs (such as Microsoft Office) to create documents as PDFs (portable document formats) so that all documents appear the same regardless of the operating system used to view them. In many cases, Acrobat installs an add-on that allows it to integrate with other programs. In addition, many third-party products provide their own plug-ins for Acrobat. As a result, Acrobat has become an essential program in most law offices.

With the advent of electronic filing in many courts (including the increasing requirement that lawyers file papers in PDF/A format), the increase in electronic discovery, and the transition of most law firms to a "less paper" environment, a program like Acrobat has become essential. With Acrobat, users may perform a wide range of functions on almost any document, regardless of how or on what operating system it was created, improving their workflow and their ability to analyze information efficiently.

The Differences between Acrobat Reader, Acrobat Standard, and Acrobat Professional

- **Acrobat Reader:** This free product does not contain most of the features discussed in this book. However, many people, including clients, use the free Reader, and it remains the global standard for viewing PDF files. With Reader, you can open all PDF documents, as well as search, digitally sign, print, and collaborate on PDF files without having Acrobat Standard or Professional installed on your computer. Acrobat Reader can also view PDF Portfolios and display media content, including video and audio files, in their native (original) formats.
- **Acrobat Standard:** This paid product contains many of the features discussed in this book, although the vast majority of the legal-specific features are only available in the Professional version. Both Standard and Professional versions allow users to edit and produce PDF documents, as well as incorporate form fields and interactivity into files produced from any application that can print. Acrobat Standard is *only* available for Windows, *not* Mac computers. If you have a Mac, you will only be able to use Acrobat Professional.

- **Acrobat Professional:** This paid product contains all of the features discussed in this book. We believe that the Professional version is essential for legal professionals because of legal-specific features such as redaction, OCR, side-by-side document comparison, Bates numbering, indexing, and the ability to automate many helpful features through "actions." The Professional version also offers print production tools and other features designed for the graphic design industry (we do not discuss those features in this book). Law firms that redact, produce, or review documents electronically, as well as firms that aspire to be paperless, should purchase Acrobat Professional. Although the cost is greater, the increase in productivity will more than pay for itself.
- Of note, with the introduction of Adobe Acrobat 2020, Adobe now fully differentiates between the perpetual desktop version (Acrobat 2020) and the version enhanced with Document Cloud services (Acrobat DC).

Why You Should Use Electronic Documents

Advantages of Using Electronic Documents

Using electronic documents is crucial to having a paperless office and has other advantages:

- **Easy Access:** Any person can access an electronic document, not only in the office, but also remotely if the office permits remote access. As a result, lawyers and staff can retrieve electronic documents instantly and then share them as desired.
- **Searchable Text:** After a document is OCRed, you can search the document, and you do not even have to have the file open to do so. This converts ordinary files into databases of information that can be used to improve productivity and results.
- **Cost Savings:** Businesses save money by using electronic documents. By storing documents electronically, whether onsite or in the cloud, firms do not need as many filing cabinets (and thus, file rooms) and can reduce or eliminate file storage costs. In addition, because files are accessible from any computer, there is less time wasted getting up to retrieve a file and locate a document, and the need for file clerks is reduced. Finally, digital storage (computer hard drive) space is far less expensive than traditional storage methods.
- **Security:** Securing confidential information is simplified when files are stored digitally. In addition, electronic documents can be encrypted with a password or other method of authentication, decreasing the possibility that the documents will be disclosed to or seen by unauthorized persons.

- **No Lost Documents:** Once a document is stored electronically, it is preserved, often forever, particularly when files are backed up regularly. As a result, it is easy to locate electronic documents, and the chances of "losing" them are dramatically reduced. Also, the common problem of having an attorney or a staff member mark up or write notes on the only original is eliminated. You don't need to fear not having a "clean" copy again.
- **Easier Document Markup:** Using comments and other features, lawyers can mark up documents, highlighting critical information, while retaining the ability to produce the documents without disclosing the comments. This is far easier than trying to produce a document that contains highlights and comments on the original document.

Why Lawyers Should Use Adobe Acrobat Professional

Acrobat DC or 2020 Professional provides all the features a law office needs—integrated e-signing services, redaction, Bates numbering, commenting, and so much more—including the ability to manage documents easily in the cloud. In addition, Acrobat includes the capabilities lawyers expect and need in a PDF program, ranging from compliance with PDF/A and PDF/X standards to the Send for Signature and Fill & Sign features, which allow users to sign documents, to its ability to edit PDFs and scanned documents almost exactly as you would in a traditional word processor.

Plus, users who purchase a subscription to Adobe's cloud services have access to the e-sign services, which allow them to sign and send documents from any device and use the Fill & Sign feature to convert most documents into a fillable form, which clients and others can fill in on virtually any device.

Finally, when you use the "Document Cloud" version of Acrobat, known as Acrobat DC, Adobe regularly updates features, including many that are featured in this edition of our book. In many cases, these additional features are incremental enhancements that make the program even better.

Chapter 2

Getting to Know Adobe Acrobat DC

Starting Adobe Acrobat

To start Acrobat, double-click on the Adobe Acrobat icon on your desktop; the icon is now red with the white Acrobat logo image (Figure 2-1). Alternatively, on Windows PCs, you can open Acrobat from your computer's Start menu by double-clicking on the Acrobat icon, or on a Mac computer, click the Applications folder in the dock and launch Acrobat from there. On either platform, if you know

Figure 2-1

which PDF file you want to open, just double-click on the file's name and it will open in Acrobat (assuming that Acrobat is listed as the default program for opening PDFs on your computer).

If you open Acrobat from its icon, or click on the Home tab on the main toolbar, you will see a list of your recently opened files on the Home tab (Figure 2-2). On the left side of the screen are three sections: Recent, Starred, and Scans. The Recent list displays by default, showing the files you have opened most recently, organized by date. On the top right of this list are two icons, providing the option of viewing the files in Thumbnail or List view. If you click on a file name, you can select (check) one or more files. To the right of the file name is a star, which you

Figure 2-2

can select so that it will appear on the list of Starred files, that is, files you want to appear every time you open Acrobat. When you select (check) more than one file name on the Recent list, you will have the option (on the right side of the screen) to either Combine Files or Remove [the files] From Recent.

When you single-click on the name of a file, a column appears on the right side of the screen, displaying the file name, the date it was last opened, and the path to the file on your computer (Figure 2-3). Below these items are a variety of options available for the file: Share, Send for Comments, Adobe Sign, Edit PDF, Export PDF, Organize Pages, Comment, Fill & Sign, and Remove From Recent.

Figure 2-3

Clicking Starred Files displays files you have selected by clicking the star to the right of the file name. If you are using Acrobat DC's cloud version, you will have the option to "Access starred files" "On all your devices" or "On this device only." (Figure 2-4) You can also check the box to "Remember my choice," an option that can be changed under Preferences>Adobe Online Services.

Figure 2-4

When you select one or more files on this list, the same options appear as on the Recent files list.

Clicking Scans displays files that you have created with the Adobe Scan app, an app available for phones and tablets that converts scanned items into PDFs.

On the Home screen beneath the options for Recent, Starred, or Scans are three sections: Files, Shared, and Sign, from which you can use the Windows Explorer dialog or Mac's Finder icon to view files. You can view Files from My Computer or from the Adobe Document Cloud, or you can Add an Account (from Box, Dropbox, Google Drive, OneDrive, or a SharePoint Site) (Figure 2-5).

Figure 2-5

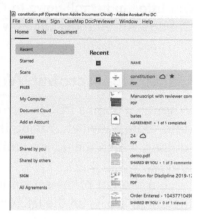

The Shared section displays files "Shared by you" or "Shared by others."

The Sign section allows you to view "All Agreements" that you have sent or have received for signature.

Making Sure Acrobat Is the Default Program for Opening PDFs

Although Acrobat is generally the default program for opening PDFs on a computer (in other words, your computer knows that it should use Acrobat when it opens a PDF), sometimes it is not. In addition, if you install a newer version of Acrobat Reader, it could be designated as the default program that opens PDFs.

On Windows-based computers, there are two ways to verify that Acrobat is the default.

- Click on a PDF file and if Acrobat is the default program, the file will display in Acrobat.
- Verify the "file associations." To view file associations, just press the Windows+Q keys and type "Default apps," and then click on Default apps. Depending upon which version of Windows you are using, you may have to select "Choose default apps by file type," "Choose default apps by protocol," or "Set defaults by app" for Windows 10, or a similar command in prior versions of Windows.

  You will see a list of file types based upon "Name." Scroll down until you see "PDF," and, if Adobe Acrobat is not listed as the default, click on either "Choose a default" or the name of the program listed, and select Adobe Acrobat from among your choices. You may have to click OK. After that, Acrobat will be your default PDF viewer. There are other file types you can and should associate with Acrobat if they are listed, specifically, PDX, the file extension Acrobat uses when creating indices, and PDFXMK, a file format used by governments and corporations for electronic documentation of sensitive data. Although most attorneys will use this format rarely, if ever, Acrobat should be the default program for viewing these documents.

On Mac-based computers, Ctrl-click on any PDF file in Finder, navigate to Get Info, and scroll down to Open With and choose Adobe Acrobat, then click on Change All. Acrobat will now be your default PDF program.

Using the Acrobat Workspace

When you open a PDF in Acrobat, you will see traditional Windows or Mac menus (File, Edit, View, etc.) along the top of the screen. Below those menus is the main toolbar, which includes a limited number of items. Users can easily customize this toolbar.

On the left of the screen is the Navigation pane. If it is not open, just click on the small arrow on the left side of the screen to open the pane (Figure 2-6). On the right side of the screen is the Tools pane, displaying only the icons for Acrobat's Tools. If it is not open and displaying the names of the Tools, just click on the small arrow on the right side of the screen to open the pane (Figure 2-7).

Figure 2-6

Figure 2-7

Opening a PDF File

There are many ways to open a PDF file in Acrobat.

- Click on the name of the file: If you are using Windows Explorer or Mac Finder, just click on the name of the file.
- From within Acrobat:
  - ❖ Click File>Open and click on the name of the file from the list displayed in that dialog, or select "View All Recent Files" and select the name of the file.
  - ❖ Click File>Open and navigate to the file using the Windows Explorer or Mac Finder window.
  - ❖ Use Ctrl+O (Windows) or Cmd+O (Mac) and navigate to the file using the Windows Explorer or Mac Finder window.
  - ❖ From the Home screen, click on the name of the file (if it is listed among your recently accessed files).

Navigating PDF Documents

The Menu Bar

We discuss most of the features on the menu bar in the context of their specific use in Acrobat. It is important for users to "play with" this bar (and other menus) to learn about Acrobat's many features. The menu bar is located across the top of the Acrobat screen and contains the File, Edit, View, Sign, Window, and Help drop-down menus.

- **The Window Menu:** Often overlooked, this dropdown helps users to arrange documents in Acrobat (Figure 2-8).

  Figure 2-8

  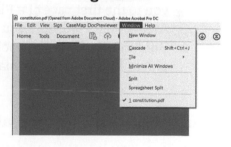

  - ❖ **Cascade (Ctrl+Shift+J for Windows and Cmd+Shift+J for Mac):** This option places each PDF window on top of another while still displaying the name of the document, so users may navigate among the PDFs by clicking on the name of the desired PDF.
  - ❖ **Tile:** This option arranges the windows so that they are next to each other. If you arrange windows Horizontally (Ctrl+Shift+K for Windows and Cmd+Shift+K for Mac), they are on top of each other. If you arrange windows Vertically (Ctrl+Shift+L for Windows and Cmd+Shift+L for Mac), they are side by side in portrait format.
  - ❖ **Minimize All Windows:** This command removes the PDF from displaying on your screen. To view a minimized PDF, go to the taskbar or dock

and select it as you would any minimized Windows or Mac OS program window.

❖ **Split:** This command creates two windows for one document and is useful for viewing two different sections of a document simultaneously. You can unsplit the windows by going to the Window menu and either unchecking Split or selecting Remove Split.

❖ **Spreadsheet Split:** This setting divides your document into four panes and is useful if you want to view column headings and row labels while scrolling through a large spreadsheet or table.

Moving from Place to Place in a PDF

There are many ways to navigate (go from one page to another) in a PDF. The easiest way is to use the Page Up and Page Down keys (Windows) or Fn+Up Arrow or Fn+Down Arrow (Mac) on your keyboard. Acrobat also offers additional options:

■ Click into the page number display dialog and enter the page number you want to view on the main toolbar in the section that displays the page you are on and the total number of pages in the document.

■ Use the Up and Down arrows on the main toolbar next to the section that displays the page you are on and the total number of pages in the document.

■ Open the Page Thumbnails view and click on the page you want to view. (Thumbnails is the first section of the Navigation pane, which is discussed later in this chapter.)

■ Go to View>Page Navigation and select the page option you want.

■ Use Ctrl+Shift+N (Windows) or Cmd+Shift+N (Mac).

■ Press the Home key (Windows) or Fn+Left Arrow (Mac), which will take you to the first page of a PDF; pressing the End key (Windows) or Fn+Right Arrow (Mac) will take you to the last page of a PDF.

■ **Bookmarks:** By using bookmarks, you can navigate from one part of a document to another. Bookmarks are discussed in greater detail in Chapter 4.

Working with Toolbars and Task Panes

Acrobat's toolbars (across the top of a document file) and task panes (on the sides of the document file) allow users to navigate between various file functions and permit users to work with all of Acrobat's many functions.

Getting to Know the Various Toolbars and Panes

■ **The Menu Bar:** Traditional menus are located across the top of the Acrobat program on the menu bar: File, Edit, View, Sign (only on Windows PCs), Window, and Help. Third-party programs such as LexisNexis CaseMap or Legal Files may add additional dropdown menu items to the menu bar.

Figure 2-9

❖ **The File Menu:** (Figure 2-9) This menu contains commands allowing users to open, save, close, and exit the program. It also allows users to reopen PDFs from the last session. There are many other options.

The Create menu allows users to create PDFs in a variety of ways. The Save As, Save as Other, and Export To menus allow users to save their PDFs in a variety of other formats, including Word format, image format (such as jpg and tiff), and multiple other types.

The Reduce File Size option will reduce the document to its smallest size, displaying the progress of the feature, and advising users either the "before and after" file size or that the file has been reduced to the smallest size possible. Users can also use the Protect With Password command to enter a "Viewing" or "Editing" password, along with optional Advanced Options to "Encrypt with Password" or "Encrypt with Certificate."

The Share File option allows users to share the open document in four ways: Get a Link to the file; Invite People to view, track, and comment online; Attach to Email; or Request Signatures.

The Properties menu contains information about the document, commonly called the "metadata" of the document. Finally, the bottom section of this menu shows recently opened documents and allows users to view all recently viewed files.

❖ **The Edit Menu:** This menu contains numerous commands, including traditional Cut, Copy, and Paste commands. It also includes the spelling and search commands, the Edit Text & Images command, and, on Windows PCs, the Preferences menu, from which users can customize a wide range of program features. On a Mac, click on Acrobat Pro DC

Figure 2-10

in the main menu to find Preferences (Figure 2-10).

Figure 2-11

- ❖ **The View Menu:** (Figure 2-11) This menu allows users to work with the current document, such as by rotating, navigating, and displaying pages. It also contains the Compare Documents or Compare Files command, from which you can compare two documents. The Read Out Loud command permits users to listen to the document.
- ❖ **The Window Menu:** This menu allows users to modify the way one or more open documents display and to open the current document in a New Window. It also displays a list of all open PDFs. See Figure 2-8 on page 11.
- ❖ **The Help Menu:** (Figure 2-12) In addition to providing access to online help, this menu allows users to verify the version of the software they are using (About Adobe Acrobat menu), to check for software updates, and to use Repair Installation (for Windows only), a helpful feature when the program is displaying error messages. On a Mac computer, the About Adobe Acrobat menu can be found by clicking on Acrobat Pro DC in the main menu.

Figure 2-12

Although Acrobat checks for updates automatically, if you want to be certain that you are using the latest version, you can do so by selecting Check for Updates.

At times, you may receive an error message (most frequently when using Acrobat's integration with Outlook or a web browser) that instructs you to repair or reinstall the software. In almost every case, if you select the Repair Installation option, Acrobat will correct the error. On a Mac computer, you must reinstall the program.

- **The Main Toolbar:** (Figure 2-13) The main toolbar, which is displayed under the menus, contains tools and commands used with PDF files. When you purchase Acrobat, this toolbar contains a limited number of commands. You can add more tools to the toolbar, add tools to the Quick Tools portion of the toolbar, and display tools you recently used. Customizing this toolbar will save time in the future.

Figure 2-13

By default, the main toolbar includes the Home, Tools, and Documents icons, as well as icons that allow users to save, print, email, navigate, and change the way they view a document. There are also limited comment tools on the default toolbar.

- ❖ **Customizing the Main Toolbar:** Acrobat allows users to add virtually any command to the main toolbar. We recommend customizing the main toolbar by adding commands that you frequently use, although you should balance the need to add tools with the program's ability to display only a limited number of tools at a time.

Figure 2-14

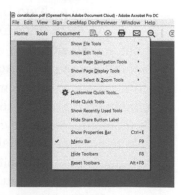

To customize the main toolbar, just drag and drop a command from almost anywhere in the program onto the toolbar. Or, right-click anywhere along the toolbar, and Acrobat will display a menu with 12 options or additional menus (Figure 2-14). To enable the various available features, you just select (check) them or permit Acrobat to display every available tool on the menu.

NOTE: Tools will not work at times depending on the security settings/editing restrictions that are placed on a PDF.

There are five default sections on the main toolbar, and users can specify which, or all, features of those tools appear by default by right-clicking on the toolbar. The top section of the menu that appears contains the following five items:

♦ **Show File Tools:** This menu allows you to display some or all of the file-saving tools. NOTE: You cannot add the Save As command to the toolbar. The Print tool is also here.

♦ **Show Edit Tools:** This menu allows you to display various editing tools, including Spell Check, Cut, Copy, Paste, Undo and Redo, and Find.

♦ **Show Page Navigation Tools:** This menu allows you to display some or all of the page navigation tools, including the icons that allow you to go directly to the first or last page of a document.

♦ **Show Page Display Tools:** This menu allows you to display some or all of the ways in which Acrobat displays a PDF, as well as the options to view a document in Full Screen mode (without toolbars or panes) and to rotate documents or pages.

♦ **Show Select & Zoom Tools:** This menu allows you to display some or all of the various tools that allow you to focus on all or a particular area of a document. It also includes the Loupe tool, which permits you to magnify a specific part of a document (in the same way a jeweler uses a loupe to view a diamond or other jewel).

  ı **Some general terms**, which explain the toolbar, are helpful to know for viewing PDFs:

    ı **Automatic:** Acrobat decides which perspective it believes is best, although it rarely is the most desirable view.

    ı **Single Page:** Acrobat displays one page at a time, and when you scroll or move to another page, it displays only that page.

    ı **Single Page Continuous:** Acrobat displays one page at a time, but when you scroll you continue to see one page until the next moves into full view.

    ı **Two-Up:** Acrobat displays two pages at a time, but you continue to see portions of pages until full pages move into view.

  ı **Zoom**

    ı **Fit Page:** Resizes the page to fit entirely in the document window.

    ı **Fit Width:** Resizes the page to fit horizontally within the width of the document window.

    ı **Fit Visible:** Resizes the page so that the text and images fit within the width of the document window.

    ı **Various Percentages:** Changes the document magnification.

❖ **You can customize other items on the main toolbar** by right-clicking anywhere on the toolbar:

♦ **Customize Quick Tools:** (Figure 2-15) When you select this option, a new dialog appears that lists by category virtually every Acrobat command. To add a tool to the toolbar, you expand the relevant section of the dialog and highlight the commands you want to place on the toolbar. Next, you click on the icon on the right of the dialog, which is a crosshair with an Up arrow, and place the items on the toolbar. Then click Save and the commands will appear on your toolbar.

Figure 2-15

♦ **Hide Quick Tools:** This command hides all of the Quick Tools you have added to the toolbar.

♦ **Show Recently Used Tools:** This displays tools you have recently used.

♦ **Hide Share Button Label:** This command removes the Share command from the toolbar.

♦ **Show Properties Bar (Ctrl+E Windows or Cmd+E Mac):** This command displays the properties bar. The properties bar is content sensitive, which means it will display different options depending on what you select in a document. For example, this tool allows you to quickly change the properties of an annotation, such as font size, color, and style. You cannot dock the properties bar or have it automatically open when starting the program.

♦ **Menu Bar (F9 Windows or Shift+Cmd+M Mac):** This command allows you to display or hide the menu bar.

♦ **Hide Toolbars (F8):** This command allows you to display or hide all toolbars, except the menu bar.

♦ **Reset Toolbars (Alt+F8 Windows or Option+F8 Mac):** This command will reset all of the toolbar settings to the Acrobat default settings.

■ **The Tools Toolsets:** When you select an Acrobat tool, such as Create PDF or Edit PDF, an additional toolbar, called the toolset, appears below the main toolbar and contains the buttons or dropdown menus that allow you to perform the tool-specific operations (Figure 2-16). You can display only the buttons, or the buttons with text, by right-clicking on the toolbar and choosing Show All Labels.

■ **Working with the Tools Pane:** (Figure 2-17) Acrobat places the various commands needed to perform tasks on the Tools pane on the right side of the program window. Acrobat's interface, including the available

Figure 2-16

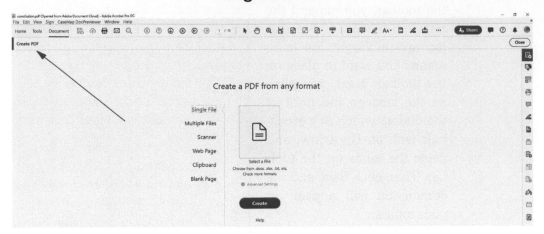

commands, will change depending on the tool selected. To select a tool, either click on its name or right-click on the name and select Open. If you do not like the default order of the tools, you can right-click on any tool and choose "Move Up" or "Move Down" to rearrange them. In addition, you can search the top box of the Tools pane and locate any tool.

When you select a tool, its options will display across the top of the program below the main toolbar. For example, when you select Edit PDF, a new pane appears below the main toolbar, as do other options, such as

Figure 2-17

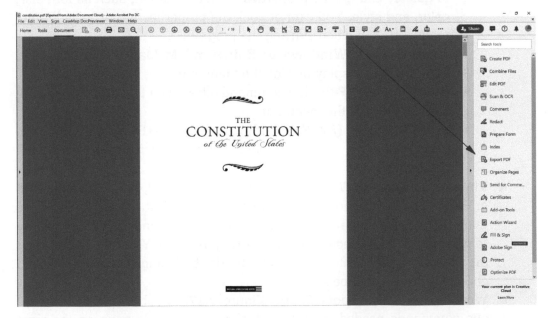

Format, Objects, and Scanned Documents, where the Tools pane had been displayed. However, if you choose Organize Pages, the Tools pane disappears. To close the options pane, click on the X at the right end of the pane.

❖ **By default, Acrobat places only the following options on the Tools pane:**

♦ **Create PDF:** Creates a PDF file from most files or scanned images.

♦ **Edit PDF:** Allows users to edit text, images, and other content and to crop pages. A note about Edit PDF: One of the often frustrating aspects of Acrobat is when the program seemingly without warning begins to OCR a document you are about to edit, using one of the features on the Edit PDF tool pane. You can change or turn off this feature by using the Settings feature on the tool pane (on the right of your screen) and/or by unchecking the "Recognize text" box on that pane.

♦ **Export PDF:** Allows users to save PDFs as Microsoft Office documents, images, HTML web pages, and other formats.

♦ **Comments:** Allows users to add, search, read, reply to, import, and export comments.

♦ **Organize Pages:** Allows users to rotate, delete, insert, replace, split, extract, and otherwise manipulate pages. The Split Page option is particularly important for lawyers who must comply with size limit requirements when electronically filing documents.

♦ **Scan & OCR:** Allows users to use Acrobat's OCR (make text searchable and editable) function, while also improving the quality of scanned documents. The Recognize Text command on this toolset is vital to being able to search the content of PDFs.

♦ **Protect:** Allows users to use security features, including encryption and password protection.

♦ **Fill & Sign:** Allows users to complete and sign forms electronically.

♦ **Prepare Form:** Allows users to create and edit PDF forms.

♦ **Adobe Sign:** Allows users to request that other persons sign documents electronically.

♦ **Send for Comments:** Allows users to share documents with other persons and to track responses.

❖ To add tools you regularly use to the Tools pane, you can go to Edit>Manage Tools, or click on Tools (located between Home and Document). Acrobat then displays all of the available tools. To add a tool to the Tools pane, left-click on the tool, drag it to the Tools pane, and drop it there. When you need to use a tool, click on its icon in the Tools pane. Acrobat will then display all of the options available for that tool on the toolset below the main toolbar.

To remove tools from the Tools pane, right-click on the name of the tool and select Remove Shortcut or View>Tools>Select a Tool>Remove.

If you are displaying the Tools screen, you can remove a tool by clicking on the X, which is not an option while viewing documents.

If you do not like the default order of the tools, you can right-click on any tool and choose "Move Up" or "Move Down" to rearrange them. In addition, you can search the top box of the Tools pane and locate any tool.

- **Working with the Navigation Pane:** (Figure 2-18) Acrobat places the tools necessary to navigate around your document on the Navigation pane on the left side of the program window.

Figure 2-18

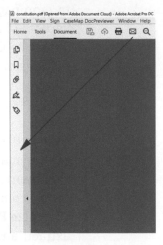

  - ❖ **By default, Acrobat places only the following options on the Navigation pane:**
    - ◆ **Security Settings:** This option displays the security restrictions, if any, in the open document. If the document has no security limitations, the padlock icon does not appear.
    - ◆ **Page Thumbnails:** This pane displays all of the pages in the document. Acrobat automatically creates thumbnail pictures of every page in a PDF when it is opened.
    - ◆ **Bookmarks Pane:** This section displays bookmarks, or links to specific points in a document. Bookmarks can be created automatically from a Table of Contents in a Microsoft Word document, for example. Users can also create bookmarks in Acrobat. In addition, users can specify what bookmarks will look like and add actions to them.
    - ◆ **Attachments Pane:** This section lists all of the items attached to the document, which can include documents in any format. Clicking on the attachment link will open the item in its native format.
    - ◆ **Tags Pane:** Tags are an often overlooked Acrobat feature. When tags are created and used, readers can view PDFs in a logical order; tags can also include more description to assist a reader. The Tags panel displays tags in a hierarchical order that shows how a document should be read. To correct or revise the reading order of a document, you can use the Reading Order tool. To review or revise the tagging structure, users must use the Tags panel.
  - ❖ To add items you regularly use to the Navigation pane, right-click on the Navigation pane and select the additional navigation devices you want to display.

Viewing PDFs

Looking at PDFs (we call it viewing) is similar to looking at documents in other programs. As with many aspects of the program, Acrobat allows users to see PDFs in a variety of ways, enabling users to customize how they use the product. Following are the standard PDF view operations.

Changing the Opening View

It is best to specify your preferred view for looking at PDFs and then modify it as needed for particular documents. To change the default document view, go to Edit>Preferences>Page Display in Windows or Acrobat Pro DC>Preferences>Page Display (Mac). In the top section, entitled "Default Layout and Zoom," you can select the page layout and zoom you prefer when you open a document. Just select your preferred view, and click OK (Figure 2-19).

Figure 2-19

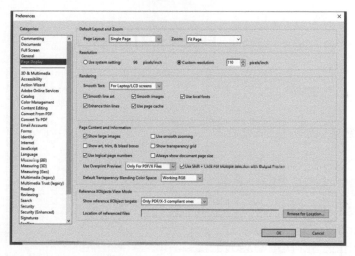

Viewing PDF Files in Read Mode

Read mode allows you to hide all of the toolbars and task panes to maximize the viewing area on your screen. In Read mode, the basic reading controls, including page navigation and zoom, are displayed in a semitransparent floating toolbar that appears near the bottom of the window. To use Read mode, go to View>Read Mode, use Ctrl+H (Windows) or Ctrl+Cmd+H (Mac), or click on the Read Mode icon on the toolbar (Figure 2-20).

    To restore the work area, you can choose View>Read Mode, use Ctrl+H (Windows) or Ctrl+Cmd+H (Mac), or click on the Close button in the floating toolbar.

Figure 2-20

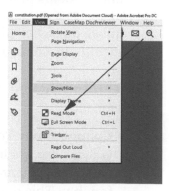

■ NOTE: At times, a PDF may open in a web browser in Read mode rather than in Acrobat itself. You can still view the document in a traditional Acrobat work area by clicking on the Acrobat icon in the toolbar. If you want to disable Read mode in the browser so that PDFs from web browsers will open in Adobe Acrobat automatically, go to Edit>Preferences (Windows) or Acrobat Pro DC>Preferences (Mac), select Internet from the categories, and uncheck "Display in Read Mode by default."

Changing User Preferences

As previously discussed, you will benefit from changing Acrobat's default settings. To do so, go to Edit>Preferences (Windows) or Acrobat Pro DC>Preferences (Mac) (or use Ctrl+K for Windows or Cmd+K for Mac) to open the Preferences dialog box. The left column of the dialog displays all of the categories of preferences, while the right side shows the specific options for each category (Figure 2-21).

Figure 2-21

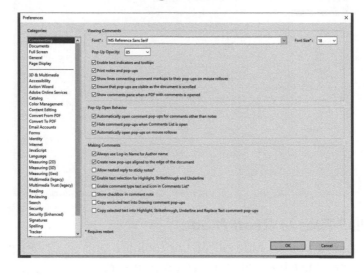

Acrobat does not give users the ability to reset the program to all default settings without delving into the installed files on a computer or reinstalling the program.

The following are the categories of Preferences most relevant to legal professionals:

■ **Commenting:** This dialog specifies how comments (such as sticky notes) will appear, including the font and font size. It is helpful to change the default commenting font to one that is large enough for you to view comfortably. This dialog also defines how comments appear, etc. (Figure 2-22.)

Figure 2-22

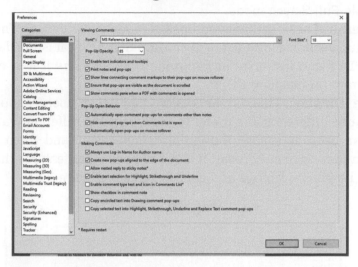

■ **Documents:** This dialog specifies the way Acrobat will open and save documents. It also provides the ability to specify how Acrobat will save files in which content has been redacted. (See Chapter 12.) This is a particularly important setting because if Acrobat does not adjust the name of a redacted document, you increase the likelihood of saving a redacted document over the "original" and losing the ability to access the preredacted version of the document. In addition, this window allows you to autosave files and automate (do so carefully) the removal of hidden information and permits Acrobat to always reduce files larger than 10 MB (Figure 2-23).

Figure 2-23

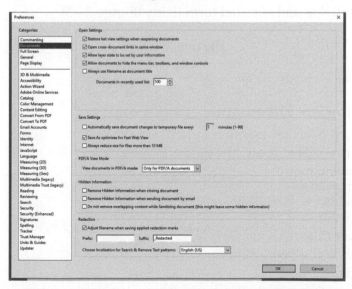

■ **Full Screen:** This setting controls how documents display when you enable Full Screen mode.

■ **General:** These settings address a variety of issues. The Application Startup section allows users to confirm that Acrobat is the default program for PDFs and instructs the program to notify users if it is not the default program for handling PDFs.

■ **Page Display:** This is the dialog that most users should customize. Because different users prefer to view pages in different ways, this dialog allows users to specify the initial default layout and zoom of documents when they open in Acrobat. It also provides other features that are particularly helpful on laptops and certain screens (Figure 2-24).

Figure 2-24

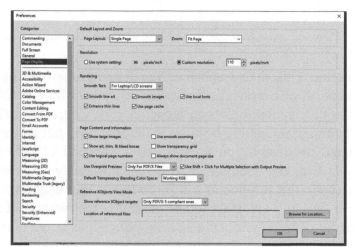

■ **Forms:** This dialog specifies the way in which Acrobat will create and work with forms and form fields. It also allows you to customize the color of form fields and required form fields (Figure 2-25).

Figure 2-25

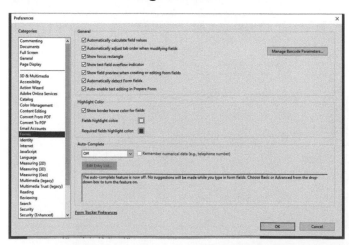

- **Identity:** This dialog contains the name of the primary user of the program, information that appears in comments and metadata and is used for online services (Figure 2-26).

Figure 2-26

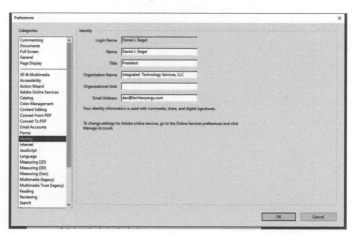

- **Internet:** This dialog specifies whether PDFs will appear in Read mode in a web browser, and it includes a link to instructions about how to set up a browser to view PDFs.

Although there are many other categories of Preferences, we do not discuss them because users will generally not change the settings of those categories.

Printing PDFs

Printing PDFs is similar to printing other documents. Many of the options in the Acrobat Print dialog box are similar to those in the Print dialog boxes of other applications. For example, you can select a printer and print a selection, a specific page, selected pages (this is best done by selecting the pages using the thumbnails), or a range of pages. You can also specify features such as paper size and orientation. Acrobat also allows users to print the current view, that is, exactly what is currently displayed on the screen.

- If your PDF file contains odd-sized pages (legal-sized paper can still be common), you can use the Size options in the Page Sizing & Handling area of the Print dialog box to reduce, enlarge, or divide pages. The Fit option scales each page to fit the printer page size; that is, pages in a PDF file are enlarged or reduced as necessary. The Poster option allows users to tile oversize pages, that is, print portions of them on several sheets of paper so that they may be assembled to reproduce the oversize image.

Another helpful feature is the ability to print multiple pages on one sheet and to print a page border around each page for easier viewing. There is also an option to either Print in grayscale (black and white) or Save ink/toner (Figure 2-27).

Figure 2-27

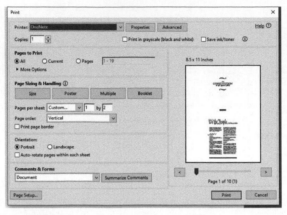

Chapter 3

Creating and Saving PDFs

Creating and saving PDF files is perhaps the most basic and most essential feature of Adobe Acrobat. When you create a PDF file, you are creating a document that others can read using any program capable of viewing PDFs, whether it is an Adobe product or a program created by another company. Because the PDF format preserves the fonts, formatting, graphics, and color of the original/source file, it should appear the same as if it were the original document from which it was created. In addition, Acrobat can create PDFs not only from "documents" but also from spreadsheets, web pages, images, and many more file types. It can also create a PDF of an entire website.

If the document you want to convert to PDF is open in its native program (for example, a spreadsheet may be opened in Excel), you can generally convert the file to a PDF without opening Acrobat. If Acrobat is already open, you can convert the file to a PDF with a couple of mouse clicks. The following are the most common ways to create PDFs from native/source files.

Create PDF Tool

This tool allows you to create a PDF from many types of files.

With Acrobat open, click Tools to open the Tools center or click on Create PDF from the Tools pane (Figure 3-1). Acrobat then displays a dialog that asks if you want to create the PDF from a single file, multiple files, a scanner, a web page, the clipboard, or a blank page. Alternatively, you can open the Create dialog by going to File>Create. Mac computers also offer the option to create the PDF from a screenshot. Next, select the appropriate option, such as Single File. After you select the relevant source type, Acrobat will offer a variety of options.

- **Single File:** Allows you to select a file through Windows Explorer or Finder.
- **Multiple Files:** Asks whether you want to Combine Files (combine multiple files into one file), Create Multiple PDF Files (make a separate PDF for each source file), or Create PDF Portfolio (create a separate PDF for each

Figure 3-1

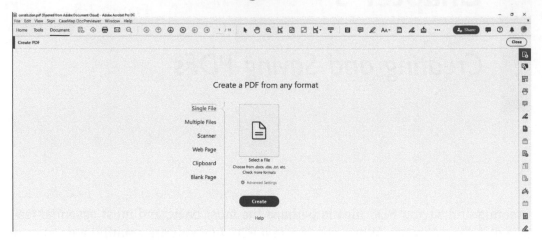

source file and display them within one file). We discuss why you could or would choose one format or the other in Chapter 4.

- **Screenshot:** Asks if you want to create a PDF from a Window Capture or a Selection Capture. If you choose Selection Capture, crosshairs appear, allowing you to choose the area to capture. In a Window Capture, a camera will appear, allowing you to choose which screen to capture. Clicking on the camera icon will create the PDF of the selected screen.
- **Scanner:** Allows you to specify the type of source file. If you have not configured a scanner, it will walk you through the Custom Scan dialog.

    NOTE: You cannot scan directly to Acrobat using a Fujitsu Scansnap or other non-TWAIN-compliant scanner.
- **Web Page:** The program will ask for the URL (website address) or source file, as well as if you want to convert just the URL address into a PDF or multiple levels of the website (in other words, pages that appear when you click on links on the specified web page).
- **Clipboard:** Creates a PDF from content you have copied either in Acrobat or another program.
- **Blank Page:** Creates a new blank page/document, which you can insert into a file or type on.

Print Command (Figure 3-2)

When Acrobat is installed on a computer, it also creates a printer known as "Adobe PDF," which appears in the list of the available printers on your computer. If you select the Adobe PDF printer, you can convert all of the pages, a limited range of pages, or a selection from the source file into a PDF in the same manner as if you were printing a paper copy of the file.

Figure 3-2

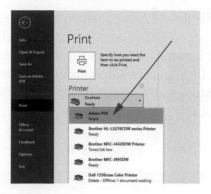

Create Command (Figure 3-3)

The Create command, available at File>Create on the main menu, allows you, as in the Create PDF tool, to (1) Create a PDF from File (Ctrl+N for Windows and Cmd+N for Mac), (2) Create a PDF from Scanner, (3) Create a PDF from Web Page (Ctrl+Shift+O for Windows and Cmd+Shift+O for Mac), (4) Create a PDF from Clipboard, (5) Combine Files into a Single PDF, (6) Create Multiple PDF Files, (7) Create a Form, (8) Create a PDF Portfolio, or (9) Create a Blank Page. On a Mac, these options are ordered differently, but they are all available. Additionally, Mac computers have the option of creating a PDF from a Screen Capture, Window Capture, or Selection Capture. Once you select what you are creating, the dialog is identical to the process with the Create PDF tool.

Figure 3-3

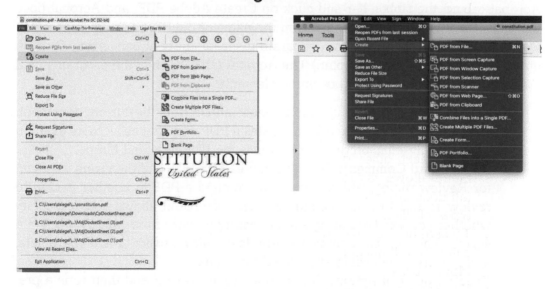

Acrobat PDFMaker (Figure 3-4)

PDFMaker is the name of the Acrobat feature that works inside numerous programs, including the Microsoft Office applications. When you install Acrobat, the PDFMaker appears in each supported application. The following discussion about converting files to PDFs from within Microsoft Office focuses on the PDFMaker, not the Print command. Most users never change these settings, which tend to be satisfactory for traditional law office documents.

Figure 3-4

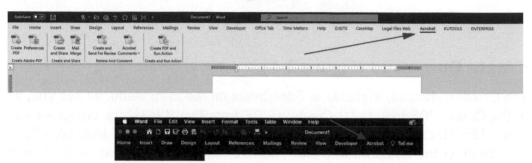

Converting Files to PDFs in Microsoft Office Using the PDFMaker

In each of the three Office applications, Acrobat installs a new Acrobat tab on the ribbon to make it easy to convert an item to a PDF. The process for converting documents, spreadsheets, and presentations to PDFs is essentially the same in Microsoft Word, Microsoft Excel, and Microsoft PowerPoint. Just select the Acrobat tab on the ribbon bar and click on Create Adobe PDF, and Acrobat does the rest. It will create your PDF, confirm the name of the PDF, and ask where you would like to store it. (There is a separate discussion about converting Outlook email to PDFs later in this chapter.) The Acrobat tab in each of the programs on a Windows PC has the following common elements:

- **Create Adobe PDF:** This option creates a PDF from the current document.
- **Create and Share:** This option creates a PDF and attaches it to an email in your default email program or includes the PDF in a Mail Merge.
- **Review and Comment:** This option creates a PDF and then runs the Send for Review dialog, which allows you to send a PDF to another person to review it and to insert comments. The command allows you to specify whether you will be sharing and collecting reviews from your own internal server. The Acrobat Comments dropdown allows users to analyze, delete, and perform other comment-related functions.
- **Create and Run Action:** This option creates a PDF and then runs a pre-defined action within Adobe.

- **Insert Media:** This command was disabled for Microsoft Word and PowerPoint users since the March 2017 update for Office 2016 Click-to-Run
  edition (Office 365).

On a Mac, the only options shown on the Acrobat tab are Create PDF and Preferences. The Preferences option does not allow you to set preferences but is more
of an informational box about the add-in. If you create a PDF using this tool, once
a PDF is created, it opens in Adobe Acrobat and you can Send for Comments,
Run Actions, or Share using standard Acrobat tools. Alternatively, you can install
the Adobe Document Cloud add-in from the Developer tab. On the Developer tab,
choose Add-ins and choose Adobe Document Cloud. If it is not automatically listed
as one of My Add-ins, you can find it in the Store. The Adobe Document Cloud
add-in adds the following items to the Home tab rather than to the Acrobat tab: Fill
and Sign, Send for Signature, Agreement Status, Create and Share Adobe PDF,
and Request Signatures.

- **Using the Print Command:** You can also use the Print command in these
  programs and select the Adobe PDF Printer. On a Mac, Adobe PDF is not
  a printer choice as it is in Windows. Rather, when the print command is
  chosen, at the bottom of the dialog box there is a PDF box with a dropdown
  arrow. Save as Adobe PDF is one of the options.

PDFMaker Conversion Settings (Windows Only)

- To view or modify these settings, open an application such as Microsoft
  Word and go to the Adobe PDF tab on the ribbon. Click on either Preferences or Configure PDF Creation Settings on the Preferences tab (depending upon which program you are using), and the Acrobat PDFMaker dialog
  opens.
- On the Settings tab, you can change the default conversion settings or
  create new conversion profiles. For example, in Outlook, you can specify
  whether to include attachments when converting email to PDF. You can
  also specify the page size, margins, and page orientation for converting
  items.
- On the Security tab, you can require a password to open documents and
  restrict editing. This dialog is similar to the security settings that you can
  apply individually to documents.

Creating Files from the Clipboard

To convert content from any file or web page to a PDF, select the content you
want to convert, and then choose Copy or Paste. Next, use the Create PDF tool or
File>Create>PDF from Clipboard and follow the prompts to create and save your
new file.

You can use this same process to add the copied material to an existing PDF. First, open the PDF you want to add the material to. Next, select the Organize Pages tool and select Insert>From Clipboard.

Converting Web Pages to PDF Format

Without any other software, Acrobat can convert a web page to PDF format. When you install Acrobat, it is capable of working with every browser, but the manner in which it interacts differs in every browser. In most cases, you will be able to use Acrobat in your browsers by installing an add-in to permit you to view downloaded PDFs (sometimes within your browser, sometimes externally, and at times you will be able to customize how Acrobat works). Generally, you can print any web page to PDF using the installed Adobe PDF printer.

Converting Websites to PDF Format (Figure 3-5)

Without any other software, Acrobat can convert an entire website or pages from a website to PDF format. To begin, select File>Create>PDF from Web Page or Ctrl+Shift+O (Windows) or Cmd+Shift+O (Mac). This displays the Create PDF from Web Page dialog box, which can be expanded to display more options if you select Capture Multiple Levels. You will be prompted to

Figure 3-5

type the URL of the website, and you are given the option to convert only the top level or multiple levels of a website. If you select Get only 1 level, you will create a PDF from what is typically only the home page of a website. To capture additional pages, such as pages you would find by navigating to dropdown menus or links, you will need to choose multiple levels. If you are not sure how many levels you need, you can choose Get entire site; however, for a large website, this can take a long time or create a very large file. If the site is too large, Acrobat will not be able to capture it.

If you do not select Stay on same path or Stay on same server, you will potentially retrieve web pages and/or files from websites other than the one you specified in the URL. For example, a website could link to a video on YouTube and the PDF you create would potentially include that outside material. After you select the site and other information, Acrobat will begin the process of capturing the website. This can be a lengthy process. When Acrobat completes the website capture, it will open a file and each web page will display as a separate bookmark in the Navigation pane. The PDF is searchable just like any other PDF file would be.

Dragging and Dropping Files (Figure 3-6)

Simply click on one or more files (regardless of the program in which they were created) and, while still holding the mouse button, drag them on top of the Acrobat icon on your desktop, the Windows task bar, the Mac dock, or elsewhere on your computer. Your computer will briefly display a message that the file is converting, and then it will automatically convert and open each document as a separate PDF file for you to save.

Figure 3-6

Saving PDF Files

By default, Acrobat saves files in a traditional PDF format. PDFs can be revised, however. Therefore, unless you add security features to the PDF, others can modify it. If you regularly need to save files to the PDF/A format, you can either do so on a file-by-file basis or change Acrobat's default conversion settings (see the previous section on Acrobat PDFMaker).

PDF Formats for Saving Documents

Using the Save as Other command, Acrobat allows users to save PDFs to a variety of other formats (Figure 3-7):

Figure 3-7

- **Reduced Sized PDF:** This command optimizes and reduces the size (the amount of space your file takes up on your computer) of a PDF. This command is generally the first step you should take if a file is large, such as files too large to attach to an email or file in an electronic filing system.
- **Certified PDF:** A Certified PDF informs recipients that the PDF originated from you and has not been accidentally or maliciously modified since you published it. If you certify a form containing prepopulated information, you can verify that recipients of the document did not modify the form data before returning it to you.
- **Reader Extended PDF:** When you enable this feature, you can allow readers *who have only the free Acrobat Reader* to (1) add comments to the document (Enable Commenting and Measuring) or (2) perform a variety of actions, including filling in forms, signing a document, and saving the document (Enable More Tools).

- **Optimized PDF:** This command brings up a dialog box that enables users to reduce the size of a PDF; specify how it saves the documents, including images; and perform other actions. Most law firms will not use this command.
- **Archivable PDF (PDF/A):** The PDF/A format is the required format for filing in *some* federal and state courts. A PDF/A is considered the desired format for long-term storage of documents. PDF/A files do not have all of the characteristics of traditional PDF files, such as object linking and encryption. The PDF/A standards are developed and maintained by a working group with representatives from government, industry, academia, and Adobe Systems Incorporated.

  Of note, when you are viewing a PDF/A formatted document, you cannot OCR it or perform other functions. In some cases, Acrobat can disregard the PDF/A setting and allow the document to revert to a traditional PDF format. However, the ability to do so depends on the settings placed on the document when it was saved as a PDF/A.
- **Press-Ready PDF (PDF/X):** This format is generally used for PDFs that are to be published or used in digital media. Lawyers will not use this format.
- **PDF/E:** This format is generally used for engineering documents. Lawyers will not use this format.

Working with Microsoft Windows Files

Virtually any file type can be converted to PDF format. As discussed previously, you can simply drag and drop the file onto the Acrobat icon and the program will convert it to PDF format. In addition, the Adobe PDF printer is available in every program on your computer from the Print command.

Using the Create Command

Another method of converting any file is to use the File>Create or Create PDF tool.

Scanning a Paper Document

- You can scan paper documents to PDFs from many types of scanners; because there are so many scanners, it is beyond the scope of this book to detail the settings for each scanner.

  NOTE: Technically speaking, scanners can be either TWAIN-compliant or non-TWAIN-compliant, which addresses how they interface with computers, etc. You cannot scan directly to Acrobat, however, using a Fujitsu Scansnap or other non-TWAIN-compliant scanner. These types of scanners still work with Acrobat but require users to scan from programs other than Acrobat.

■ In Windows, you can choose presets to optimize the quality of your scanned document and define your own conversion settings. In most cases, scanner preset settings will work well to scan common law office documents such as letters and briefs.

■ To create a PDF, go to File>Create>PDF from Scanner to open the Scan dialog box. Click to begin scanning. When prompted, click OK to confirm that the scan is complete. The PDF of the scanned document will then appear in Acrobat. Next, save the scanned document by going to File>Save As (Ctrl+Shift+S for Windows or Cmd+Shift+S for Mac) (Figure 3-8).

Figure 3-8

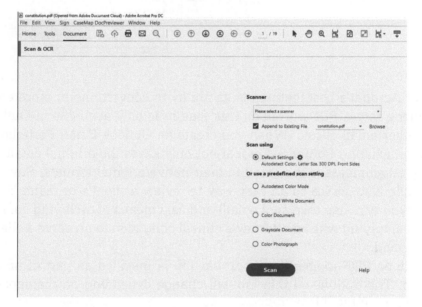

■ To view the scanner's conversion settings, go to File>Create>PDF from Scanner>Configure Presets. This dialog box allows you to specify multiple options, including single-sided or double-sided scanning, paper size, whether to prompt for more pages, file size, and whether to OCR the file while scanning.

NOTE: If you allow Acrobat to OCR documents while scanning, (1) it will slow the scanning process, and (2) you are limited to Searchable Image or Editable Text and Image settings, not the preferred Searchable Image (Exact) setting for law offices.

The crucial differences in these settings for law firms are discussed in Chapter 6. Click Save and then click Close to exit the dialog box.

Creating PDFs from Microsoft Outlook Emails (Figure 3-9 and Figure 3-10)

This feature is only available on Windows computers. Unfortunately, the only Acrobat add-in available to Mac users is Adobe Sign. Individual emails, or groups of emails, can be saved as PDF, but the functions described below for saving emails with attachments in native format, as a portfolio, are not an option.

<table>
<tr><td align="center">**Figure 3-9**</td><td align="center">**Figure 3-10**</td></tr>
<tr><td></td><td></td></tr>
</table>

One of Acrobat's best features is its ability to convert one or more emails, or email folders, into a PDF Portfolio. This feature is only available in Outlook and not with other email clients. When you create an Outlook Email Portfolio, or add emails to an existing Portfolio, Acrobat not only saves the original email but also saves any attachments to the email in their native/original formats. Saving email as a Portfolio also serves as an easy way to review a client's or matter's communications (you can also save sent email) and as a means of archiving communication, thus complying with an attorney's ethical obligation to preserve a client's file, including email.

The Adobe PDF toolbar or ribbon bar tab is installed as part of an Acrobat installation. The options on this tab will change depending on the specific task you are doing.

- **When Sending Email:** When a user creates a new email message, the Attach File via Link command appears on the ribbon, allowing the sender to attach Adobe Document Cloud file links to an email, which is a helpful option for larger files.
- **Viewing Email Messages in Outlook:** There are three sections on the Adobe PDF section of the ribbon when viewing messages in the Reading pane. Only the Convert section appears when reading an email in its own window.
  - ❖ **Convert:** There are two options in this section. The Convert Selected Messages option converts one or more selected email messages to PDF. The Convert Selected Folders option converts one or more selected folders to PDF. These options allow users to either create a new PDF or to append the selected messages or folders to an existing PDF. The Append command is particularly handy because it allows you to add

messages relating to a specific topic or matter to an existing PDF. In addition, when you append messages or folders, Acrobat only appends messages or folders that were not previously included in the PDF. This means that there are no duplicate messages stored in the PDF.

When you use the Selected Folders option, Acrobat displays a dialog box showing all of the folders in Outlook and allows you to choose whichever folder or folders you wish to include.

Whether you are creating a new PDF from one or more emails or one or more folders, Acrobat then allows you to specify the location where you want to save the file and the name you want to use. Acrobat will then convert the emails and will show you the progress of the conversion.

Acrobat creates a Portfolio from the emails rather than one single PDF file. You can change this setting (we do not recommend doing so) by unchecking Output Adobe PDF Portfolio when creating a new PDF file in the Settings tab of the Change Conversion Settings dialog. The Portfolio contains not only the email messages but also any attachments to the emails in their native format. The default view lists the number of attachments to a particular email but does not automatically display any links to open them. There are two ways to display attachments. The first is to use the View menu on the main menu and choose View>Show/Hide>Navigation Panes>Attachments. Acrobat then displays the Attachment pane to the left of the email message. Alternatively, you can select Open Document to display the specific email message as a single PDF outside of the Portfolio. Once the single email is open, you will need to open the Navigation pane on the left and click on the paper clip to view the available attachments. When you choose an attachment, it will open in the default program on your computer for that file type.

The content of the Portfolio is fully searchable, so you could find a specific email just by remembering and searching for a word or phrase in it. To do so, select Edit>Search Entire Portfolio from the main menu or Ctrl+Shift+F. Saved messages are also date-stamped with the date that messages were sent or received, not the date on which they were saved.

- **Change Conversion Settings:** This setting allows you to specify various settings, including the Portfolio's compatibility with earlier versions of Acrobat. Generally, users do not need to change these settings, particularly the settings that specify that the results should be displayed in a Portfolio. Because emails may contain links, the default setting is to block external content. The Security option allows the Portfolio's creator to require a password to open the document as well as an option that would prevent or limit editing and printing of the Portfolio.

- **Archive:** This setting allows users to automatically archive email at specified intervals. While this can be a handy setting, in most cases users will prefer to select the email to be saved rather than allow the software to do so.

Saving/Exporting PDF Files to Other Formats

In addition to saving PDFs in various PDF formats, users can save PDFs in other document formats. The quality of these results varies and often depends on the source from which the PDF was created. Thus, a spreadsheet created in Microsoft Excel and converted to PDF will easily save back to an .xls format, and a PDF created from Microsoft Word will seamlessly convert back to a .doc document. On the other hand, documents created from scanners may not produce equally satisfactory results. The command appears in the Export To menu at File>Export To.

This command allows Acrobat to save PDFs in the following formats (Figure 3-11):

- Microsoft Word (.docx) format
- Microsoft Word 97-2003 (.doc) format
- Spreadsheet: Microsoft Excel (.xlsx) format
- Spreadsheet: XML spreadsheet (.xls) format
- Microsoft PowerPoint Presentation (.pptx) format
- Image (picture) formats: JPEG, JPEG2000, TIFF, PNG
- HTML: Web page format
- Rich Text Format: This is a generic text format that is compatible with most word processing programs, including Notepad.
- Text (Accessible): Each line from the PDF becomes a line (with a hard return) in the generic document.
- Text (Plain): Each paragraph retains its formatting (hard returns are inserted at the end of each paragraph).
- There are also options for saving in a PostScript (.ps) format, which is primarily used in publishing and is not relevant for most Acrobat users.

Figure 3-11

Chapter 4

Arranging and Manipulating PDFs

One of Acrobat's best features is that it provides many ways to work with PDF files so that users can choose the methods they prefer.

Working with Thumbnails (Figure 4-1)

Page thumbnails, which are miniature previews of the pages in a document, provide access to many features (generally by right-clicking on a thumbnail), allowing users to edit PDFs easily. You access thumbnails from the left navigation panel, selecting the image showing two overlapping documents.

Figure 4-1

Page thumbnails allow you to click on a page's image and go directly to the selected page or to adjust the view of the page. Thumbnails make it simple to rearrange pages. All you have to do is to move, copy, or delete a page thumbnail. When you do, you will also move, copy, or delete the specific page or pages in the document.

Rearrange Pages

With this option, you select a page by clicking on it and moving it to another location in a document. If you want to move multiple pages, use the Ctrl key (Windows) or Cmd key (Mac) to select individual pages or use the Shift key to select a range of pages to move.

Copy Pages (Figure 4-2)

With this option in Windows, you select one or more pages and then press the Ctrl key while holding down the left mouse key. Move the cursor to the location where you want to place the copied pages and release the mouse and Ctrl keys. The selected pages will be copied to the new location. On a Mac, press the Cmd key while holding down the mouse on the page(s) you wish to copy. Right-click to copy and paste.

Figure 4-2

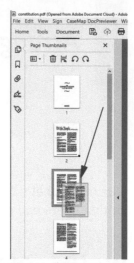

Right-Clicking on Thumbnails (Figure 4-3)

When you right-click on the thumbnails, you have many options, which are also available from the Organize Pages tool on the Tools pane:

- **Insert Pages:** This option allows you to add pages to the PDF.
  - ❖ **From File:** This allows you to add pages from a file you locate through Windows Explorer.
  - ❖ **From Clipboard:** This allows you to insert pages that were cut or copied to the clipboard.
  - ❖ **A Blank Page:** This allows you to add a blank page to a document. This is a helpful command, for example, if you are printing double-sided and want a particular page to be blank.
- **Extract Pages:** This option allows you to extract or remove pages from the open PDF. You have three options:
  - ❖ If you do not check either option, the extracted pages will be extracted as a single new file and the pages will remain in your original document.
  - ❖ **Delete Pages after Extraction:** This option deletes the extracted pages from the original document.
  - ❖ **Extract Pages as Separate Files:** This option makes each of the extracted pages a separate single-page file.
- **Replace Pages:** This option allows you to replace pages in the displayed document with pages from another document. You can select the specific pages to be removed and the specified pages to be inserted in their place.
- **Delete Pages (Ctrl+Shift+D for Windows or Cmd+Shift+D for Mac):** This option allows you to delete pages in the displayed document.

Figure 4-3

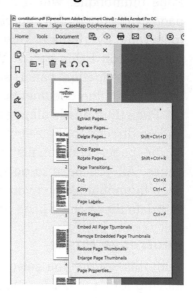

- **Crop Pages:** This option allows you to crop (reduce the margins on) one or more specified pages. This feature gives users the option to draw a box around the area to be cropped or to use measurements that display on the page being cropped. This can be useful when you need to remove fax headers from a document, for example.
  - ❖ You may draw a box on a page, and double-click to bring up the Set Page boxes dialog, from which you can change the crop settings. Using this method, Acrobat displays your selected area. The other two methods do not display a selection until you change the margins or other crop settings.
  - ❖ You can double-click on a page to bring up the Set Page boxes dialog.
  - ❖ You can right-click on a thumbnail to bring up the Crop (or other) dialog.
- **Rotate Pages (Ctrl+Shift+R for Windows or Cmd+Shift+R for Mac):** This option allows you to rotate one or more specified pages. This dialog allows users to rotate pages 90 degrees clockwise or counterclockwise, or 180 degrees, and allows the user to specify whether to rotate even and/or odd pages, as well as pages that are currently displayed in landscape or portrait.
- **Page Transitions:** This dialog allows users to specify what animation or effects occur when moving from one page to another. Users can specify the range of pages to which the transition applies.
- **Cut (Ctrl+X for Windows or Cmd+X for Mac):** This option allows you to cut a page (virtually deleting it) and then paste it in a different location or in multiple locations in the file.
- **Copy (Ctrl+C for Windows or Cmd+C for Mac):** This option allows you to copy a page (leaving the original in its current location) and then paste it in a different location or in multiple locations in the file.
- **Paste (Ctrl+V for Windows or Cmd+V for Mac):** This option pastes (inserts) pages you have copied or pasted into a different location or in multiple locations in the file.
- **Page Labels:** This dialog is used to change the page numbering that appears on the toolset for a given page or range of pages. Note that page numbers or Bates numbers on the document do not change as a result of this dialog.
- **Print Pages:** This setting allows users to print one or more specified pages.
- **Embed All Page Thumbnails:** Embedded page thumbnails do not need to be redrawn every time the Pages pane is opened. Embedding page thumbnails uses approximately 3 KB of space per page thumbnail, but it saves time for subsequent users (particularly with very large documents) because Acrobat does not have to recreate the thumbnails when the document is opened.
- **Remove Embedded Page Thumbnails:** This option removes embedded page thumbnails from the document.

- **Reduce Page Thumbnails:** This option allows users to reduce the displayed size of each page thumbnail, up to the smallest size permitted in the dialog. The top of the dialog also has icons that access all of the navigation options.
- **Enlarge Page Thumbnails:** This option allows users to enlarge the displayed size of each page thumbnail.
- **Page Properties:** This dialog specifies the order of pages when tabbing from one page to another.

Working with Bookmarks (Figure 4-4)

A bookmark is a link that takes the reader to a different view or page in a document. Bookmarks are generated automatically during PDF creation from tables of contents that are created by Word and other programs. You can also create additional bookmarks; mark a location in a PDF to which you want to return; or jump to a location in the PDF, another document, or a web page. Bookmarks can also perform actions, such as executing a menu item or submitting a form.

Figure 4-4

When a PDF contains bookmarks, readers can click on any bookmark to immediately move from one location in a document to another. Bookmarks can simply mirror a document's table of contents or index. They can also be created to serve a particular user's needs. For example, if you had a PDF containing 1,000 pages of hospital records from a lengthy hospitalization, you could create bookmarks for the Discharge Summary, each Operative Report, and every Consultation, avoiding the need to search or scroll through the document to view desired information.

At the top of the Bookmarks pane is a dropdown menu that allows users to (1) expand the current bookmark, (2) expand all top-level bookmarks, (3) highlight the current bookmark, (4) hide the Bookmarks pane after it is used, (5) change the size of the bookmarks text (options are Small, Medium, or Large), (6) go to a highlighted bookmark, (7) print sections of the document, (8) delete bookmarks, and (9) rename bookmarks. There are fewer options when a file does not have any bookmarks.

Depending on the security levels of the document, you can cut, delete, rename, or specify the destination of a bookmark by right-clicking on the bookmark in the pane.

Adding a Bookmark (Figure 4-5)

Either click on the Add Bookmark icon or right-click on the location you want to bookmark and select Add Bookmark (Ctrl+B for Windows or Cmd+B for Mac), and a new bookmark will appear. You can then include any information you like to describe the bookmark.

Figure 4-5

Working with Attachments (Figure 4-6)

Attachments include any file included with a document (such as an attachment to an email) or any file attached to the PDF.

Figure 4-6

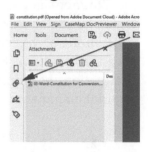

Adding an Attachment (Figure 4-7)

You can add an attachment from the dropdown menu on the Attachments panel or choose Tools>Edit PDF>More>Attach File. In either instance, a Windows File Explorer or Mac Finder menu opens where you can choose the file you wish to attach. This file does not have to be a PDF file. Navigate to the file and click Open. Save your PDF file. The file you selected is now attached to your PDF and will remain available even if the attached file is moved or deleted from its own location.

Figure 4-7

Viewing an Attachment

Just click on the attachment and it will open in its native format (provided your computer is capable of opening the specific type of file).

If you right-click on an attachment, you can also open the attachment (Figure 4-8). There are also other options:

Figure 4-8

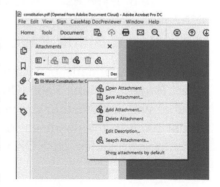

- **Save Attachment:** This option saves the attachment to a location on your computer.
- **Add Attachment:** This option adds a new attachment to the document.
- **Delete Attachment:** This option removes the attachment from the document.
- **Edit Description:** This option changes the description of the attachment.

- **Search Attachments:** Also available in the small toolbar at the top of the Attachment pane, this option searches all attachments for specific content. The results will not include images or un-OCRed/nonsearchable items.
- **Show Attachments by Default:** Acrobat automatically displays attachments for all documents containing them.

Dragging and Dropping Files between Different PDFs (Figure 4-9)

Another way to add pages to a PDF is to open two or more PDFs, making sure that the Thumbnails pane is open in each document. Next, select the pages you want to add to another document, and left-click and drag and drop the pages in the destination file at the location you want them to appear (a locator bar appears to display the location). Release your mouse and your pages will be inserted at the destination location. This copies the pages but does not remove them from the original document.

Figure 4-9

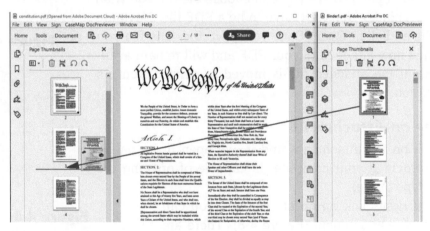

Inserting a Blank Page (Figure 4-10)

With the Thumbnails pane open, right-click on a thumbnailed page and select Insert Pages>A Blank Page (Ctrl+Shift+T for Windows or Cmd+Shift+T for Mac). Acrobat will ask whether you want to insert the blank page before or after the first or last page in the document or before or after another specified page. After you indicate your choice, click OK and Acrobat will insert the blank page.

Figure 4-10

Combining Files

It is very easy to combine or merge multiple files. When you do so, you will have the option of creating one document or a Portfolio, which keeps the documents separate but in the same PDF (as if the chapters of a book were printed separately but were bound together). To create a PDF Portfolio, see "Creating a PDF Portfolio" later in this chapter. For example, consider a client with medical records from five providers. If you combine them into one document, the result is an electronic "stack" of documents. If you combine them into a Portfolio, the result is one electronic document that has separate folders, allowing you to view each of the five providers' records independently and without having to search through the stack.

In addition, Acrobat allows you to combine types of files. To do so, you must have the programs installed that support the documents' "native" formats, thus permitting them to be converted to PDFs. For example, if you do not have Word installed on your computer, you will not be able to include those files in a combined PDF. If you do, you can assemble all of the documents for inclusion in a brief, including Microsoft Word documents, email messages, spreadsheets, and photographs. When combining the files, Acrobat allows you to select specific pages from each document and to rearrange them.

Acrobat Standard and Professional both allow you to combine multiple files into one file. Acrobat Professional also allows you to combine the files in a PDF Portfolio. In addition to the ability to organize documents easily, a PDF Portfolio permits users to include documents in their native/original format, such as Word or Excel.

Selecting Files to Combine

- **Using Windows Explorer** (Figure 4-11) *(This option is not available in Finder on a Mac. If you wish to combine files into a PDF, you should combine the files from within Acrobat as discussed below.)*
  - ❖ Go to the folder that holds the documents you want to combine and select the files to combine.
  - ❖ Right-click on the highlighted files and select Combine files in Acrobat.

Figure 4-11

- ❖ The Combine Files dialog will appear, displaying the selected files.
- ❖ Under Options at the top right of the dialog, you can specify the File Size (small, medium, or large) and whether the output file is a Single PDF or a PDF Portfolio. Review the other options to determine if any applies, and then click OK and return to the Combine Files dialog.
- ❖ Using the Add Files dropdown menu, you can select other files to combine. This menu allows you to add files, add folders (all documents in the folders), or add other types of files.
- ❖ To change the order in which the files are combined, highlight a file name and either drag it or click Move Up or Move Down.
- ❖ You can sort the list by clicking on the name of a column. If you click again, the items will be sorted in reverse order.
- ❖ Next, click on Options to verify if you want the output file to be a Single PDF. There are other options that you should review to determine if they apply. Click OK and return to the dialog.
- ❖ Along the bottom of the dialog, you can adjust the slide to reduce or enlarge the size of the previewed documents. You can also remove files by selecting one or more files and choosing Remove. You can select multiple files by clicking on Ctrl and clicking on the chosen files, or by selecting Select Multiple, which allows you to select files to remove without using the Ctrl key. Click Remove to remove files from the list of selected files.
- ❖ You can rearrange the files into the order you want them combined by clicking on a file and dragging and dropping it where you want it (between other displayed files).
- ❖ Click Combine Files and Acrobat will create the new file. Name and save it.
- **From within Acrobat** (Figure 4-12 through Figure 4-14)
  - ❖ Go to File>Create and select Combine Files into a Single PDF.
  - ❖ The Combine Files dialog will appear, displaying the selected pages.
  - ❖ Using the Add Files dropdown menu, you can select other files to combine. This menu allows you to add files, add folders (all documents in the folders), or add other types of files.
  - ❖ To change the order in which the documents appear (which can be relevant when assigning Bates numbers or establishing reading order), highlight a file name and either drag it or click Move Up or Move Down.

Figure 4-12

Figure 4-13

Figure 4-14

❖ You can sort the list by clicking on the name of a column. If you click again, the items will be sorted in reverse order.

❖ Next, click on Options to verify if you want the output file to be a Single PDF. There are other options that you should review to determine if they apply. Click OK and return to the dialog.

❖ Along the bottom of the dialog, you can adjust the slide to reduce or enlarge the size of the previewed documents. You can also remove files by selecting one or more files and choosing Remove. You can select multiple files by clicking on Ctrl and clicking on the chosen files, or by selecting Select Multiple, which allows you to select files to remove without using the Ctrl key. Click Remove to remove files from the list of selected files.

❖ You can rearrange the files into the order you want them combined by clicking on a file and dragging and dropping it where you want it (between other displayed files).

❖ Click Combine Files and Acrobat will create the new file. Name and save it.

Arranging Pages in an Existing PDF

■ Acrobat makes it easy to arrange pages in a PDF. Just open the Page Thumbnails pane on the left side of the screen, and you can view all of the pages in your file.

Figure 4-15

❖ To move one page, click on it and drag it and drop it in the location in the document where you want it to be.

❖ To move multiple pages, you have two options (Figure 4-15):

◆ Select multiple pages by using the Ctrl key (Cmd key on a Mac) and clicking on the selected pages.

◆ Highlight a range of pages by clicking on the first page to be moved and, using the Shift key, selecting the last page to be moved.

❖ Next, move the highlighted pages (as one group) to the location in the document where you want them to be.

Copying Pages in an Existing PDF

■ Acrobat makes it easy to copy one or more pages in your documents. Just open the Page Thumbnails pane on the left side of the screen, and you can view all of the pages in your file.

❖ In Windows, to copy one page, click on it and, while holding down the Ctrl key, drag it and drop it in the location in the document where you want a copy of the page to appear.

❖ To copy multiple pages, you have two options:

♦ Select multiple pages by using the Ctrl key and clicking on the selected pages.

♦ Alternatively, you can highlight a range of pages by clicking on the first page to be moved and, holding down the Shift key, selecting the last page to be moved.

❖ While holding down the Ctrl key, drag and drop the selected pages (as one group) to the location in the document where you want them to be.

❖ On a Mac, press the Cmd key while holding down the mouse on the page(s) you wish to copy. Right-click to copy and paste.

Creating a PDF Portfolio (Acrobat Professional only)

■ A PDF Portfolio contains multiple files assembled into one PDF and can include various types of files. For example, a PDF Portfolio can include text documents, email, spreadsheets, and PowerPoint presentations, each in its original format (Word, Excel, Outlook Memo, etc.). In addition, you can open, edit, and review each file separately. Portfolios are a more effective way of presenting information than displaying them in a single PDF, even if the PDF has bookmarks.

Perhaps the best way to explain the difference between creating one PDF from multiple files and creating a Portfolio from multiple files is to imagine that you have five file folders full of paper. You want all of these files to be "one." You can choose to remove all the paper from the individual file folders and put them in an expandable redweld, or you can leave the papers in their individual files and simply place the five folders in the redweld, each containing the original documents. Both serve the same purpose; you have one folder, but the organization of the first is virtually nonexistent. You can add sticky notes or other items to help organize your pile of paper (this would be similar to adding bookmarks to a PDF file), but leaving the individual folders intact, as a Portfolio would do, creates a much more manageable system.

■ The process for creating a PDF Portfolio is the same as combining files, except that when you create a Portfolio, you have the additional option about how the resulting PDF Portfolio will display.

❖ **Selecting files to combine**

♦ **Using Windows Explorer (Figure 4-16)** *(This option is not available in Finder on a Mac. If you wish to combine files into a PDF, you should combine the files from within Acrobat as discussed below.)*

Figure 4-16

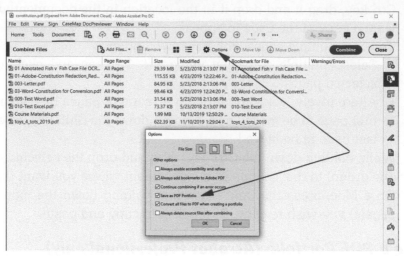

I Go to the folder where the documents you want to combine are
   stored and select the files to combine.
I Right-click on the highlighted files and select Combine files in
   Acrobat.
I The Combine Files dialog will appear, displaying the selected
   pages.
I Under Options at the top right of the dialog, you can specify the
   File Size (small, medium, or large) and whether the output file is
   a Single PDF or Portfolio. Review the other options to determine
   if any applies, and then click OK and return to the Combine Files
   dialog.
I Using the Add Files dropdown menu, you can select other files to
   combine. This menu allows you to add files, add folders (all documents in the folders), or add other types of files.
I To change the order in which Bates numbers are assigned, highlight a file name and either drag it or click Move Up or Move
   Down.
I You can sort the list by clicking on the name of a column. If you
   click again, the items will be sorted in reverse order.
I Next, click on Options to verify if you want the output file to be a
   Portfolio. There are other options that you should review to determine if they apply. Click OK and return to the dialog.
I Along the bottom of the dialog, you can adjust the slide to reduce
   or enlarge the size of the previewed documents. You can also
   remove files by selecting one or more files and choosing Remove.
   You can select multiple files by clicking on Ctrl and clicking on
   the chosen files, or by selecting Select Multiple, which allows you

to select files to remove without using the Ctrl key. Click Remove to remove files from the list of selected files.

ı You can rearrange the files into the order you want them combined by clicking on a file and dragging and dropping it where you want it (between other displayed files).

ı Click Combine Files and Acrobat will create the new file. Name and save it.

♦ **From within Acrobat**

ı Go to File>Create>PDF Portfolio (Figure 4-17 and Figure 4-18).

Figure 4-17

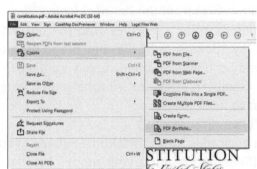

Figure 4-18

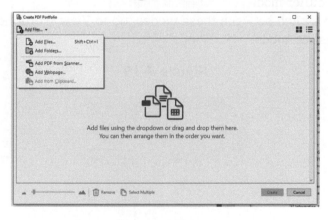

ı The Combine Files dialog will appear displaying the selected pages. Alternatively, you can drag and drop files into the Create PDF Portfolio dialog.

ı Using the Add Files dropdown menu, you can select other files to combine. This menu allows you to add files, add folders (all documents in the folders), or add other types of files.

ı To change the order in which the files are combined, highlight a file name and either drag it or click Move Up or Move Down.

▪ You can sort the list by clicking on the name of a column. If you click again, the items will be sorted in reverse order.

▪ Next, click on Options to verify if you want the output file to be a Portfolio. There are other options that you should review to determine if they apply. Click OK and return to the dialog.

▪ Along the bottom of the dialog, you can adjust the slide to reduce or enlarge the size of the previewed documents. You can also remove files by selecting one or more files and choosing Remove. You can select multiple files by clicking on Ctrl and clicking on the chosen files, or by selecting Select Multiple, which allows you to select files to remove without using the Ctrl key. Click Remove to remove files from the list of selected files.

▪ You can rearrange the files into the order you want them combined by clicking on a file and dragging and dropping it where you want it (between other displayed files).

▪ Click Combine Files and Acrobat will create the new file. Name and save it.

❖ **Portfolio Views** (Figure 4-19)

♦ You can view files in a Portfolio in either Layout (Preview) mode or Details (Files) mode. In Layout mode, Acrobat displays the files in the left Navigation pane. In Details mode, Acrobat displays the file below the secondary toolbar. You can work with the component files in either mode.

♦ To switch between these modes, go to View>Portfolio and select the desired mode.

Figure 4-19

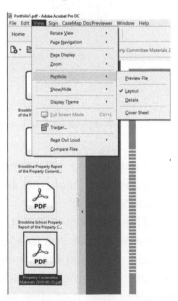

❖ **Displaying Information in a Portfolio** (Figure 4-20)

  ♦ Right-clicking on the thumbnails displays many other options, including the ability to extract files from a Portfolio or to reduce the size of a file using the Reduce File Size dialog. In addition, you can add files, folders, and other items to the Portfolio by right-clicking on the Thumbnails pane. If you select Portfolio Properties from the options, you can specify the information that will display about the files in the Portfolio.

  ♦ If you hover your mouse over the displayed file, a toolbar appears at the bottom of the screen that allows you to save, print, or navigate through the file. This is the same toolbar that appears when you display PDFs in a web browser.

Figure 4-20

Chapter 5

Numbering Pages and Adding Backgrounds

Acrobat allows you to add headers, footers, watermarks (background graphics and text), and other information to a PDF.

Using Headers and Footers

With Acrobat, you can add a header and a footer to one or more documents at a time. Headers and footers can include a variety of information, such as a date and copyright information.

Headers and footers can vary within a PDF, and you can have more than one header or footer on a page. They are also editable, so that if a document changes, you can update a header or footer with only a mouse click or two.

You can also specify the location of the headers and footers on the page. In addition, Acrobat allows you to save headers and footers and use the patterns you created in other documents.

Adding Headers and Footers

Adding a Header or Footer to an Open Document

- Open a PDF file and go to Tools>Edit PDF. Select Header & Footer>Add to display the Add Header and Footer dialog. Formatting options appear in the panel on the right side of the document (Figure 5-1).

Figure 5-1

NOTE: When creating headers and footers, you should enter information by completing the form from top to bottom, going line by line.

■ If your file has a header or footer, or Acrobat perceives that it has one that may have been added by another program, it will ask whether to Replace Existing or Add New. Click Add New (Figure 5-2).

Figure 5-2

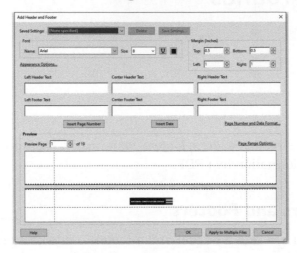

■ If you are using a Saved Setting, you would select it now. If not, proceed to the Font section to specify the font and size you want. These properties apply to any header or footer created with this specific dialog. You must apply headers or footers separately if you want to have different fonts or font sizes.

■ In the Margin section, determine whether the margins are acceptable. Note that the top and bottom margins are set at 0.5 inch because most documents have one-inch margins for the text.

■ Click on Appearance Options and adjust the following options as needed:
  ❖ Shrink document to avoid overwriting the document's text and graphics: This setting reduces the size of the PDF to ensure that any header or footer does not overlap existing content.
  ❖ Keep position and size of header or footer text constant when printing on different page sizes: This setting prevents the header or footer from being resized or repositioned when the PDF is printed on a large or nonstandard-sized page.

■ If your header or footer includes a page number or date, click on the hyperlink for Page Number and Date Format. In this dialog, you specify the format of the date and page number.

■ Type in the text of the headers and footers in the box corresponding to where you want the text to appear. If you want to insert a page number or a date, you must place your cursor in the applicable box before clicking on Insert Page Number or Insert Date.

❖ As you insert header or footer text, you will see a preview of the text appear in the page thumbnails at the bottom of the dialog box. Acrobat permits you to include page numbers and dates in the same area.

■ If you want to save these settings for future use, click Save Settings and name your settings before applying the header or footer content.

■ If you want to apply the same header or footer to other PDFs, click Apply to Multiple Files. Click Add Files. Using the Add Files dropdown menu, you can select other files to include when applying the header or footer. This menu allows you to add files, add folders (all documents in the folders), or add other types of files.

❖ You can sort the list by clicking on the name of a column. If you click again, the items will be sorted in reverse order.

❖ When you click OK, the Output Options dialog appears. From this dialog you can specify whether the documents are stored in their original folder or in a different folder you specify. You can also specify whether Acrobat maintains the original file names, overwrites the existing files, or adds a suffix or prefix to the file name. Click OK and Acrobat applies the header or footer.

■ If you do not want to apply the header or footer to other files, click OK and Acrobat will insert the header and footer into your PDF.

Adding Headers and Footers with No Document Open (Figure 5-3)

One of the many benefits of using Acrobat is its ability to allow users to perform many functions on files, even when the files are not open. This means you can, for example, add footers, OCR, and do various other actions even without having a particular file open.

Figure 5-3

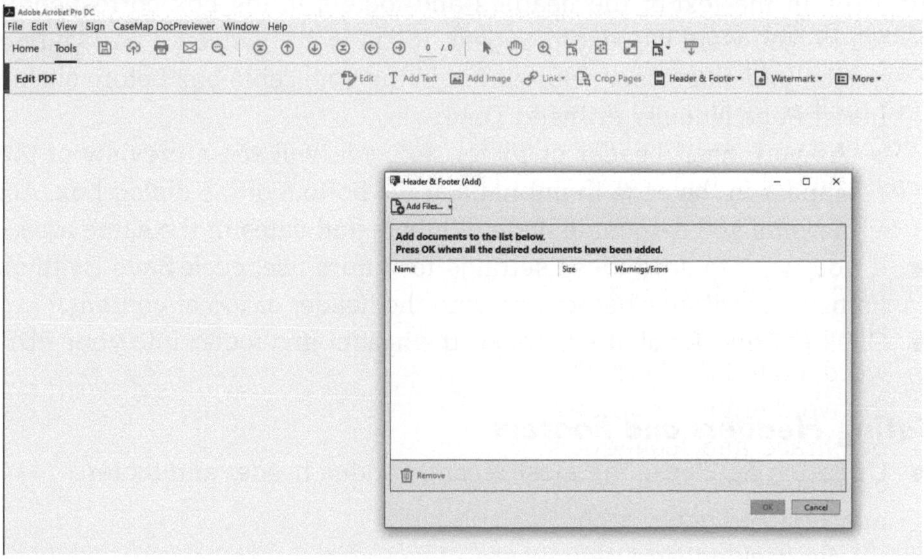

- Go to Tools>Edit PDF. Select Header & Footer>Add to display the Header & Footer (Add) dialog. Using the Add Files dropdown menu, select the files you will be using. This menu allows you to add files, add folders (all documents in the folders), or add other types of files.
- You can sort the list by clicking on the name of a column. If you click again, the items will be sorted in reverse order.
- When you click OK, you will see the Add Header and Footer dialog.

  NOTE: When creating headers and footers, you should enter information by completing the form from top to bottom, going line by line.
- If you are using a Saved Setting, you would select it now. If not, proceed to the Font section to specify the font and size you want. These properties apply to any header or footer created with this specific dialog. You must apply headers or footers separately if you want to have different fonts or font sizes.
- In the Margin section, determine whether the margins are acceptable. Note that the top and bottom margins are set at 0.5 inch because most documents have one-inch margins for the text.
- Click on Appearance Options and adjust the following options as needed:
  - ❖ Shrink document to avoid overwriting the document's text and graphics: This setting reduces the size of the PDF to ensure that any header or footer does not overlap existing content.
  - ❖ Keep position and size of header or footer text constant when printing on different page sizes: This setting prevents the header or footer from being resized or repositioned when the PDF is printed on a large or nonstandard-sized page.
- If your header or footer includes a page number or date, click on the hyperlink for Page Number and Date Format. In this dialog, you specify the format of the date and page number.
- Type in the text of the headers and footers in the box corresponding to where you want the text to appear. If you want to insert a page number or a date, you must place your cursor in the applicable box before clicking on Insert Page Number or Insert Date.
  - ❖ As you insert header or footer text, you will see a preview of the text appear in the page thumbnails at the bottom of the dialog box. Acrobat permits you to include page numbers and dates in the same area.
- If you want to save these settings for future use, click Save Settings and name your settings before applying the header or footer content.
- Click OK and Acrobat will insert the header and footer into your PDF.

Updating Headers and Footers
- Updating applies to the most recently added header and footer.

- Open the PDF file containing the header and footer, and select Tools>Edit PDF. Select Header & Footer>Update from the Edit PDF toolset.
- Change the settings as needed. Click OK and Acrobat will update the header or footer.

Adding Another Header and Footer

- Open the PDF file containing the header and footer. Select Tools>Edit PDF. In the Edit PDF toolset, select Header & Footer>Add, and then click Add New in the message that appears.
- Type in the text of the new header and footer. Select any new formatting options. Click OK and Acrobat will add the additional header or footer.

Replacing All Headers and Footers

- Replacing applies to the most recently added header and footer.
- Open the PDF file containing the header and footer. Select Tools>Edit PDF. In the Edit PDF toolset, select Header & Footer>Add, and then click Replace Existing. Select your new formatting options. Click OK and Acrobat will replace the prior header and footer with the new one.

Removing All Headers and Footers

- You can remove the headers and footers from one or more documents in one process.
  - ❖ Removing all headers and footers from one document:
    - ♦ Open the PDF file containing the header and footer. Select Tools>Edit PDF. In the Edit PDF toolset, select Header & Footer>Remove. Acrobat will ask if you are sure you want to permanently remove the header and footer information. When you click Yes, Acrobat will remove the header and footer information.
  - ❖ Removing all headers and footers from multiple documents:
    - ♦ Close all open PDFs, and then select Tools>Edit PDF. In the Edit PDF toolset, select Header & Footer>Remove to display the Header & Footer (Remove) dialog.

      Using the Add Files dropdown menu, select the files you will be using. This menu allows you to add files, add folders (all documents in the folders), or add other types of files. Click OK to display the Output Options dialog.

      Next, determine where you want to save the revised documents and whether they will keep the original file names or if Acrobat should add a prefix or suffix to the file names. Click OK and Acrobat will remove the headers and footers from the documents.

Using Watermarks and Other Background Features (Figure 5-4 and Figure 5-5)

Watermarks are extremely useful. They allow you to place phrases, such as "Draft," "Copy," or "Attorney-Client Privilege," or images in front of or behind the text of your documents. Also, like headers and footers, you can save them, allowing you to quickly insert them on other documents without having to recreate the settings.

Figure 5-4

Figure 5-5

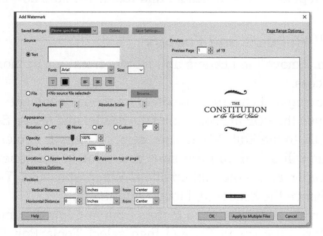

Adding a Watermark or Other Background to an Open Document

■ Open a PDF file and go to Tools>Edit PDF. Select Watermark>Add to display the Add Watermark dialog. Formatting options appear in the panel on the right side of the dialog as you add them.

NOTE: When creating watermarks, you should enter information by completing the form from top to bottom, going line by line.

■ If your file has a watermark, or Acrobat perceives that it has one that may have been added by another program, it will ask whether to Replace Existing or Add New. Click Add New.

- If you are using a Saved Setting, you would select it now. If not, proceed to the Source section to specify the text to insert and font and related settings for it. These properties apply to the watermark created with this specific dialog. You must apply multiple watermarks separately. In this section, you would specify if you want a page of a file to appear as the watermark, selecting the source file and the page of the file. You also specify the scale (percent of the page it covers) under Absolute Scale.
- In the Appearance section, determine whether the watermark is horizontal, rotated 45 degrees or some other degree, how dark it is relative to the page (Opacity), and its scale to the page. You also specify whether it appears behind or in front of the page's content.
  - ❖ Above the previewed page is Page Range Options, which allows you to place the watermark on All Pages, a page range, or some other subset of pages.
  - ❖ Click on Appearance Options and adjust the following options as needed:
    - ♦ Show when printing
    - ♦ Show when displaying on the screen
      - ı Both of these options are selected by default.
    - ♦ Keep the position and size of watermark text constant when printing on different page sizes: This setting prevents the watermark from being resized or repositioned when the PDF is printed on a large or nonstandard-sized page.
  - ❖ In the position section, you can specify where the watermark appears relative to the page, both horizontally and vertically.
- If you want to save these settings for future use, click Save Settings and name your settings before applying the watermark content.
- If you want to apply the same watermark to other PDFs, click Apply to Multiple Files. Click Add Files. Using the Add Files dropdown menu, you can select other files to apply a watermark. This menu allows you to add files, add folders (all documents in the folders), or add other types of files.
  - ❖ You can sort the list by clicking on the name of a column. If you click again, the items will be sorted in reverse order.
  - ❖ When you click OK, the Output Options dialog appears. From this dialog you can specify whether the documents are stored in their original folder or in a different folder you specify. You can also specify whether Acrobat maintains the original file names, overwrites the existing files, or adds a suffix or prefix to the file name. Click OK and Acrobat applies the watermark.
- If you do not want to apply the watermark to other files, click OK and Acrobat will insert the watermark into your PDF.

Adding a Watermark with No Document Open (Figure 5-6)

- Go to Tools>Edit PDF. Select Watermark>Add to display the Watermark (Add) dialog. Using the Add Files dropdown menu, select the files you will be using. This menu allows you to add files, add folders (all documents in the folders), or add other types of files.
- You can sort the list by clicking on the name of a column. If you click again, the items will be sorted in reverse order.
- When you click OK, you will see the Add Watermark dialog.

    NOTE: When creating watermarks, you should enter information by completing the form from top to bottom, going line by line.
- If your file has a watermark, or Acrobat perceives that it has one that may have been added by another program, it will ask whether to Replace Existing or Add New. Click Add New.
- If you are using a Saved Setting, you would select it now. If not, proceed to the Source section to specify the text to insert and font and related settings for it. These properties apply to the watermark created with this specific dialog. You must apply multiple watermarks separately. In this section, you would specify if you want a page of a file to appear as the watermark, selecting the source file and the page of the file. You also specify the scale (percent of the page it covers) under Absolute Scale.
- In the Appearance section, determine whether the watermark is horizontal, rotated 45 degrees or some other degree, how dark it is relative to the page (Opacity), and its scale to the page. You also specify whether it appears behind or in front of the page's content.

Figure 5-6

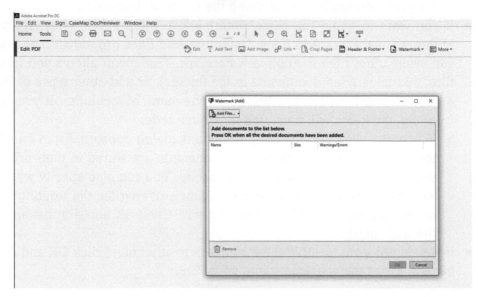

- ❖ Above the previewed page is Page Range Options, which allows you to place the watermark on All Pages, a page range, or some other subset of pages.
- ❖ Click on Appearance Options and adjust the following options as needed:
  - ♦ Show when printing
  - ♦ Show when displaying on the screen
    - ı Both of these options are selected by default.
  - ♦ Keep position and size of watermark text constant when printing on different page sizes: This setting prevents the watermark from being resized or repositioned when the PDF is printed on a large or nonstandard-sized page.
- ❖ In the position section, you can specify where the watermark appears relative to the page, both horizontally and vertically.
- ■ If you want to save these settings for future use, click Save Settings and name your settings before applying the watermark content.
- ■ If you do not want to apply the watermark to other files, click OK and Acrobat will insert the header and footer into your PDF.
- ■ Click OK and Acrobat will insert the watermark into your PDF.

Updating a Watermark

- ■ Updating applies to the most recently added watermark.
- ■ Open the PDF file containing the watermark and select Tools>Edit PDF. Select Watermark>Update from the Edit PDF toolset.
- ■ Change the settings as needed. Click OK and Acrobat will update the watermark.

Adding Another Watermark

- ■ Open the PDF file containing the watermark. Select Tools>Edit PDF. In the Edit PDF toolset, select Watermark>Add, and then click Add New in the message that appears.
- ■ Create your new watermark. Select any new formatting options. Click OK and Acrobat will add the additional watermark.

Replacing a Watermark

- ■ Replacing applies to the most recently added watermark.
- ■ Open the PDF file containing the watermark. Select Tools>Edit PDF. In the Edit PDF toolset, select Watermark>Add, and then click Replace Existing. Select your new formatting options. Click OK and Acrobat will replace the prior watermark with the new one.

Renumbering Pages (Figure 5-7 and Figure 5-8)

This section discusses renumbering the pages as they appear in Acrobat's page number display on the main toolbar, not renumbering the actual pages of the document. For example, you could renumber pages such as a table of contents with small roman numerals, such as i, ii, etc., and then renumber the content starting at page 1. Although this feature applies only to the numbering that displays on the toolbar, there are circumstances when this is helpful to readers.

By default, Acrobat numbers pages starting from page 1, regardless of whether those page numbers correspond with a document's actual page numbering. Users may modify how Acrobat numbers pages, however, using arabic numbers and roman numerals.

To renumber pages, open the Page Thumbnails view on the left panel.

From the dropdown menu, select Page Labels or right-click on a thumbnail and select Page Labels to display the Page Numbering dialog.

First, select the pages to renumber. You can renumber all pages, a range of pages, or those that you have selected in the Thumbnails pane.

Next, go to the Numbering section, and decide whether to create a new numbering section or to extend the numbering from the preceding section of your document. If you begin a new section, you will select the Style (how the page numbers appear, such as arabic numbers), any prefix to include with the numbers, and the starting number.

Click OK and Acrobat will apply the selected page numbering format.

Figure 5-7

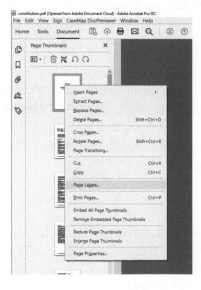

Figure 5-8

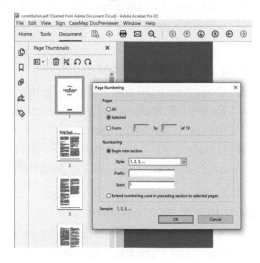

Chapter 6

OCRing (Converting PDFs to Make the Text Searchable) and Searching OCRed PDFs

Documents created directly from text-based programs, including Microsoft Word, Corel WordPerfect, and Microsoft Excel, are automatically searchable when Acrobat or other PDF conversion programs create a PDF from the source file. Although some scanners can make the text searchable while scanning, most do not, which means you can see the letters on the pages but cannot search for them as you would in Word, WordPerfect, or other programs. The solution is called OCR (optical character recognition).

OCR is a technology that converts different types of documents, such as scanned paper documents, PDF files, or images captured by a digital camera, into editable and searchable data. For example, imagine that you have scanned a contract that a client has provided for your review. You scan it, but all the scanner does is create an image or picture of the document. To be able to search the actual text within the picture, you need OCR software that can analyze the letters on the image and convert them into words, permitting users to search the content of the document.

The quality of the results of searching an OCRed document depends upon the quality of the image itself and the quality of the software performing the OCR process, often known as the OCR engine. The ability to OCR—that is, to make images into searchable text—is one of Acrobat's most important features for legal professionals and is an essential part of a paperless practice. Acrobat's OCR quality continues to improve as Adobe releases updates.

OCRing converts scanned images into a format in which you can search within or for specific documents using a keyword or phrase. For example, you could effortlessly search hundreds of contracts and locate a specific name or provision in moments without having to read through extensive files. Acrobat can search for a word, a word pattern, or multiple words and do so in one or many documents, including documents in different folders or locations on your computer or in your office's network, in virtually the amount of time it takes to type the phrase and click your mouse.

OCR is the process by which a program such as Acrobat analyzes the pattern of pixels in an image and searches for letters or numbers that are the "same" as the images. Acrobat then replaces portions of the image with characters and identifies characters that may have been analyzed incorrectly. This conversion of an image into machine-encoded text is the crucial first step in the process of converting scanned images into searchable, annotatable documents. Advances in Acrobat's OCR capabilities have greatly improved the quality of the results, although poor-quality copies, distorted text, and stray marks can lead to less than satisfactory results. Fortunately, with Acrobat DC, the process has improved, and Acrobat DC offers users the ability to edit the underlying OCR text.

Determining If a Document Has Been OCRed

Checking Manually for Text

- If you look at text in a document and search for a visible word using the Find command at Edit>Find (Ctrl+F for Windows or Cmd+F for Mac), the word should appear and be highlighted. If it does not, then the document has not been OCRed. Adobe notifies users if a document has not been OCRed with a dialog box called "No searchable text," from which you can with one click begin to OCR the document (Figure 6-1).

Figure 6-1

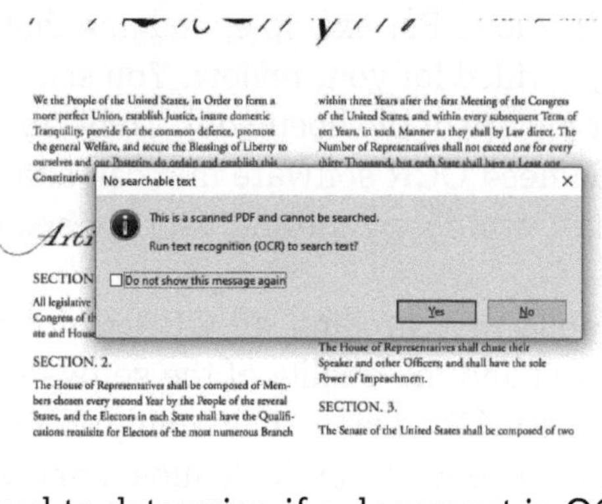

- Another method to determine if a document is OCRed is to use the Accessibility Check. To run the Accessibility Check, go to the Accessibility tool and select Accessibility Check. Verify that Create Accessibility Report is checked. Uncheck all of the other options except "Document is not image-only PDF." Click the Start Checking button. The report displays on the left of your screen. Expand the Document section. If the PDF is not OCRed, the second line will have a green check and state, "Image-only PDF—Passed." If it passes, the document is not OCRed and you should begin the OCR process (Figure 6-2).

Figure 6-2

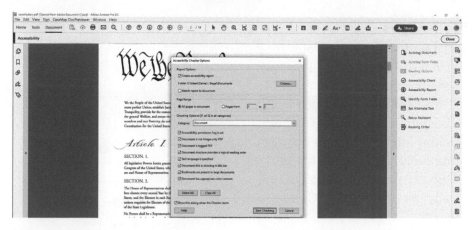

Making Scanned Text Editable and Searchable (OCRing It)

Go to the Tools pane, click on Scan & OCR, and choose Recognize Text. If you are in a file, the toolbar will open (Figure 6-3). If you are not in a file, you are prompted to either select a file, scan a document, or select text in multiple files. If you are in a file, you can select whether to OCR the currently open file or multiple files (Figure 6-4 and Figure 6-5).

Figure 6-3

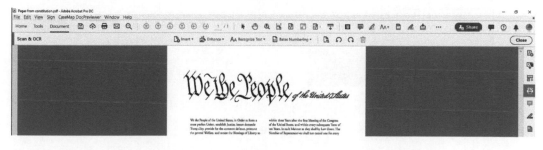

Figure 6-4

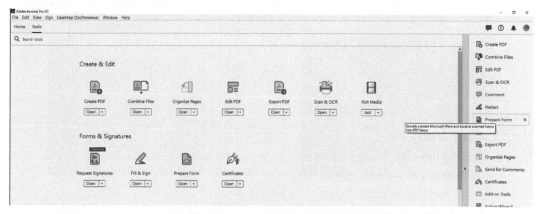

Figure 6-5

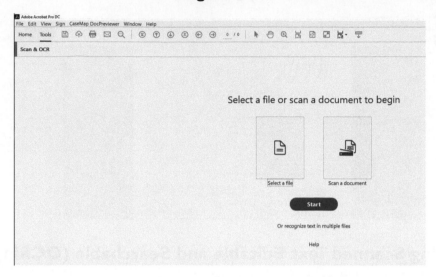

- If you select In This File (Figure 6-6), the Recognize setting bar will appear below the Scan & OCR tool on your screen. To change the existing settings before OCRing or to verify those settings, click on the Settings button (Figure 6-7).

Figure 6-6

Figure 6-7

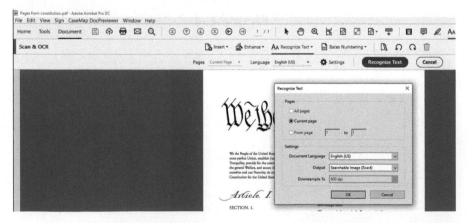

■ If you select In Multiple Files (Figure 6-8), Acrobat will display a dialog that allows you to Add Files (individually), Add Folders (scanning entire locations), or Add Open Files. You can use these options until all of the files you select are listed in the dialog box. If you selected any files in error, you can click Remove. Next click OK to continue.

Acrobat then asks where you want it to save the output (the OCRed files) and whether you want to keep the original file names or add information before or after the names. Finally, you can select whether to "Overwrite existing files" (save the OCRed file in place of the original). When you select OK, the Recognize Text dialog appears.

Figure 6-8

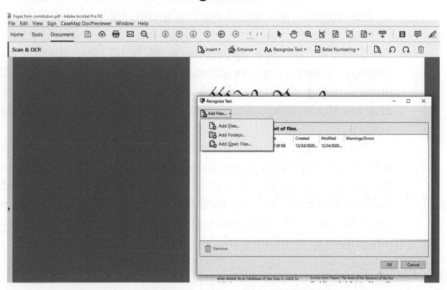

■ **General Settings: Why It Is Crucial for Attorneys to Review the OCR Output Setting**
  ❖ There are three settings for Recognize Text. The Document Language setting allows users to specify the document's native language, and the Downsample To setting specifies the quality of the output. Generally, users do not change the default settings of English and 600 dpi (the standard printer quality setting, which is acceptable for most PDFs).
  ❖ **The Output Setting Is Crucial**
    ◆ There are three Output styles (Figure 6-9):
      ı Searchable Image: This setting will "tweak" the image by deskewing it so that the document appears plumb and true. It also recognizes images, recognizes text and places an invisible text layer on top, and discards whitespace. This means that an OCRed image may appear differently from the non-OCRed version.

Figure 6-9

- Searchable Image (Exact): This setting does not "tweak" the image or discard whitespace, which means the image displays exactly the same after it is OCRed. Thus, the OCRed version of a document looks identical to the non-OCRed version.

- Editable Text and Images: Called "ClearScan" in previous versions of Acrobat, this Output style replaces every character with an outline character; that is, Acrobat creates a custom font to match the appearance of the pixels. However, this output style could replace a zero (0) with an O or a one (1) with an l.

♦ **To ensure that the appearance of legal documents does not change in any way, we strongly recommend scanning all documents using the Searchable Image (Exact) setting. Once you change the setting, Acrobat will remember it for all future OCR output.**

NOTE: While Acrobat is running the OCR, it cannot do anything else. Thus, if you try to open a second PDF file, it will not open until the OCR is complete. If you have a very large file that needs to be OCRed and need to keep working with other PDFs, we suggest that you run the OCR when you can give Acrobat time to complete it and not hinder your other work.

Editing OCR Text

Acrobat DC includes a feature that allows users to look "behind the visible text" and edit the OCRed content to correct any mistakes made by Acrobat when it OCRed the document. By using the following procedure, you can correct those OCR errors, that is, when Acrobat mistakenly identifies characters:

- Open the document.
- Open the Scan & OCR tool, and view the Scan & OCR toolset.
- Click the Recognize Text dropdown menu, and select Correct Recognized Text (Figure 6-10).

Figure 6-10

- The secondary toolset appears.
- Acrobat highlights suspected OCR errors and advises you that if any possible "suspects" have been located, they are highlighted (Figure 6-11).

Figure 6-11

- You may select an error. Click Accept if the result is correct. If the result is incorrect, click into the field and type the correct text (it will appear in the "recognized as" box on the toolset). Click Accept (Figure 6-12).

Figure 6-12

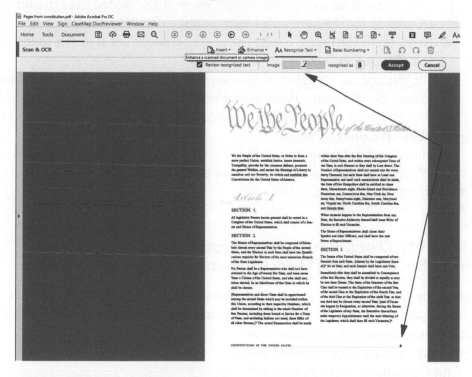

- Alternatively, you may select the Review recognized text checkbox, and Acrobat will begin the review process at the first suspected error in the document.
- Review any other errors using the same process.
- Click Close to finish.

What If a Document Cannot Be OCRed? (Undocumented Solution)

There are times when the security settings of a document prohibit users from OCRing the file. If you need to have an OCRed version of the file, your first inclination may be to print the document, scan it, and then OCR it. That solution will work, but it takes time and, potentially, a lot of paper. Another solution that *may* work, depending on the document's security settings, is to export it—convert it to another format (generally an image format)—and recreate it. Here's how:

- Convert the PDF to JPEG (or other image) format and back, and rerun the OCR process. This process will work unless there are security settings that prevent exporting the document.
  - ❖ To do this, select File>Save As.
  - ❖ Go to File>Export to>Image>JPEG, and select the location on your computer where you want to export the document.
  - ❖ Name the output file and click on Save. Unless prohibited by the document's security settings, Acrobat will create a separate image file for each page of the document, with "_Page_XXX" added to each output file (X stands for the number of each page).
  - ❖ Next, go to the folder where the output files are located and select all of the output files.
  - ❖ Right-click on the selected files and select Combine Files in Acrobat.
  - ❖ When the Combine Files dialog appears, click on Options to confirm that the files will be combined into a single PDF. Click OK, and then click on Combine Files.
  - ❖ Name and save the output file.
  - ❖ When the combined files open as a PDF, run the Recognize Text command and proceed.

What If My Documents Are Mostly Handwritten and Cannot Be OCRed? (Undocumented Solution)

Acrobat cannot generally convert handwriting or poor-quality documents into searchable text. At times, you may be able to use the Correct Recognized Text command. However, when the document is of very poor quality, the handwriting cannot be OCRed, or an image cannot be OCRed, there is an alternative that permits users to search for the text.

Figure 6-13

- Open the Comment toolset (Figure 6-13).

- Click the Add Sticky Note tool (or click Ctrl+6 for Windows or Cmd+6 for Mac).
- Drag your cursor to the location in the document where the suspect text appears and click.
- A Comment dialog box will appear and display the name of the Acrobat user. In the box, type the correct text (Figure 6-14).

Figure 6-14

- Save the document.

To Locate the Additional Text

- Open the Find (Ctrl+F for Windows or Cmd+F for Mac) or Advanced Search (Ctrl+Shift+F for Windows or Cmd+Shift+F for Mac) dialog.
  - ❖ Using the Find dialog, type the desired text in the dialog box, click the gear icon in the search box and select "Include Comments," and then click Previous or Next (Figure 6-15). Your results should include the text in the comment box. Note that the comment box appears in the Comment panel on the right of the document.

Figure 6-15

  - ❖ Using the Advanced Search dialog, type the desired text in the dialog box, select "Include Comments," and then click Search. From this dialog, you can search within one or many documents by selecting "In the current document" or the "All PDF Documents in" dialog.

Searching PDF Documents

With Acrobat you can search for one or all instances of a word, phrase, or part of a word in OCRed documents in seconds. For example, you can run a simple search for one term in one file, or run a more advanced search looking for various words or phrases in one or more PDFs. In addition, when this feature is combined with Acrobat's editing feature, you can selectively replace text in the documents; only the Find toolbar (Edit>Find) includes the Replace With option, however.

You can run a search using either the Search window or the Find toolbar. In both cases, Acrobat will search the PDF, as well as form fields and digital signatures. You can also search within bookmarks and comments.

Searching Individual Documents

- Use the Find tool (Figure 6-16): To search for a word, phrase, or part of a word, go to Edit>Find (Ctrl+F for Windows or Cmd+F for Mac) and type in the word or phrase you want. Acrobat will find the word (or part of a word) or phrase and highlight it. In addition, the Find tool reports how many exact matches are in the document, and now provides the option of replacing the word you searched for with another word or phrase.

  By clicking Next, you can see the next instance of the word or phrase. By selecting the wheel adjacent to the word you searched for, you are presented with other options: Whole Words, Case Sensitive, Include Bookmarks, and Include Comments. Users may also choose Open Full Acrobat Search to use the Advanced Search tool.

Figure 6-16

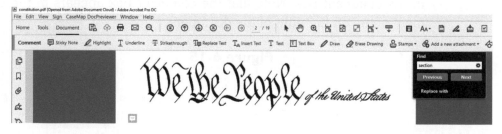

- Use the Advanced Search tool (Figure 6-17): This feature allows users to search the current opened document for a word or phrase and allows the search to be Case-Sensitive, to be limited to Whole words only, or to Include Bookmarks and Include Comments. When searching bookmarks and comments, Acrobat examines items in the Bookmarks and Comment panels. To assure accuracy, save the document before running a search so that all content is included within the results.

Figure 6-17

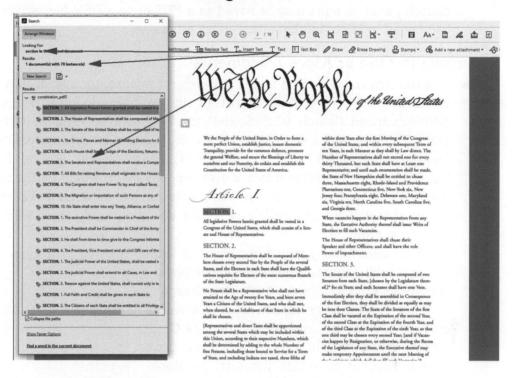

The Advanced Search also has an Arrange Windows button that rearranges your document and search windows so that you can see both clearly side by side. If you select the Show More Options dialog at the bottom of the Advanced Search window, you may include Proximity, Stemming, and Attachments.

A Proximity search looks for two or more words separated by no more than the specified number of words set in the Search preferences. This option is available only for a search of multiple documents or indexes and when Match All of the words is selected.

Stemming locates words that contain part (the stem) of a specified search word. For example, a search for "asking" will find instances of "ask," "asked," and "asks." This option applies to single words and phrases when you search the current PDF, a folder, or an index. You may not use wildcard characters (*, ?) in Stemming searches. Stemming is not available if either Whole Words Only or Case-Sensitive is selected.

When you select an Attachment search, Acrobat will search the current PDF or other attached PDFs (up to two levels deep).

The results will display below the dialog, with the search term appearing in bold typeface. Simply click on each result and Acrobat will display the result in whichever document it is located, with the search term highlighted.

You can save your results by clicking on the Save (diskette) icon on the Search panel. Results may be saved as a PDF or as a CSV file, which can be viewed in Microsoft Excel and other programs.

Searching in One or More Documents

■ Use the Advanced Search tool: To search for a word, phrase, or part of a word in your current document or in multiple documents, go to Edit>Advanced Search (Ctrl+Shift+F for Windows or Cmd+Shift+F for Mac). This displays a dialog that allows you to search in the current document or to search All PDF Documents in (1) My Documents, (2) Your Desktop, (3) Your PC, or (4) in a location you specify by browsing for the folder using Windows Explorer. The Advanced Search has an Arrange Windows button that will automatically arrange the document and search windows on your screen.

After determining which document or location you will search, type the word or phrase you are looking for (Figure 6-18). Searches may be Case-Sensitive, be limited to Whole words only, or Include Bookmarks and Include Comments. When searching bookmarks and comments, Acrobat examines items in the Bookmarks and Comment panels. To assure accuracy, save the document before running a search so that all content is included within the results.

Figure 6-18

If you select the Show More Options dialog at the bottom of the Advanced Search window, you may include Proximity, Stemming, and Attachments (Figure 6-19).

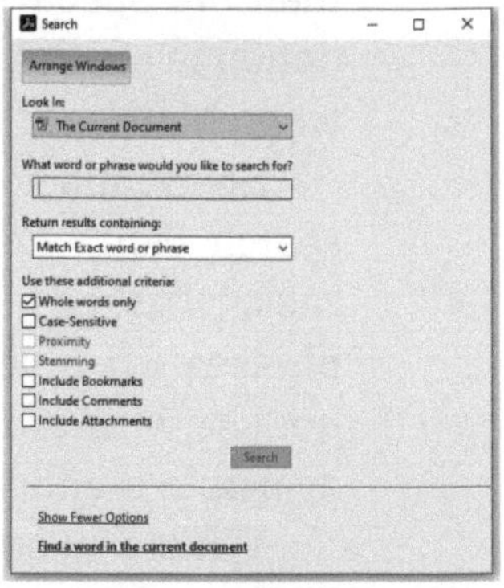

A Proximity search looks for two or more words separated by no more than the specified number of words set in the Search preferences. This option is available only for a search of multiple documents or indexes and when Match All of the words is selected.

Figure 6-19

Stemming locates words that contain part (the stem) of a specified search word. For example, a search for "asking" will find instances of "ask," "asked," and "asks." This option applies to single words and phrases when you search the current PDF, a folder, or an index. You may not use wildcard characters (*, ?) in Stemming searches. Stemming is not available if either Whole Words Only or Case-Sensitive is selected.

When you select an Attachment search, Acrobat will search the current PDF or other attached PDFs (up to two levels deep).

The results will display below the dialog, with the search term appearing in bold typeface. Simply click on each result and Acrobat will display the result in whichever document it is located, with the search term highlighted.

You can save your results by clicking on the Save (diskette) icon on the Search panel. Results may be saved as a PDF or as a CSV file, which can be viewed in Microsoft Excel and other programs.

Chapter 7

Editing and Displaying PDF Content

Editing Text in an Existing PDF

You can edit or delete the actual text in virtually any OCRed PDF file—unless the document's security settings prohibit it. (Document security is discussed in depth in Chapter 15.) Assuming you are able to make changes, you may either click on Edit PDF from the Tools pane (without a file open) (Figure 7-1) or open the PDF file and select Edit PDF from the Tools pane to begin editing the file (Figure 7-2). The Format pane opens on the right and the Edit PDF toolbar opens above, just below the main toolbar.

Figure 7-1

Figure 7-2

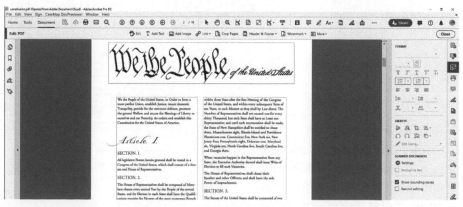

If the document you are opening is a scanned document that has not been OCRed, Acrobat DC will automatically run OCR to convert the document into an editable image (if you have "Recognize text" checked). Alternatively, if you have the feature unchecked (our recommended setting) (Figure 7-3), or the document is already OCRed, you must begin the OCR process manually, as described in Chapter 6.

Figure 7-3

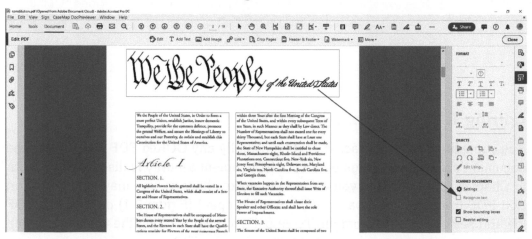

Once the document is OCRed, you will see boxes around any text that can be edited (Figure 7-4). Select Edit from the toolbar, place your cursor in the document, and begin typing as you would in any word processing file. You can also delete any text by either backspacing over the text or, if you want to delete an entire box, selecting the box and pressing the Delete key.

Figure 7-4

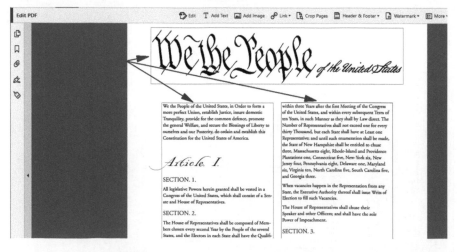

Acrobat will automatically attempt to match the fonts in the original document and will "reflow" the paragraph. When your changes are complete, be sure to save your file.

Replacing Multiple Occurrences of Text in an Existing PDF (Figure 7-5)

■ Acrobat DC contains a Find and Replace feature that is similar to the one available in word processing programs. To use this tool, open your PDF file and select Edit>Find from the main menu. Type the text you wish to find in the Find box. When you choose the dropdown arrow for Replace With, Acrobat will OCR the page. When it is complete, you will see boxes around any text that is able to be edited. Type the replacement text you wish to use in the "Replace with" box and select Replace. Adobe will then highlight the next instance of the text you wish to find, and you can choose either Replace Next to make the replacement or Next to skip it. When your changes are complete, be sure to save your file.

Figure 7-5

Adding Text in an Existing PDF (Formerly Known as the Typewriter Tool)

You can add text to virtually any PDF file, unless the document's security settings prohibit it. Assuming you are allowed to make changes, to add text to the existing text, open the PDF file and select Tools>Edit PDF from the Tools pane. The Format pane opens on the right and the Edit PDF toolbar opens above, just below the main toolbar.

If the document you are opening is a scanned document that has not been OCRed, Acrobat DC will automatically run OCR to convert the document into an editable image (if you have "Recognize text" checked). Alternatively, if you have the feature unchecked (our recommended setting), or the document is already OCRed, you must begin the OCR process manually, as described in Chapter 6.

Once the document is OCRed, you will see boxes around any text that is able to be edited. Select Add Text from the toolbar (Figure 7-6). Because you are not attempting to edit any existing text with this tool, the boxes disappear, allowing you to begin typing wherever you wish. Place your cursor in the document and begin typing as you would in any word processing file. The text you are typing appears in a text box that Acrobat creates as you type.

The default font used by Acrobat is Minion Pro in 12 points. If you want to choose a different font type and/or size, highlight the text, and in the Format pane, you can choose from any number of fonts and sizes. Acrobat also provides standard text formatting options such as bold, italics, underline, superscript, text alignment, line spacing, and paragraph spacing.

When your changes are complete, be sure to save your file.

Figure 7-6

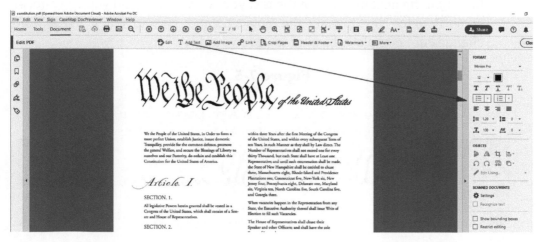

Editing, Adding, and Replacing Images in an Existing PDF

Acrobat DC allows you to make simple changes to images in a PDF file, such as replacing images, adding images, or making adjustments to the position or size of existing images.

Adding Images

■ To add an image to your document, open the PDF file and select Edit PDF from the Tools pane. The Format pane opens on the right and the Edit PDF toolbar opens above, just below the main toolbar.

If the document you are opening is a scanned document that has not been OCRed, Acrobat DC will automatically run OCR to convert the document into an editable image (if you have "Recognize text" checked). Alternatively, if you have the feature unchecked (our recommended setting), or the document is already OCRed, you must begin the OCR process manually, as described in Chapter 6.

Once the document is OCRed, you will see boxes around any text that is able to be edited. Select Add Image from the Edit PDF toolbar. A Windows File Explorer or Mac Finder box opens where you can choose the image you wish to insert (Figure 7-7). Select Open and a thumbnail of the image appears with your mouse pointer. Left-click where you want the image to appear in your document. You can move the image by selecting it and dragging it around the page. Shift-dragging the image constrains its movement up or down or left or right. The image can also be resized by dragging the sizing handles (the small boxes) that appear around the image. Remember, to keep the image's original aspect ratio, shift-drag the sizing handles! If you do not retain these settings, the document will not display correctly; that is, its proportions will be distorted (Figure 7-8).

Figure 7-7

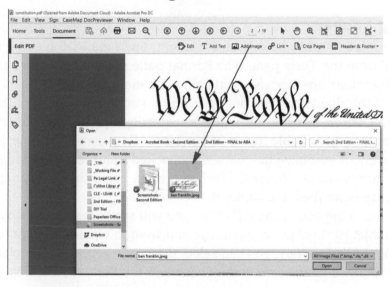

Figure 7-8

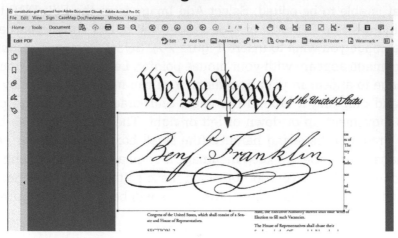

Replacing Images

■ To replace an image in your document, open the PDF file and select Edit PDF from the Tools pane. The Format pane opens on the right and the Edit PDF toolbar opens above, just below the main toolbar.

If the document you are opening is a scanned document that has not been OCRed, Acrobat DC will automatically run OCR to convert the document into an editable image (if you have "Recognize text" checked). Alternatively, if you have the feature unchecked (our recommended setting), or the document is already OCRed, you must begin the OCR process manually, as described in Chapter 6.

Once the document is OCRed, you will see boxes around any text that's editable. Right-click on the image you wish to replace and choose Replace Image. Alternatively, you can select the image you wish to replace and use the Replace Image icon under Objects in the Format pane (Figure 7-9).

Figure 7-9

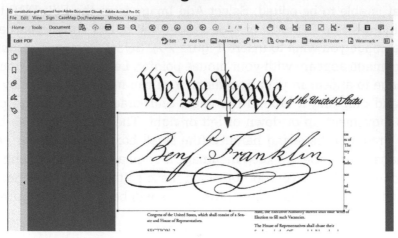

A Windows File Explorer or Mac Finder box opens where you can choose the new image. Select Open and the existing image is replaced with the new one.

Editing Images

■ Acrobat is not an image-editing application like Photoshop, but you can make simple changes to images to enhance the look of your PDF file. If you desire to use other image-editing tools, you can right-click on the image and select Edit Using> and choose the tool you want. Alternatively, Acrobat includes tools for making changes, which are also found by selecting the image and then right-clicking on the image, after which a dialog displays adjacent to the image, containing the following tools, some of which only display in certain circumstances (Figure 7-10):

Figure 7-10

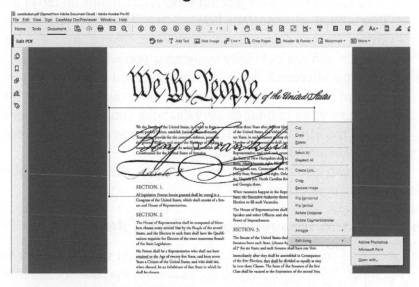

❖ **Cut:** This deletes the image and allows you to paste it in a different location in the document.

❖ **Copy:** This copies the image and allows you to paste it in a different location in the document.

❖ **Delete:** This removes the image from the file.

❖ **Select All:** This command selects all items on the page.

❖ **Deselect All:** This command deselects all items on the page.

❖ **Create Link:** This creates a dialog that allows you to create a link (click on) from the items to a page, a different file, or a web page.

❖ **Crop:** When selected, the image handles change from small boxes to corners and lines. You can drag these handles to crop the image.

❖ **Replace Image:** This allows you to replace an existing image with another image. This has been already discussed fully in "Replacing Images" earlier.

❖ **Flip Horizontal:** This flips the image horizontally on the vertical axis.

❖ **Flip Vertical:** This flips the image vertically on the horizontal axis (essentially turns the image upside down).

❖ **Rotate Counterclockwise and Rotate Clockwise:** These rotate the image 90 degrees in the selected direction.

❖ **Align Objects:** This aligns multiple images in the document. Select the images you wish to align by Ctrl-clicking them, and then choose Align Left, Align Right, Align Top, or Align Bottom. There are also options for Align Vertical Center and Align Horizontal Center, but you will likely never need these.

❖ **Arrange Objects:** This option allows you to move an image in front of or behind text or other images.

♦ **Bring to Front:** This will place the image on top of any text or images.

♦ **Send to Back:** This will place the image behind any text or images. This can be useful for placing a signature image on top of a signature line without covering the line.

♦ **Bring Forward and Send Backward:** These are used for stacked images and are not likely something you will need to use.

❖ **Edit Using Microsoft Paint** (or other installed applications you have on your computer): You can use Paint or other applications to make more substantive edits to images. Any changes you make will appear and be saved in the PDF file only. The original image where it is stored on your computer remains unchanged.

You can also right-click on an object to find the same options.

Copying Text and Images from a PDF File

There are many reasons to copy text from a PDF file for use in another document, such as in Microsoft Word. It is easy to do, assuming that the document's security settings do not prohibit it. Also, you may wish to copy an image from a PDF file. To select the text or image you wish to copy, the PDF file needs to be OCRed. If your document's security settings do not permit you to OCR, see "What If a Document Cannot Be OCRed? (Undocumented Solution)" for an undocumented solution to this problem.

■ **Copying Text**

❖ In order to copy text from a PDF file, open your PDF file. If the file is already OCRed, you will be able to see this when you try to select text. In an OCRed file, when you attempt to select text, the mouse pointer will become a vertical line (Figure 7-11). This line can be dragged along the text. In a non-OCRed file, when you are attempting to select text, the mouse pointer becomes a cross hair (Figure 7-12) that will draw a box around the text you are attempting to select.

Figure 7-11

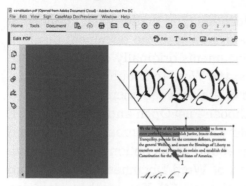

Figure 7-12

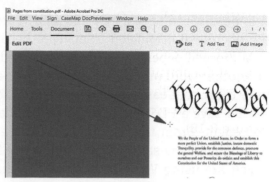

* If you need to OCR your document, go to the Tools pane, click on Scan & OCR, and then choose Recognize Text. You can select whether to OCR the currently open file or multiple files.

* Once your document is OCRed, you can drag your mouse pointer along the text you want to copy, right-click, and select either Copy or Copy with Formatting. Generally, if you are copying for use in a word processing file, Copy is sufficient, as you would want to use your word processor's built-in Paste options.

■ **Copying Images**

* To copy an image, select the image, and then right-click and select Copy (Figure 7-13). It will be pasted to your clipboard. You can then use the Paste feature of Acrobat, Word, or your other application and paste the image into your document. For example, you could insert a picture of an accident scene into a brief, rather than referring the reader to an exhibit.

Figure 7-13

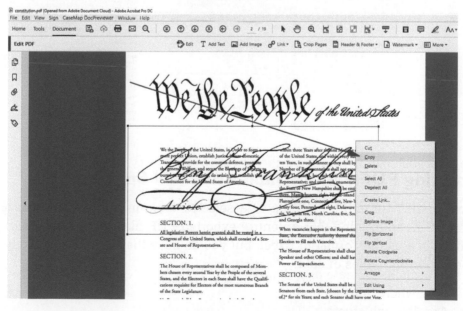

Saving PDF Files as Word Documents

It is possible to save a PDF file as a Word document, no matter what application the document originated from. That being said, how well the document displays in Word will depend on how it originated. Documents originally created in Word or another word processing program will export to Word in a much cleaner format than those that came from other applications or are scanned documents.

To save a PDF file to Word, in Acrobat choose File>Open and open your PDF document. From the main menu, choose File>Export To>Microsoft Word>Word Document. This saves the file to a .docx format and is the option generally used. If you are using Word 2003 or earlier, instead of Word Document, choose Word 97-2003 Document, which will save a .doc file (Figure 7-14). You are then prompted to name and save your file in your preferred location. Word will open your document automatically as long as you have the View Result check box ticked under the Save as type dialog box.

Alternatively, open the PDF and choose Export PDF from the Tools pane. Here you are given the option to export your file to Microsoft Word in either the .docx or .doc format. Click the Export button to complete the process.

Figure 7-14

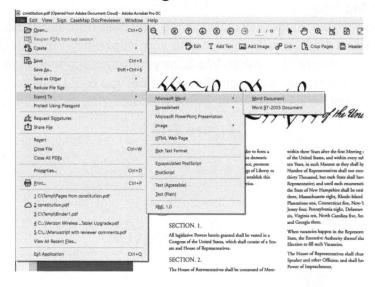

Extracting PDF Files or Tables to Excel Spreadsheets

You can export an entire PDF file or a selected table in a PDF file as an Excel worksheet. Keep in mind that an entire exported PDF file will not necessarily be formatted in a usable format in Excel, but you do have the ability. Most likely, you will be exporting tables of data.

Exporting a Table to Excel

To export a table, in Acrobat choose File>Open and open your PDF document. In order to select the table, drag your mouse around the table so that the entire table is selected. Right-click the selected table and choose Export Selection As. In the Export Selection As dialog box, choose Excel Workbook from the Save as type dropdown menu. Name the file and save it to your desired location, and click Save. Excel will open your document automatically as long as you have the View Result check box ticked under the Save as type dialog box.

Exporting an Entire PDF File to Excel

If you do want to export an entire PDF file to an Excel spreadsheet, in Acrobat choose File>Open and open your PDF document. From the main menu, choose File>Export To>Spreadsheet>Microsoft Excel Workbook (Figure 7-15). This saves the file to an .xlsx format. The Windows File Explorer window opens and allows you to navigate to the folder where you want to save your file. Name the file and click Save. Excel will open your document automatically as long as you have the View Result check box ticked under the Save as type dialog box.

Alternatively, open the PDF and choose Export PDF from the Tools pane. Here you are given the option to export your file to Spreadsheet. Click the Export button to complete the process.

Figure 7-15

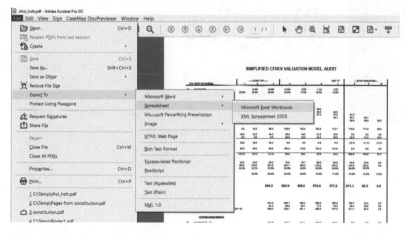

Creating and Managing Links

Links are a method of letting you move to specific locations within your PDF document, to other electronic documents including attachments to your PDF, or to websites. Using links allows a reader of a PDF file to move around easily and to have immediate access to information referenced in the PDF when it comes from an outside source. Thus, you can create a link to an exhibit in a contract, to an online location where a reader can view the original version of a decision, and so on.

Creating Links

When you add links to a PDF, you allow users to go from either text or an image in the document to another place, such as a web page. For example, you could add a link that would take the reader to a court opinion, statute or regulation, or other item relevant to the matter. If you are filing the document in a court that allows e-briefs, you could (or might be required to) link your document with the source documents.

■ To create a link in a PDF document, select the text or area of the document you want to link to (Figure 7-16), right-click on the selected text or area, and select Create Link (Figure 7-17). If you want to link to an image, right-click on the image and select Create Link. In either instance, the Create Link dialog opens and you can choose options for your link's appearance, such as whether the link is visible or highlighted, what color it is highlighted in, etc. (Figure 7-18) This is also where you will specify the Link Action:

Figure 7-16

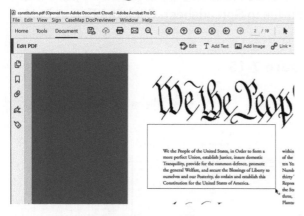

Figure 7-17

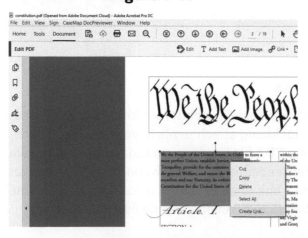

Figure 7-18

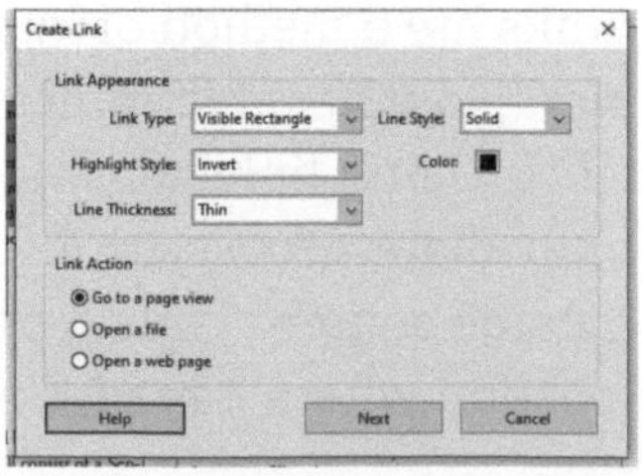

❖ **Go to a Page View:** Click Next and the Create Go to View dialog box opens. Here, you are instructed to use your mouse or scroll bars to navigate to the page where you want to set the link destination (Figure 7-19). The destination can be within the current document or in a file attachment. Navigate to the desired location and click Set Link when you are done. To test your link, select the Hand Tool.

Figure 7-19

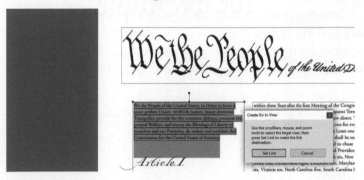

❖ **Open a File:** Select the destination file from the Windows File Explorer or Mac Finder window and click Open (Figure 7-20). If the file is a PDF, the Specify Open Preference dialog opens, where you can specify how the document should open (for example, in a new window or within an existing window). Click OK. To test your link, select the Hand tool.

Figure 7-20

❖ **Open a Web Page:** In the Edit URL dialog box, type the URL of the destination web page and click OK (Figure 7-21). To test your link, select the Hand tool.

Figure 7-21

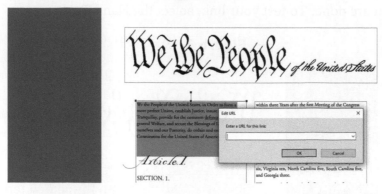

Managing Links

■ **Editing Links:** Once a link is created, you can move, resize, or change the appearance of the link, edit the link action, or delete the link by right-clicking on the linked area or image (Figure 7-22).

Figure 7-22

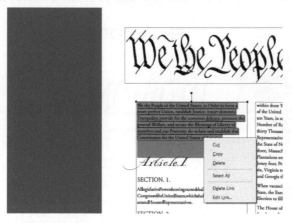

❖ **Move or Resize a Link:** Select the linked image. Place the mouse pointer over the link rectangle and the handles will appear. To move the link rectangle, drag it to the new location. To resize the link rectangle, drag one or more of the boxes that appear in the corners and the middle of each side when you click your mouse into the link box.

❖ **Change the Appearance of a Link:** Select the linked image or text, right-click, and select Edit Link. Place the mouse pointer over the link rectangle and the handles will appear. Double-click the link rectangle. In the Appearance tab of the Link Properties dialog box, you can modify the color, line thickness, visibility, etc.

❖ **Edit the Link Action:** Select the linked image or text, right-click, and select Edit Link. In the Actions tab of the Link Properties dialog box, select the listed action you want to change, and click Edit.

❖ **Delete a Link:** Select the linked image or text. Either use the Delete key or right-click and select Delete from the menu.

Adding Multimedia Files to a PDF

You can easily add audio or video files to your PDF. These files can be added directly to the PDF or linked to files on the Internet. Acrobat Professional DC supports the following multimedia types: mov, M4V, 3GP, mp3, and mp4.

To add a multimedia file, open the PDF. Choose Edit>Manage Tools, or click on Tools and select Rich Media (Figure 7-23). Acrobat then displays all of the available tools. From the Rich Media toolbar, select the Add Video, the Add Sound, or the Add SWF tool and drag it to the location where you want it. You can also choose Select Object from the toolbar and select an object in a document to which you want to add multimedia.

Figure 7-23

After you select where to locate the multimedia item, drag your mouse pointer or double-click an area where you want the sound or video to appear. The Insert dialog box opens, where you can browse to find the file you want to insert or type the URL of the Internet location of the file.

By selecting Show Advanced Options, you can specify when the content is enabled or disabled, how it is played back, etc. Choose OK when you are done.

Exporting PDF Content to Use in a PowerPoint Presentation

Acrobat DC allows you to export a PDF file to Microsoft PowerPoint. Each page of the PDF becomes its own slide that is editable, while keeping as much of the original formatting and layout as possible. From the main menu, choose File>Export To>Microsoft PowerPoint Presentation (Figure 7-24).

Figure 7-23

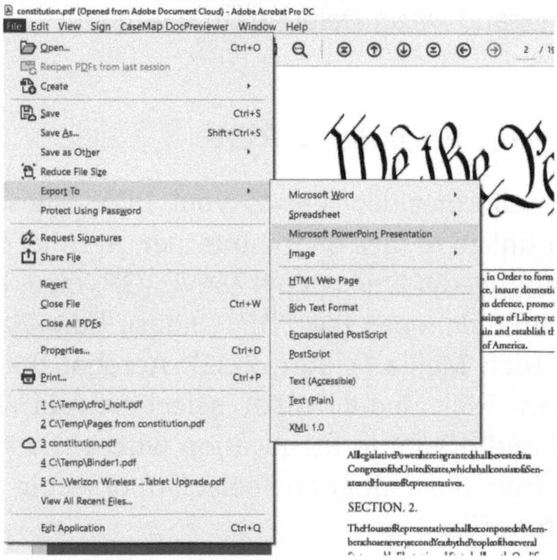

The Windows File Explorer or Mac Finder window opens and allows you to navigate to the folder where you want to save your file. You should note the Settings button under the Save as dialog. The Settings will allow you to either include Comments in your export or not, and to run Text Recognition or not. Name the file and click Save. PowerPoint will open your document automatically as long as you have the View Result check box ticked under the Save as dialog box.

Alternatively, open the PDF and choose Export PDF from the Tools pane. Here you are given the option to export your file to Microsoft PowerPoint. You should note the Settings icon next to PowerPoint presentation. The Settings will allow you to either include Comments in your export or not, and to run Text Recognition or not. Click the Export button to complete the process.

Chapter 8

Adding and Working with Comments

Adding Comments

Adding comments to a PDF file can be useful, whether you are adding comments as notes for yourself while reading or as part of a collaborative effort with a team. In either case, adding comments to a PDF document is relatively easy. You will be able to add comments to any PDF document as long as the security settings do not prohibit it. To begin, open your PDF document and select Comment from the Tools pane (Figure 8-1).

Figure 8-1

The Comment toolbar will open at the top of your document. Acrobat offers commenting tools similar to the physical tools you are already familiar with, such as sticky notes and highlighting, but there are also a number of other tools.

There are additional features on the Comment toolbar. One is the Push Pin, which becomes active when you select the pin to either keep the tool selected or disengage it. When active, your comment settings will remain unchanged for subsequent comments until you disengage it. In addition, for comments that use color, such as the Highlight Text tool, there is a solid colored circle on the Comment toolbar, from which you can quickly select the color in which the Comment type selected will appear. This color will remain the preferred color until you change it (Figure 8-2).

Figure 8-2

If your comments contain an "@" symbol, Acrobat will invite any user named after the symbol to view the file after it is uploaded to the Adobe Document Cloud (Figure 8-3).

Figure 8-3

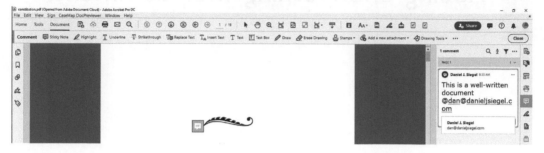

The Commenting Tools

- **Sticky Note Tool:** This tool creates sticky notes just as you would with paper documents. Click where you want the note to appear and type. You will notice that the note contains the author's name (the name listed in your Preferences—for Windows, Edit>Preferences>Identity, or for Mac, Acrobat Pro DC>Preferences>Identity) as well as the date and time the comment was made. In the right top corner are three ellipses that display additional options for the comment, including Copy Text, Edit, Delete, Set Status, Properties, and Add Checkmark. The Set Status function allows users to change the status of the comment to None, Accepted, Cancelled, Completed, or Rejected (Figure 8-4). The Add Checkmark option allows users to place a checkmark in the box, such as to demonstrate when it has been reviewed.

Figure 8-4

- **Highlight Text Tool:** This tool acts like a highlighter pen. You can select specific text to highlight, and you can draw anywhere on the page. By double-clicking the highlight, you can add a comment to it (Figure 8-5).

Figure 8-5

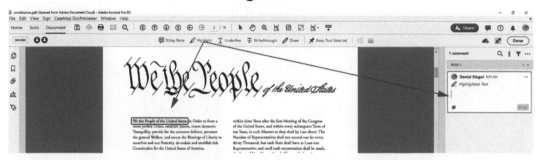

- **Underline Tool:** This tool marks text that should be underlined. This tool will only work on a PDF that has been OCRed. If you use the Underline tool on un-OCRed text, Adobe will ask you if you want to OCR the document. By double-clicking the underline, you can add a comment to it (Figure 8-6).

Figure 8-6

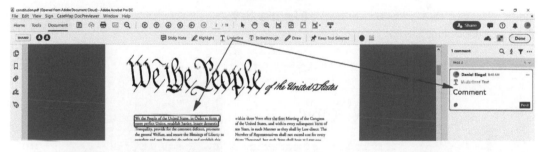

- **Strikethrough Tool:** This tool marks text that should be deleted. This tool will only work on a PDF that has been OCRed. If you use the Strikethrough tool on un-OCRed text, Adobe will ask you if you want to OCR the document. By double-clicking the strikethrough text, you can add a comment to it (Figure 8-7).

Figure 8-7

■ **Replace Text Tool:** This tool marks text to be removed and specifies what text should replace it. This tool will only work on a PDF that has been OCRed. If you use the Replace Text tool on un-OCRed text, Adobe will ask you if you want to OCR the document (Figure 8-8).

Figure 8-8

■ **Insert Text Tool:** This tool indicates where text needs to be added at the insertion point and what text should be inserted. This tool will only work on a PDF that has been OCRed. If you use the Insert Text tool on un-OCRed text, Adobe will ask you if you want to OCR the document (Figure 8-9).

Figure 8-9

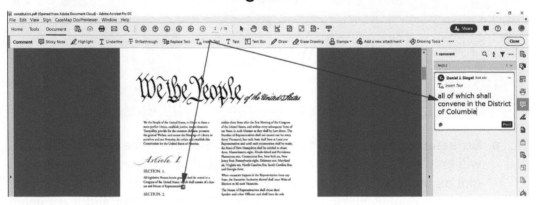

- **Add Text Comment Tool:** This tool allows you to type text that will appear directly on the page just as if you were editing the document. Unlike using the Edit PDF tool, this comment will not change the document (Figure 8-10).

Figure 8-10

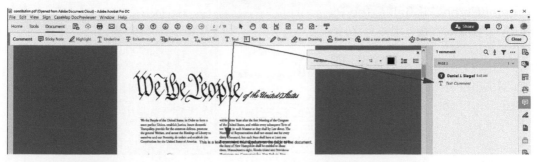

- **Text Box Tool:** This tool allows you to create a text box that you can type in anywhere on the page. Select the tool and drag your cursor to create a box where you can insert your text (Figure 8-11). This box will remain visible on the page.

Figure 8-11

- **Pencil Tool (Draw Free Form):** This tool allows you to draw free-form lines and shapes. You can use this tool to circle text or otherwise indicate any areas of text you wish to highlight (Figure 8-12).

Figure 8-12

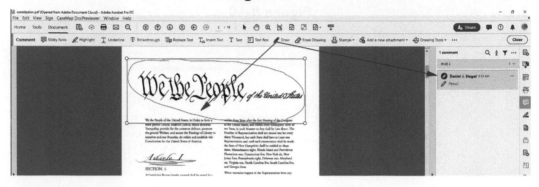

- **Eraser Tool:** This tool allows you to erase any drawing on the page.
- **Stamp Tool:** This tool acts as an electronic rubber stamp, stamping Approved, Draft, Confidential, Sign Here, Witness, etc. You can also create custom rubber stamps (Figure 8-13).

Figure 8-13

- **Attach File Tool:** This tool allows you to attach a file to the PDF or to Record Audio to attach to the file (Figure 8-14).

Figure 8-14

- **Drawing Tool:** This tool is similar to the Pencil tool, but it allows you to draw straight lines as well as exact shapes such as arrows, rectangles, and ovals (Figure 8-15).

Figure 8-15

Reviewing Comments

A list of all comments added to the document is shown in the Comments pane on the right (Figure 8-16). As you review a comment, you can add a checkmark to it to indicate that you have reviewed that comment or replied to it, or for any other reason that is appropriate for you. You can also reply to the comment by typing a reply in the Type your reply dialog box.

Figure 8-16

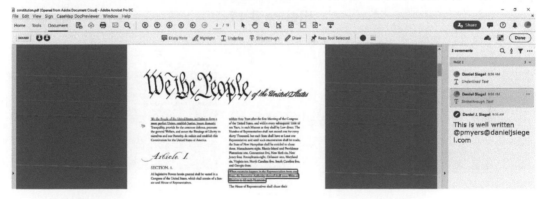

- **Sorting Comments:** By default, the comments are listed in the order they appear in the PDF. You can sort the comments by Page, Author, Date, Type, Status, and Color by using the Sort button in the Comments pane.
- **Filtering Comments:** You can filter the comments by Reviewer, Type, Status, and Color by using the Filter button in the Comments pane.
- **Deleting Comments:** You can delete a comment either by highlighting the comment on the PDF and using the Delete key or by right-clicking on the comment in the Comments pane and selecting Delete.
- **Searching Comments:** You can search the comments by typing a word or phrase in the Search box in the Comments pane.

- **Setting Status of Comments:** You can mark a comment's status as None, Accepted, Cancelled, Completed, or Rejected by right-clicking on the comment in the Comments pane.
- **Options Menu:** You can expand or collapse the comments in the Comments pane by using the Options menu, which is displayed next to the Sort and Filter icons above the comments list (displayed as "...").

Changing the Appearance of Comments

You can change the appearance of your comments by right-clicking on the comment either on the PDF or in the Comments pane and selecting from the available options. The Properties dialog box allows you to change things such as color and opacity as well as the way your name appears.

Summarizing Comments

You can prepare a summary of the comments from the Options menu, which is displayed next to the Sort and Filter icons above the comments list. The Options menu allows you to Create a Comment Summary or Print with Comment Summary, which will print the document with the comments visible (Figure 8-17).

Figure 8-17

When you choose Create a Comment Summary, you are given various options for how much information is displayed. In the Create a Comment Summary dialog box, you can choose among various layouts that either do or do not include the original document. For example, you can choose to print Comments Only, or the document with the comments printed as a list on a separate page. You can also choose how to sort the comments and whether to print pages with no comments (Figure 8-18).

Figure 8-18

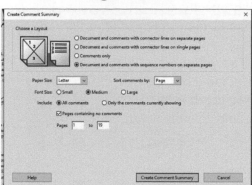

Review Process

Using the Acrobat Word Round Trip (a Great Way to Send a Document to One or More People for Review)

There are many ways to send a document to another person for review. Many attorneys prefer not to send Word documents to another attorney because they are concerned about relying on Track Changes in the event the other attorney makes changes that do not appear in the returned document. Acrobat has many options to avoid this concern. Among the easiest is the Acrobat Word Round Trip, in which one party converts a Word document into a PDF and sends it to another person (who only needs the free Acrobat Reader), who adds any proposed changes or comments and returns the document to the sender. When the sender receives the PDF with the proposed revisions, he or she can open the PDF in Word and review the suggestions using Track Changes. Here is how to do it.

- **Windows:** Open a document in Microsoft Word. Go to the Acrobat tab on the ribbon bar. In the Review and Comment section, click on Create and Send for Review. You can also do this by using the Send for Comments tool. Acrobat opens an Explorer window. Name and save the document (as a PDF) in your desired location.
- Acrobat will create a PDF of your document.
- After the document opens in Acrobat, it will display the "share your file" dialog (Figure 8-19). By default, Invite People is chosen. Enter the email addresses of the recipients to whom you are sending the document to review. A message is already included, which may be modified.

Figure 8-19

- Acrobat will then upload the document to the Acrobat cloud and send a link to the recipient to use to add comments, etc. The recipient may also download the document.
- When you reopen the document, it will notify you that the recipient has proposed revisions or included comments, which you may accept or reject.
- **Mac:** Open a document in Microsoft Word. On the Home tab on the ribbon bar, choose Create and Share Adobe PDF. Acrobat will open a Save window where you can name your PDF document and decide where to save it.
- Acrobat will create a PDF of your document.

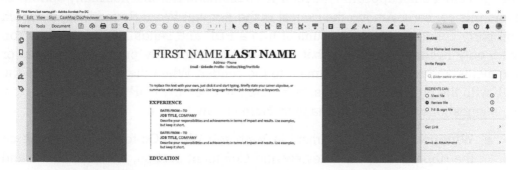

- After the document opens in Acrobat, it will display a Share with Others dialog where you enter email addresses of your recipients as well as a message, if you desire to add one.

- Acrobat will send a link to each recipient that they can use to add comments, etc. The recipient may also download the document.
- When you reopen the document, it will notify you that the recipient has proposed revisions or included comments.

Chapter 9

Creating an Index of One or More PDFs

An index is a searchable database of either one document or multiple documents. When you create an index of a document or group of documents, you will dramatically reduce the time necessary to locate words or phrases. For example, you could create an index of medical records, pleadings, etc. and search the index for keywords rather than opening every document or using the Search tool every time.

If you index one document, Acrobat embeds the index in the document, which means it will be included when you share the PDF with others. There are no extra steps required.

- Creating an Embedded Index (in One PDF)
    - ❖ With the document open in Acrobat DC, go to Tools>Index. (Figure 9-1) Acrobat will display the Index toolset. Click Manage Embedded Index, (Figure 9-2) and click Embed Index.

Figure 9-1

Figure 9-2

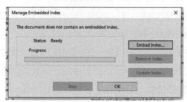

After saving the document (if it has not been saved), Acrobat will create the index and advise you that "The document contains a valid embedded index." Click OK and you are done. (Figure 9-3)

Figure 9-3

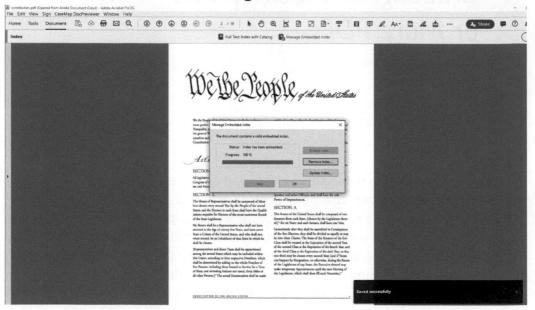

- Updating or Removing an Embedded Index in a PDF

Figure 9-4

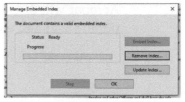

  - ❖ Go to Tools>Index, and view the Index toolset. Click Manage Embedded Index. (Figure 9-4) Select either Update Index or Remove Index, and follow the prompts. Updating an index is helpful if you correct OCRed content, or add or remove pages or content.

- **Indexing Multiple PDFs: Creating and Using a Full Text Index with Catalog Feature** (*this feature is only available in Acrobat Professional*)
  - ❖ You can include a group of PDFs in one "catalog" and create one index, which will be in a separate index (PDX extension) file, for all of the documents. By creating a catalog, users can search through multiple documents very quickly. If you share the documents with others, you can include the index with the PDFs.

    Catalogs may include the text of the documents, comments, bookmarks, form fields, tags, object and document metadata, attachments, document information, digital signatures, image XIF (extended image file format) metadata, and custom document properties.

❖ Creating an Index
  ◆ To create an index, save all of the documents you want to catalog in one or more folders/directories. You will be able to exclude sub-folders, but not individual files, that you do not want to index. If the files include scanned documents, they must be OCRed. You can also add information to a file's document properties to improve its searchability.
  ◆ When you create a new index, Acrobat creates a file with the .pdx extension and creates a new support folder, which contains one or more files with .idx extensions. The IDX files contain the index entries. Users who want to use the index must be able to access all of these files.
  ◆ Next, go to Tools>Index, and Acrobat will display the Index toolset. Click Full Text Index with Catalog, and you will see the Catalog dialog box. (Figure 9-5) Click New Index. Type the name of the index in the New Index Definition dialog box. Type a description of the index in the Index Description box. If necessary, click on Options to determine if you want to exclude words (in the Stop Words section) or numbers from the index or do not want Acrobat to prompt you for changed documents when searching.

Figure 9-5

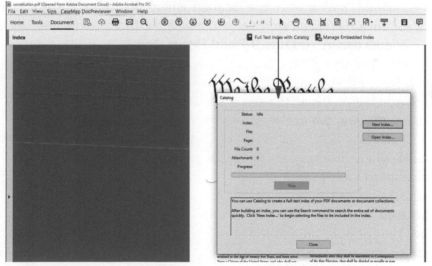

In the "Include these directories" box, click Add, select a folder containing the PDF files to include in the index, and click OK. (Figure 9-6) Repeat this step if you want to include more folders. By default, Acrobat includes all folders nested under an included folder in the index. You may include folders from multiple servers or disk drives,

Figure 9-6

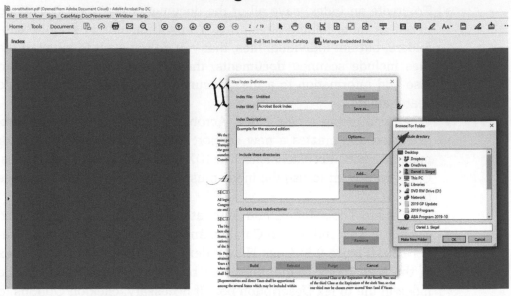

provided you do not intend to move the index or any items in the document collection. In the "Exclude these subdirectories" box, click Add to select any nested folder containing PDFs you want to exclude from the index. Click OK and repeat the process, as needed. Click Build, and specify the location where the index file will be created. Click Save, and Acrobat will create the index and state, "Index build successful." (Figure 9-7 and Figure 9-8)

Figure 9-7   **Figure 9-8**

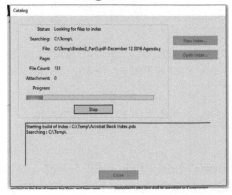

❖ Revising an Index
- ◆ You can update, rebuild, or purge/delete an existing index.
- ◆ Go to Tools>Index to view the Index toolset. Click Full Text Index with Catalog to view the Catalog dialog box. In the Catalog dialog box, click Open Index. Locate and select the index definition file (PDX) for the index, and click Open. Make any changes in the Index Definition dialog box, and then click the function you want Acrobat to perform:
  - ▪ **Build:** This function creates a new IDX file using the existing information and updates it by adding new entries and marking changed or outdated entries as invalid.
  - ▪ **Rebuild:** This function creates a new index by overwriting the existing index folder and its contents (the IDX files).
  - ▪ **Purge:** This function deletes the index contents (the IDX files) without deleting the index file itself (PDX).
- ◆ Changing Catalog Preferences
  - ▪ One benefit of this feature is the ability to apply your preferences to all indexes you build in the future. Alternatively, you can override some of these preferences when preparing an individual index. To do so, select your new options while building an index and follow the prompts.
  - ▪ Go to Edit>Preferences for Windows or Acrobat Pro DC>Preferences for Mac and select the Catalog category. Next, specify your preferences. Many of the available options are identical to those used in the index-building process.

❖ Searching an Index
- ◆ Either from the File>Open dialog or by clicking on the index (.pdx) file, (Figure 9-9) you will open the index as well as the Advanced

Figure 9-9

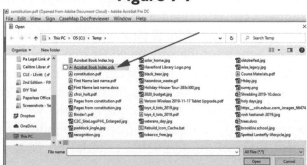

Search dialog. (Figure 9-10) From this window, type the word or phrase you are looking for. Searches may be Case-Sensitive, may be limited to Whole words only, or may Include Bookmarks and Include Comments. When searching bookmarks and comments, Acrobat examines items in the Bookmarks and Comment panels. To assure accuracy, save the document before running a search so that all content is included within the results.

Figure 9-10

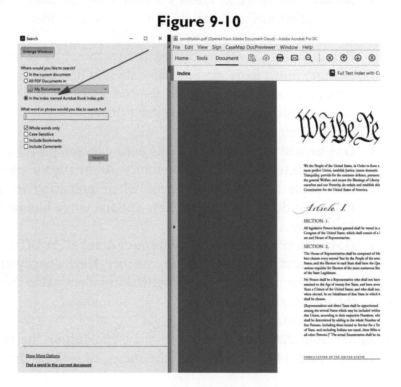

♦ The Advanced Search also has an Arrange Windows button that rearranges your document and search windows so that you can see both clearly side by side. If you select the Show More Options dialog at the bottom of the Advanced Search window, you may include Proximity, Stemming, and Attachments. Even more helpful is the ability to search an index with different criteria. You can (1) Match Exact word or phrase, (2) Match Any of the words, (3) Match All of the words, or (4) do a Boolean query. The index search allows users to select three of 12 additional criteria: (1) Date Created, (2) Date Modified, (3) Author, (4) Title, (5) Subject, (6) Filename, (7) Keywords, (8) Bookmarks, (9) Comments, (10) JPEG Images, (11) XMP Metadata, and (12) Object Data. (Figure 9-11)

♦ After specifying the criteria you desire, click Search. The results will display below the dialog, with the search term appearing in bold typeface. Simply click on each result and Acrobat will display the result in whichever document it is located, with the search term highlighted. (Figure 9-12)

♦ You can save your results by clicking on the Save (diskette) icon on the Search panel. Results may be saved as a PDF or as a CSV file, which can be viewed in Microsoft Excel and other programs.

Figure 9-11   Figure 9-12

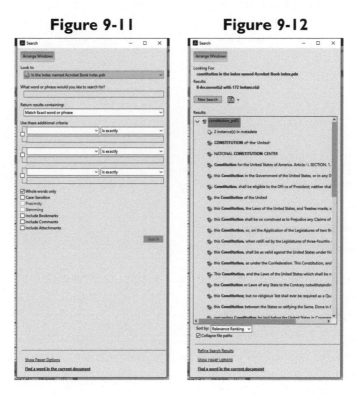

Chapter 10

Creating, Modifying, and Working with Forms

Every law office uses forms, whether they are government documents clients must complete or an intake questionnaire created in Word. In a law office, forms are also useful for obtaining information from clients or standardizing documents. The problem with forms is that many offices still open a form, print it out, and then fill it in either by hand or by typing the necessary information. Adobe Acrobat allows you to create fillable forms from existing PDF documents.

Adobe Acrobat eliminates the hassle of manually completing forms by allowing users to transform virtually any document into a form that can be filled out or into a form that can be used over and over. Consider various Social Security forms. For example, every lawyer who represents a Social Security disability claimant must prepare various forms and submit them to the Social Security Administration. By converting the static forms into ones with fillable form fields, you can avoid typing all of the firm and attorney information every time and save time in the process.

Forms can be modified in a number of ways, distributed, and tracked. This chapter outlines many of the basics and some advanced aspects of creating Acrobat forms, which can even be used by persons who only have the free Acrobat Reader or are using the mobile Acrobat Reader app. For more advanced information about creating forms, visit the Acrobat Help area of the program. There are also many excellent YouTube videos to assist.

Converting PDF Files to Interactive Forms

You can convert any type of PDF into a fillable form, whether it is an existing form that you have scanned or a document you first created in Microsoft Word that you wish to make into a fillable form. First, open your PDF file and from the Tools pane, select Prepare Form. The only exception are PDFs with security settings that prohibit changing the document.

Acrobat will offer three options: Single File, Scanner, or Create New. (Figure 10-1) Generally, Acrobat displays the document you are working on and its name

Figure 10-1

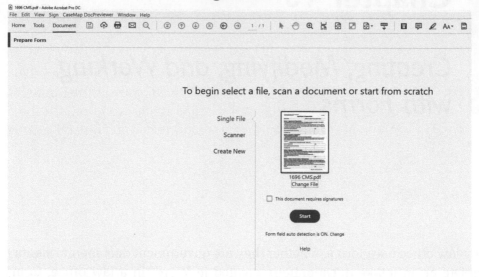

above the Change File option. If this is the correct document, click Start. If you select Change File, you can use Windows File Explorer or Mac Finder to browse and locate the file you want to convert into a form. When the correct document is displayed, click Start.

If you select "Scanner," a scanner-like interface appears. Once you scan a document, Acrobat will begin the process of creating a form. Finally, "Create New" will open a new blank document, which can be used to create a form "from scratch."

NOTE: We recommend scanning and saving any paper documents you want to convert into a form before attempting to create a fillable form. This will allow you to create the form and then work with it, discarding any changes if you discover that you need to start over.

After you select Start, Acrobat will analyze the document and add form fields where it feels they are appropriate based on the text of the document and its analysis of locations with blank lines. (Figure 10-2)

NOTE: This autodetection is set by default. You can check this default setting, and change other settings, by modifying Forms preferences in Edit>Preferences>Forms for Windows or Acrobat Pro DC>Preferences for Mac.

The Prepare Form toolbar appears above your document, and the Forms pane will display to the right. The Prepare Form toolbar contains the tools for creating different types of fields, the Pin tool, a Help button, and a Preview button, which allows you to view the form as it will display to an end user and then easily go back into Edit mode.

The Forms pane displays a list of the fields that Acrobat has added. (Figure 10-3) Adjacent to the FIELDS title are two dropdown menus. The right dropdown sorts your tabs (form fields) alphabetically or in tab order. The left dropdown menu

Figure 10-2

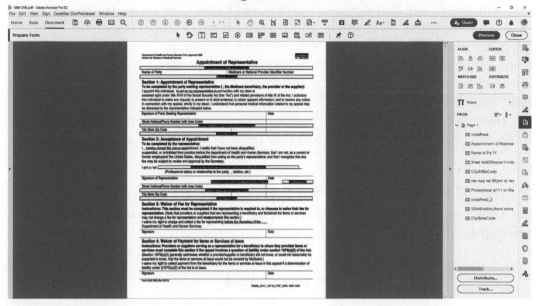

Figure 10-3

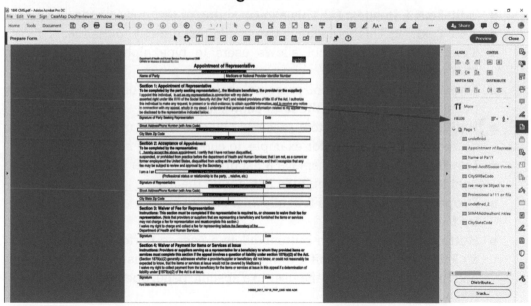

is the Reading Order tool, which allows you to specify in what order users will go as they move between tabs. If you enable Show Tab Numbers, it may be easier to arrange tabs as you edit the document. You can sort (Order) the tabs (form fields) by Structure, by Row, or by Column to make it easier for the end user.

When you review the document and the form fields that Acrobat has inserted, you will likely note that Acrobat has inserted fields where you do not need them or has not inserted them where you do need them. You can manually add form fields by using the tools on the Prepare Form toolbar or by right-clicking on the document and choosing one of the field types from the menu. You can easily delete fields by selecting the field and pressing the Delete key or by right-clicking on a field and choosing Delete.

NOTE: If a document has been password protected to prevent editing, or Reader-Enabled, you will not be able to add new fields or modify the existing fields.

Types of Form Fields (The types of fields correspond to the numbers listed under the fields in Figure 10-4.) (Figure 10-4)

Figure 10-4

- **Edit Text & Images:** [1] This allows editing of text and images.
- **Add Text:** [2] This tool allows you to add text directly to the file.
- **Text Field:** [3] This tool allows users to type alphabetic or numeric characters.
- **Check Box:** [4] This tool presents choices for the user; multiple check boxes can be selected if the form allows it.
- **Radio Button:** [5] This tool presents choices for the user; only one radio button can be selected (for example, to choose yes or no).
- **List Box:** [6] This tool displays a list of options a user can select; you can enable a user to select multiple items from the list.
- **Dropdown List:** [7] This tool allows a user to choose an item from a pop-up menu.
- **Button:** [8] These action buttons allow a user to perform functions such as Print, Reset, or Submit a form. They can also be used to perform other actions, such as moving the user to a specific page, opening a file, or opening a web page.
- **Image Field:** [9] The image field allows the user to select an image to upload and include in the document.
- **Add a Date Field:** [10] The Add a Date field is the same as a text field that requires the user to input a date in a specific format, without the extra steps.
- **Digital Signature:** [11] This tool allows a user to digitally sign a document.

- **Barcode Field: [12]** This tool encodes the data that is inputted on a form and creates a barcode. This field is not likely to be used by attorneys and will not be discussed in this book.

  NOTE: Whenever you add a form field to a document, you always have a Properties box that provides you with multiple options and settings for the form field. Because these properties boxes and options are so similar for all types of form fields, we are not showing what each looks like, but you should review the properties when you add form fields to ensure that your fields display the way you want them to.

Using Text Fields

Most legal professionals will use text fields in every document. Learning how to create and modify them is crucial to creating documents that not only look good but are also user-friendly.

To add a text field, choose the Text Field button from the Prepare Form toolbar or right-click on the document and choose Text Field from the menu. (Figure 10-5 and Figure 10-6) Place your cursor on the page where you wish the field to appear and left-click. A box will appear that will prompt you to add a Field Name. A default name such as "Text1" will appear in the box. You should not keep this default name but should instead add a descriptive, meaningful name for the field. (Figure 10-7)

Figure 10-5

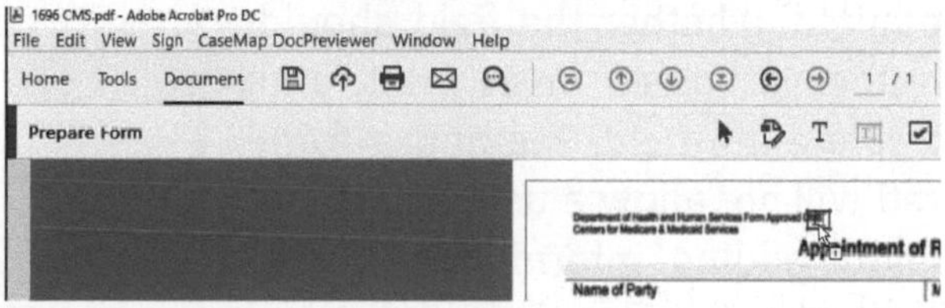

Figure 10-6

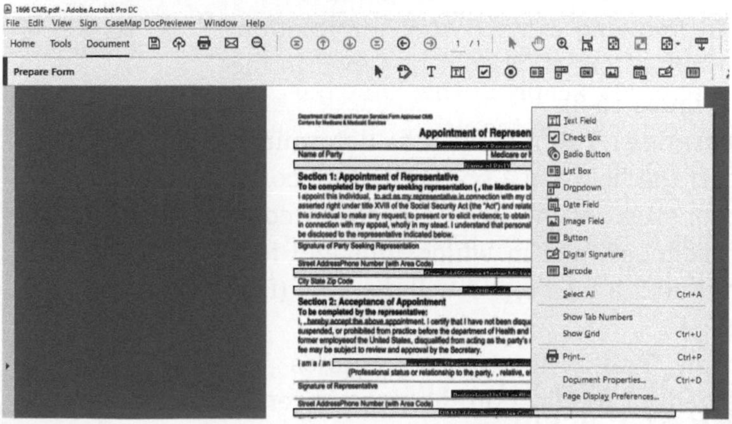

Figure 10-7

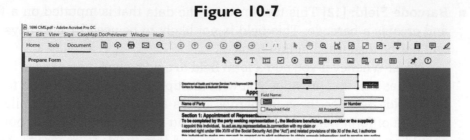

NOTE: If fields have the same name, when users type into the form field, the text they type will populate in the other fields with the same name. This can be useful if the form has areas where text needs to be repeated (such as a name, address, birthdate, etc.). Be careful when naming your fields to choose unique names that are not already in use in the document.

If you check the box for "Required field," the user must fill in the field.

If the field is not properly sized, you can drag the handles on the field to the correct size.

You can open the Text Field Properties box by double-clicking on the field or by right-clicking and choosing Properties. There are eight tabs that contain various properties that you can modify. (Figure 10-8)

- **General Tab:** This tab displays the current name of the field, a Tooltip box, and options for whether to make the field Read Only or Required, whether the field should be visible either in screen or in print, and whether to rotate the field. Making a form field required will not allow a user to submit a form without adding information to the field. Adding text to the Tooltip will display text over the field when a user's mouse pointer hovers over it. This device aids a user in knowing exactly what information, and in what format, should be typed in the box. (Figure 10-8)

Figure 10-8

- **Appearance Tab:** This tab determines whether the field has a border or a fill color, the properties of the border such as color and thickness, and in which font and font size the text a user types will display. (Figure 10-9)

Figure 10-9

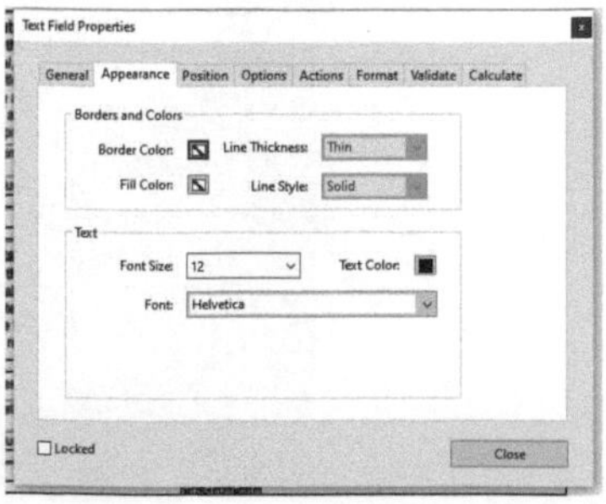

- **Position Tab:** This tab determines the placement of the field on the page in terms of inches, points, etc. This property can be used to ensure that your fields are aligned or that they are in the same position as other text on the page. (Figure 10-10)

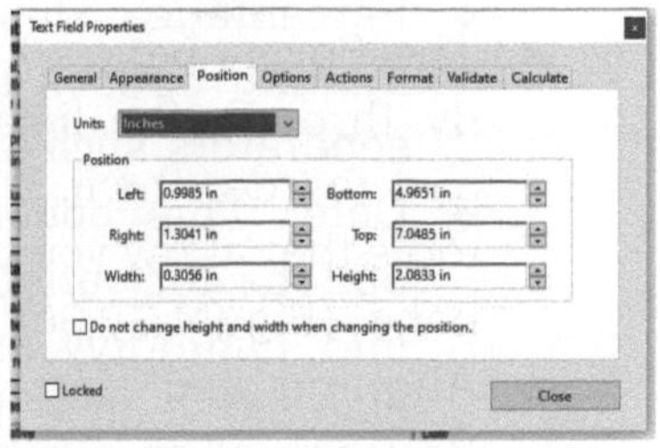

■ **Options Tab:** This tab determines the alignment (Left, Center, Right) of the text a user types as well as whether the text is spell checked. You can limit the number of characters that can be typed and allow for multiline or scrolling of long text. The multiline option allows users to type hard returns in their text. Scrolling will allow a user to type a long string of text, but will not allow for hard returns. If a user types a string of text that exceeds the box, the text that exceeds the field's dimensions will not be visible in the field. By checking the box to Allow Rich Text Formatting, you can enable your users to add formatting such as bold or italics to their text. (Figure 10-11)

Figure 10-10

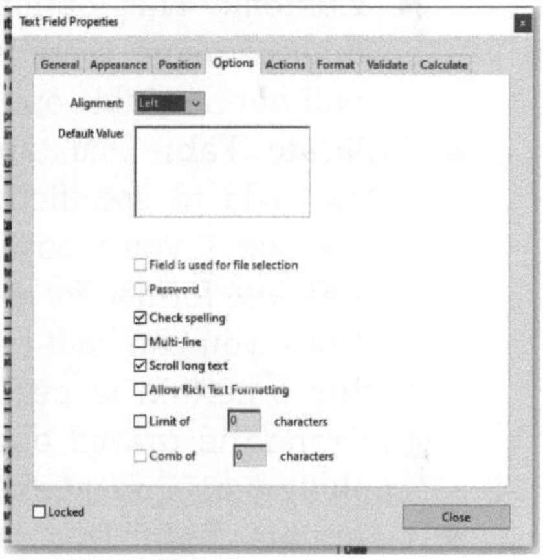

■ **Actions Tab:** This tab allows you to associate actions with the form field such as moving the user to a specific page, opening a file, or opening a web page. You can also use an action to submit the form when the user completes the final field. To add an action, you choose the trigger (Mouse Down is a click, Mouse Up is releasing after a click, Mouse Enter is moving the pointer over the button, and Mouse Exit is moving the pointer away from the button) and then use the Add button to add the desired action. Although you can use this feature with a text field, it is more commonly used when inserting an action button, discussed later in this chapter. (Figure 10-12)

Figure 10-11

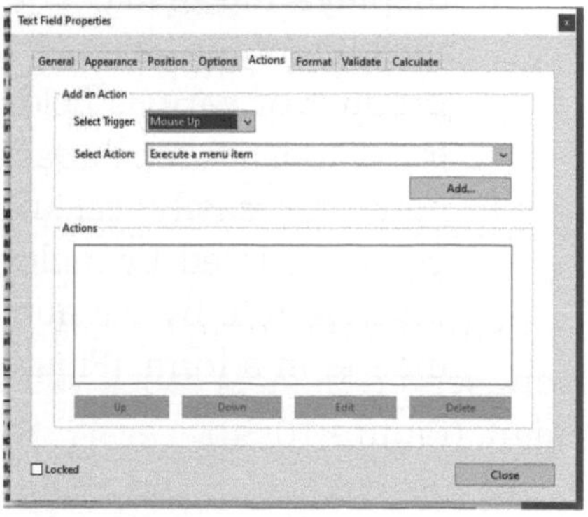

■ **Format Tab:** This tab automatically formats the information a user enters in a specific way. (Figure 10-13)

Figure 10-12

❖ None: This option applies no formatting.

❖ Number: This option provides number formatting options similar to those found in Microsoft Excel for decimal places, separators such as commas and periods, currency symbols and locations of those symbols, and negative number style (with or without parentheses or red text).

Figure 10-13

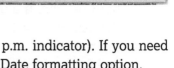

❖ Percentage: This option provides formatting options for decimal places and separators such as commas and periods.

❖ Date: This option provides formatting options for various date styles, such as m/d, mm/dd/yy, or yyyy-mm-dd. You can also use a style that combines date and time if you need to display both.

❖ Time: This option provides formatting options for various time styles, such as HH:MM or h:MM:ss tt (where tt is the a.m. or p.m. indicator). If you need to combine date and time, you should use the Date formatting option.

❖ Special: This option provides formatting options for Zip Code, Zip Code +4, Phone Number, and Social Security Number.

❖ Custom: This option provides further options using JavaScripts. Most lawyers will not need this option.

Figure 10-14

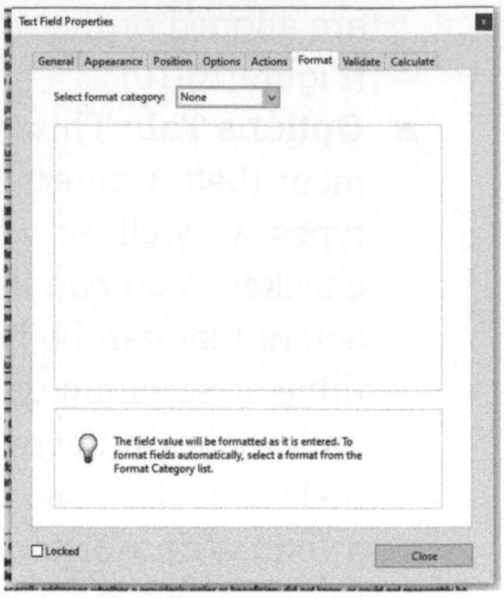

■ **Validate Tab:** This tab restricts entry in a text field to specified ranges, values, or characters. If you choose to use a number or percentage format, for example, on the Format tab, you can limit the entry to numbers within a certain range. The option to limit the range is grayed out when it does not apply to your Format style. (Figure 10-14)

Figure 10-15

■ **Calculate Tab:** This tab performs mathematical operations on field entries and displays the result. You can easily display the sum of the value of various fields, or the product of various fields. This can be used for expense reimbursement forms where you can easily calculate the amount to be reimbursed by multiplying a predefined mileage rate by the number of miles a user inserts in a form. (Figure 10-15)

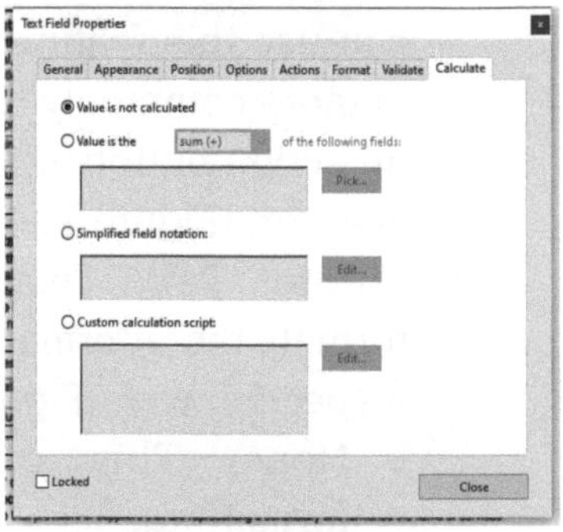

How to set up calculated fields:[1]

To add text fields

1. Double-click the field where you want to display the result to open the Properties dialog box.
2. Click the Calculate tab.
3. To add the values entered into fields, click the "Value is the" radio button.
4. Pick Sum from the pop-up menu.
5. Click Pick to open a list of the fields in your form, select the fields you want to add, and click OK to list the fields in the dialog box.

To multiply values

1. Double-click the field where you want to display the result to open the Properties dialog box.
2. Click the Calculate tab.
3. To multiply the values entered into fields, click the "Value is the" radio button.
4. Pick Product from the pop-up menu.
5. Click Pick to open a list of the fields in your form, select the fields you want to multiply, and click OK to list the fields in the dialog box.

To subtract one field from another

1. Open the Properties for the results field.
2. Click the Calculate tab.
3. Now click the Simplified Field Notation radio button.
4. Click Edit to open the Javascript Editor.
5. Type the expression in the editor, such as Field1-Field2. Make sure not to add any spaces.
6. Click OK and you'll see the expression show on the dialog box.

To divide two fields

1. In the Calculate tab for the results field, choose Simplified Field Notation, and click Edit.

---

1. These instructions for creating calculated fields are from https://acrobatusers.com/tutorials /how-do-i-use-basic-calculations-in-a-form/, which offers excellent guidance on these operations, and many other Adobe Acrobat features and functions.

2. In the JavaScript Editor, type FieldB/FieldA. Again, make sure you don't have any spaces. Click OK and you'll see the expression on the Properties dialog box.

3. Click Preview to toggle the Preview mode to test your work. You won't have any surprises with adding, subtracting, or multiplying, but a division calculation can cause display problems.

■ **Locked Button:** This choice appears on the bottom of each tab. If you check this box, the form field properties cannot be changed. Checking the box on one tab locks the options on all of the other tabs. If you need to make changes to the field properties, simply uncheck the box.

You can change the properties of multiple fields at one time by Ctrl-clicking or Cmd-clicking on the fields, right-clicking on one field, and choosing Properties. Note that, depending on the properties of the fields you select (the type of field, etc.), all of the options will not be available.

Using Check Box Fields

To add a check box field, choose the Check Box Field button from the Prepare Form toolbar or right-click on the document and choose Check Box from the menu. Place your cursor on the page where you wish the field to appear and left-click. A box will appear that will prompt you to add a Field Name. A default name such as "Check Box1" will appear in the box. You should not keep this default name but rather add a descriptive, meaningful name for the field. (Figure 10-16)

Figure 10-16

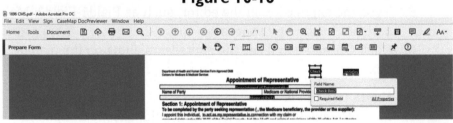

NOTE: If fields have the same name, when users type into the field, the text they type will populate in the other fields with the same name. This can be useful if the form has areas where text needs to be repeated (such as a name, address, birthdate, etc.). Be careful to choose unique names when naming your fields to avoid using names that are already in use in the document.

If you check the box for Required Field, this field will have to be completed by the user for the form to be complete.

If the field is not properly sized, you can drag the handles on the field to the correct size.

You can open the Check Box Properties box by double-clicking on the field or by right-clicking and choosing Properties. There are five tabs that contain various properties that you can modify.

Figure 10-17

- **General Tab:** This tab displays the current name of the field, a Tooltip box, and options for whether to make the field Read Only or Required, whether the field should be visible either in screen or in print, and whether to rotate the field. Making a form field required will not allow a user to submit a form without adding information to the field. Adding text to the Tooltip will display text over the field when a user's mouse pointer hovers over it. This device aids a user in knowing exactly what information, and in what format, should be typed in the box. (Figure 10-17)

Figure 10-18

- **Appearance Tab:** This tab determines whether the field has a border or a fill color, the properties of the border such as color and thickness, and in which font and font size the text a user types will display. (Figure 10-18)

Figure 10-19

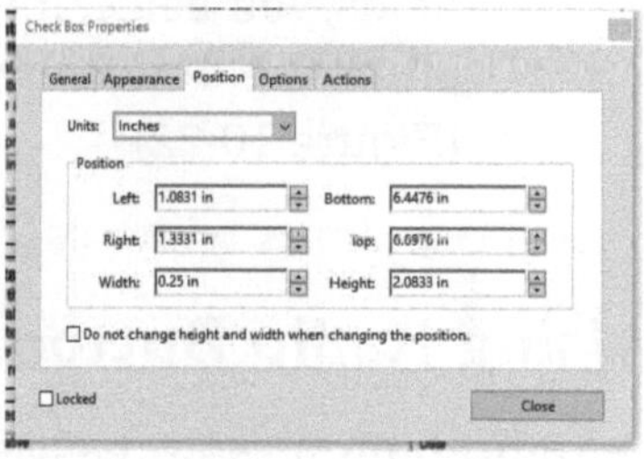

- **Position Tab:** This tab determines the placement of the field on the page in terms of inches, points, etc. This property can be used to ensure that your fields are aligned or that they are in the same position as other text on the page. (Figure 10-19)

Figure 10-20

- **Options Tab:** This tab determines the Check Box style (whether the user's choice is displayed as a checkmark, a circle, a star, etc.) as well as whether the box should be checked by default or not. The Export Value is set as Yes by default, but depending on what the check box signifies, you can change this value. (Figure 10-20)

- **Actions Tab:** This tab allows you to associate actions with the form field such as moving the user to a specific page, opening a file, or opening a web page. You can also use an action to submit the form when the user completes filling out the document. To add an action, you choose the trigger (Mouse Down is a click, Mouse Up is releasing after a click, Mouse Enter is moving the pointer over the button, and Mouse Exit is moving the pointer away from the button) and then use the Add button to add the desired action.

Although you can use this feature with a Check Box field, it is more commonly used when inserting an action button, discussed later in this chapter. (Figure 10-21)

Figure 10-21

- **Locked Button:** This choice appears on the bottom of each tab. If you check this box, the form field properties cannot be changed. Checking the box on one tab locks the options on all of the other tabs. If you need to make changes to the field properties, simply uncheck the box.

Figure 10-22

You can change the properties of multiple fields at one time by Ctrl-clicking on the fields, right-clicking on one field, and choosing Properties. Note that depending on the properties of the fields you select (the type of field, etc.), all of the options will not be available. (Figure 10-22)

Using Radio Button Fields

A radio button requires users to select one entry from a predefined set of two or more options. Thus, you must always add at least two radio buttons to a document.

- To add a radio button field, choose the Radio Button Field button from the Prepare Form toolbar or right-click on the document and choose Radio Button from the menu. Place your cursor on the page where you wish the button to appear and left-click. A box will appear that will remind you that when using radio buttons, you must have more than one. It will prompt you to add a Radio Button Choice Name. A default name such as "Choice1" will appear in the box. You should not keep this default name but rather add a descriptive, meaningful name for the field. You will then enter a name for the Group Name. You then click the Add Another Button link, place your cursor on the page where you wish the second radio button to appear, and provide a name for this choice. You should confirm that the Group Name is the same as was listed for your first radio button. All radio buttons in a set must have the same Group Name. (Figure 10-23)

Figure 10-23

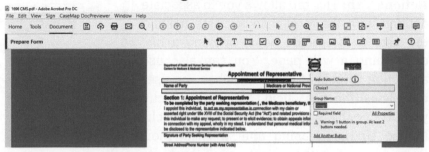

If you check the box for "Required field," this field will have to be completed by the user for the form to be complete.

You can open the Radio Button Properties box by double-clicking on the field or by right-clicking and choosing Properties. There are five tabs that contain various properties that you can modify.

- **General Tab:** This tab displays the current name of the field, a Tooltip box, and options for whether to make the field Read Only or Required, whether the field should be visible either in screen or in print, and whether to rotate the field. Making a form field required will not allow a user to submit a form without adding information to the field. Adding text to the Tooltip will display text over the field when a user's mouse pointer hovers over it. This device aids a user in knowing exactly what information, and in what format, should be typed in the box. (Figure 10-24)

Figure 10-24

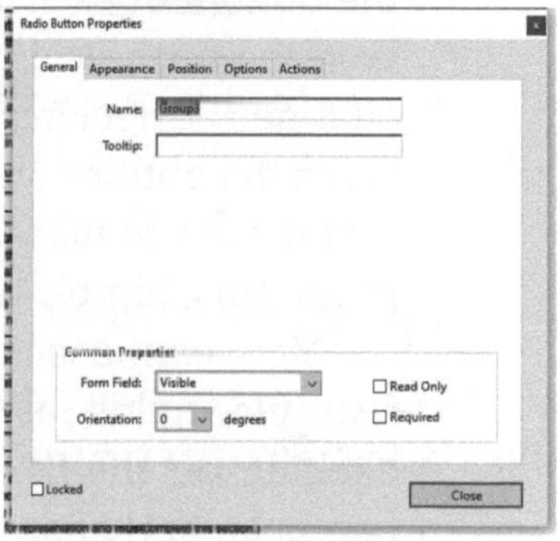

- **Appearance Tab:** This tab determines whether the field has a border or a fill color, the properties of the border such as color and thickness, and in which font and font size the text a user types will display. (Figure 10-25)

Figure 10-25

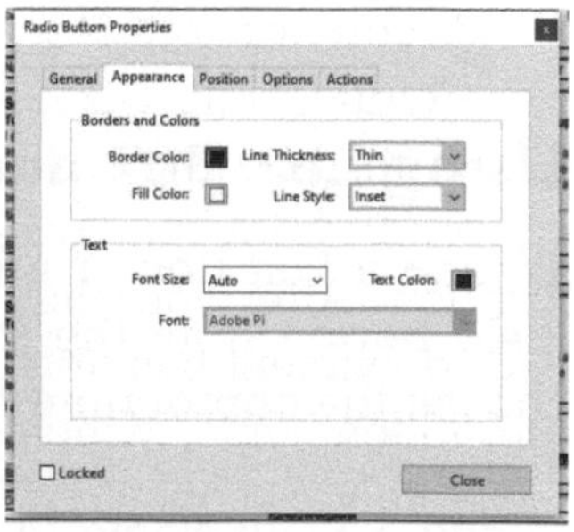

- **Position Tab:** This tab determines the placement of the field on the page in terms of inches, points, etc. This property can be used to ensure that your fields are aligned or that they are in the same position as other text on the page. (Figure 10-26)

- **Options Tab:** This tab determines the Radio Button Style (whether the user's choice is displayed as a checkmark, a circle, a star, etc.) as well as whether the button is checked by default or not. (Figure 10-27)

Figure 10-26

- **Actions Tab:** This tab allows you to associate actions with the form field such as moving the user to a specific page, opening a file, or opening a web page. You can also use an action to submit the form when the user completes the final field. To add an action, you choose the trigger (Mouse Down is a click, Mouse Up is releasing after a click, Mouse Enter is moving the pointer over the button, and Mouse Exit is moving the pointer away from the button) and then use the Add button to add the desired action. Although you can use this feature with a Radio Button field, it is more commonly used when inserting an action button, discussed later in this chapter. (Figure 10-28)

Figure 10-27

- **Locked Button:** This choice appears on the bottom of each tab. If you check this box, the form field properties cannot be changed. Checking the box on one tab locks the options on all of the other tabs. If you need to make changes to the field properties, simply uncheck the box.

Figure 10-28

You can change the properties of multiple fields at one time by Ctrl-clicking on the fields, right-clicking on one field, and choosing Properties. Note that depending on the properties of the fields you select (the type of field, etc.), all of the options will not be available.

Using List Box and Dropdown Fields

To add a List Box or a Dropdown field, choose either the List Box or Dropdown Field button from the Prepare Form toolbar or right-click on the document and choose the appropriate item from the menu. Place your cursor on the page where you wish the field to appear and left-click. A box will appear that will prompt you to add a Field Name. A default name such as "List Box 1" or "Dropdown1" will appear in the box. You should not keep this default name but rather add a descriptive, meaningful name for the field.

NOTE: If fields have the same name, when users type into the field, the text they type will populate in the other fields with the same name. This can be useful if the form has areas where text needs to be repeated (such as a name, address, birthdate, etc.). Be careful to choose unique names when naming your fields to avoid using names that are already in use in the document. Then you can complete the last sentence as it is duplicative.

If you check the box for Required Field, this field will have to be completed by the user for the form to be complete.

If the field is not properly sized, you can drag the handles on the field to the correct size.

You can open the List Box or Dropdown Properties box by double-clicking on the field or by right-clicking and choosing Properties. There are either six (List Box) or seven (Dropdown) tabs that contain various properties that you can modify. The tabs are generally common to both types of field. Because many of the property tabs are similar to those displayed earlier in this chapter, only those unique to these fields are displayed.

- **General Tab:** This tab displays the current name of the field, a Tooltip box, and options for whether to make the field Read Only, whether the field should be visible either in screen or in print, and whether to rotate the field. Making a form field required will not allow a user to submit a form without adding information to the field. Adding text to the Tooltip will display text over the field when a user's mouse pointer hovers over it. This device aids a user in knowing exactly what information, and in what format, should be typed in the box.

- **Appearance Tab:** This tab determines whether the field has a border or a fill color, the properties of the border such as color and thickness, and in which font and font size the text a user types will display.

- **Position Tab:** This tab determines the placement of the field on the page in terms of inches, points, etc. This property can be used to ensure that your fields are aligned or that they are in the same position as other text on the page.

- **Options Tab:** This tab is the vital one for creating a list. In the line marked Item, you type the various choices for the list. You then click Add to add them to the Item List below. If you wish to remove an item, simply highlight it and click Delete.

  The Item List displays the choices available to the user. The item that appears highlighted on the list is the default choice. Depending on your form's purpose, you may want to add a None choice to your list. The Up and Down buttons allow you to reorder the list display, or you can click the Sort Items box to quickly alphabetize or numerically sort your list.

Clicking the Multiple Selection option (only available when using the List Box field) allows users to choose more than one item. Clicking the box Commit Selected Value Immediately saves the value as soon as a user selects it rather than only when the user moves to another field.

Clicking the Allow User to Enter Custom Text and Check Spelling options (only available when using the Dropdown field) allows a user to type text other than one of the presented choices and will spell check the entered text.

- **Actions Tab:** This tab allows you to associate actions with the form field such as moving the user to a specific page, opening a file, or opening a web page. You can also use an action to submit the form when the user completes the final field. To add an action, you choose the trigger (Mouse Down is a click, Mouse Up is releasing after a click, Mouse Enter is moving the pointer over the button, and Mouse Exit is moving the pointer away from the button) and then use the Add button to add the desired action. Although you can use this feature with a List Box or a Dropdown field, it is more commonly used when inserting an action button, discussed later in this chapter.

- **Selection Change Tab (List Box only):** This tab specifies what to do when the list box selection changes. You can choose Do Nothing or choose to execute a JavaScript. Most likely you will not use this function. (Figure 10-29)

Figure 10-29

- **Format Tab (Dropdown only):** This tab automatically formats the information a user enters in a specific way. (Figure 10-30)
  - ❖ None: This option applies no formatting.
  - ❖ Number: This option provides number formatting options similar to those found in Microsoft Excel for decimal places, separators such as commas and periods, currency symbols and locations of those symbols, and negative number style (with or without parentheses or red text).

Figure 10-30

  - ❖ Percentage: This option provides formatting options for decimal places and separators such as commas and periods.
  - ❖ Date: This option provides formatting options for various date styles, such as m/d, mm/dd/yy, or yyyy-mm-dd. You can also use a style that combines date and time if you need to display both.
  - ❖ Time: This option provides formatting options for various time styles, such as HH:MM or h:MM:ss tt (where tt is the a.m. or p.m. indicator). If you need to combine date and time, you should use the Date formatting option.

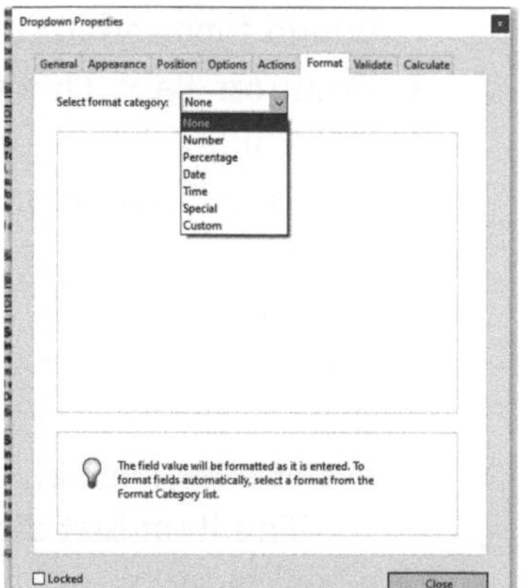

- ❖ Special: This option provides formatting options for Zip Code, Zip Code +4, Phone Number, and Social Security Number.
- ❖ Custom: This option provides further options using JavaScripts. Most lawyers will not need this option.
- **Validate Tab (Dropdown only):** This tab restricts entry in a text field to specified ranges, values, or characters. If you choose to use a number or percentage format, for example, on the Format tab, you can limit the entry to numbers within a certain range. The option to limit the range is grayed out when it does not apply to your Format style. (Figure 10-31)
- **Calculate Tab (Dropdown only):** This tab performs mathematical operations on field entries and displays the result. You can easily display the sum of the value of various fields, or the product of various fields. This is useful for expense reimbursement forms where you can easily calculate the amount to be reimbursed by multiplying a predefined mileage rate by the number of miles a user inserts in a form. (Figure 10-32)

  Figure 10-31

  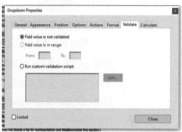

  There is also a Locked Button (similar to what appears elsewhere in the program). This choice appears on the bottom of each tab. If you check this box, the form field properties cannot be changed. Checking the box on one tab locks the options on all of the other tabs. If you need to make changes to the field properties, simply uncheck the box.

  Figure 10-32

  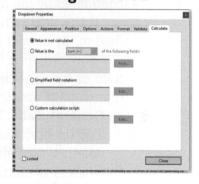

  You can change the properties of multiple fields at one time by Ctrl-clicking on the fields, right-clicking on one field, and choosing Properties. Note that depending on the properties of the fields you select (the type of field, etc.), all of the options will not be available.

Using Action Buttons

Buttons can open a file, play a movie or sound, submit information to a web server, or perform other functions that links and bookmarks do not. Every form field has an Actions tab that can execute the same types of functions as an action button. However, there are times when using an action button makes more sense, such as when you are providing an option to submit, print, or reset a form. Because many of the property tabs are similar to those displayed earlier in this chapter, only those unique to these fields are displayed. An action button can do the following:

■ Activate a single action or a series of actions.

■ Change its appearance in response to mouse actions.

■ Be copied across many pages.

■ Mouse actions can activate different button actions. For example, Mouse Down (a click), Mouse Up (releasing after a click), Mouse Enter (moving the pointer over the button), and Mouse Exit (moving the pointer away from the button) can all start a different action for the same button.

❖ To add an action button, choose the Button option from the Prepare Form toolbar or right-click on the document and choose Button from the menu. Place your cursor on the page where you wish the button to appear and left-click. A box will appear that will prompt you to add a Field Name. A default name such as "Button1" will appear in the box. You should not keep this default name but rather add a descriptive, meaningful name for the field.

NOTE: If fields have the same name, when users type into the field, the text they type will populate in the other fields with the same name. This can be useful if the form has areas where text needs to be repeated (such as a name, address, birthdate, etc.). Be careful to choose unique names when naming your fields to avoid using names that are already in use in the document.

If you check the box for Required Field, this field will have to be completed by the user for the form to be complete.

If the field is not properly sized, you can drag the handles on the field to the correct size.

You can open the Button Properties box by double-clicking on the field or by right-clicking and choosing Properties. There are five tabs that contain various properties that you can modify.

♦ **General Tab:** This tab displays the current name of the field, a Tooltip box, and options for whether to make the field Read Only, whether the field should be visible either in screen or in print, and whether to rotate the field. Adding text to the Tooltip will display text over the field when a user's mouse pointer hovers over it. This device aids a user in knowing exactly what information, and in what format, should be typed in the box.

♦ **Appearance Tab:** This tab determines whether the field has a border or a fill color, the properties of the border such as color and thickness, and in which font and font size the text a user types will display.

♦ **Position Tab:** This tab determines the placement of the field on the page in terms of inches, points, etc. This property can be used to ensure that your fields are aligned or that they are in the same position as other text on the page.

♦ **Options Tab:** This tab determines how your button is displayed: as a Label only, an Icon only, or a combination of both in various configurations. Depending on which option you choose, you will be able to enter the text of the label and/or browse to your computer for an appropriate icon. A preview of the icon will appear in this window. The Advanced dialog allows you to change the way the icon is scaled to fit inside the button.

♦ The Button Behavior determines how the button displays when clicked. None keeps the button appearance the same, Push specifies how the button looks as a mouse either hovers over or clicks the button, Outline highlights the button border, and Invert reverses the dark and light shades of the button.

♦ **Actions Tab:** This tab allows you to associate an action with the button such as moving the user to a specific page, opening a file, or opening a web page. You can also use an action to submit the form when the user completes the final field. To add an action, you first choose the trigger. Mouse Down is a click, Mouse Up is releasing after a click, Mouse Enter is moving the pointer over the button, and Mouse Exit is moving the pointer away from the button. In most cases, you will want to use Mouse Up. There are other triggers, such as Page Visible and Invisible, Page Enter and Exit, and On Focus, that are used only with media clips; however, you will not customarily use these triggers, so we only briefly mention them here.

You will then use the Add button to add the desired action such as opening a web page, submitting the form, or resetting the form.

■ **Using the Submit a Form Action (Figure 10-33)**

The "Submit a form" action allows a user to click on a button and open an email window in a user's default email client with a predetermined email recipient and the form as an attachment. The user then adds any message and sends the email to the prespecified email address.

❖ When using the "Submit a form" action, you are prompted to enter a URL. (Figure 10-34)

Figure 10-33	**Figure 10-34**

❖ You can collect form data either on a server or as attachments to email. Which option you choose will depend on the purpose of the form. If you are using the form to assemble data from a number of sources to be merged together, you may want to use the server option. If you are sending a form to a specific client and want to see the responses on the form, you may want to use the email attachment option.

♦ To collect form data on a server, type the location in the "Enter a URL for this link" box: for example, \\[server]\[folder]\[subfolder]\.

♦ To collect form data as attachments to email, type mailto: followed by the email address: for example, mailto:nobody@techlawyergy.com.

❖ You would then choose the Export format (FDF, HTML, XFDF, or PDF, which will return the entire file with user input). You can choose which fields are returned and whether to convert dates into a specific format. This tool is used when the form contains a "Submit a form" action that exported the form data into FDF, HTML, or XFDF format. This option is available to firms that desire to only export the data and not preserve the forms. Most firms will not use this option. For more information, go to https://helpx.adobe.com/acrobat/using/collecting-pdf-form-data.html.

❖ When you are finished, click Close.

NOTE: When sending a form or other document to another person for completion or for commenting, you must advise the recipient to save the document to his or her computer before completing the form or adding comments. If the recipient simply opens the email attachment without saving it, adds information, and merely hits the Save button, the document will only be stored temporarily, the recipient will not be able to find the revised version, and all of the changes will be lost. Reopening the attachment opens the blank document again.

■ **Locked Button:** This choice appears on the bottom of each tab. If you check this box, the form field properties cannot be changed. Checking the box on one tab locks the options on all of the other tabs. If you need to make changes to the field properties, simply uncheck the box.

You can change the properties of multiple fields at one time by Ctrl-clicking or Cmd-clicking on the fields, right-clicking on one field, and choosing Properties. Note that depending on the properties of the fields you select (the type of field, etc.), all of the options will not be available.

Adding Digital Signatures to a Form

A digital signature (not to be confused with a digital certificate) is a method of validating the authenticity of a PDF or other document, that is, assuring the recipient that the document is valid and has not been tampered with. It also demonstrates that the sender has approved the contents of the document. The term "digital signatures" as discussed here does *not* mean the insertion of a jpg or other image of your scanned signature into a document, which essentially is no different than inserting any other image into a PDF, and reflects no level of security or authenticity. (Digital signatures are discussed in greater detail in Chapter 16.)

To add a Digital Signature field, choose the Digital Signature button from the Prepare Form toolbar or right-click on the document and choose Digital Signature from the menu. Place your cursor on the page where you wish the field to appear and left-click. It will prompt you to add a Field Name. A default name such as "Signature1" will appear in the box. You should not keep this default name but rather add a descriptive, meaningful name for the field.

If you check the box for Required Field, this field will have to be completed by the user for the form to be complete.

You can open the Digital Signature Properties box by double-clicking on the field or by right-clicking and choosing Properties. There are five tabs that contain various properties that you can modify. Because many of the property tabs are similar to those displayed earlier in this chapter, only those unique to these fields are displayed.

- **General Tab:** This tab displays the current name of the field, a Tooltip box, and options for whether to make the field Read Only or Required, whether the field should be visible either in screen or in print, and whether to rotate the field. Making a form field required will not allow a user to submit a form without adding information to the field. Adding text to the Tooltip will display text over the field when a user's mouse pointer hovers over it. This device aids a user in knowing exactly what information, and in what format, should be typed in the box.
- **Appearance Tab:** This tab determines whether the field has a border or a fill color, the properties of the border such as color and thickness, and in which font and font size the text a user types will display.
- **Position Tab:** This tab determines the placement of the field on the page in terms of inches, points, etc. This property can be used to ensure that your fields are aligned or that they are in the same position as other text on the page.
- **Actions Tab:** This tab allows you to associate actions with the form field such as moving the user to a specific page, opening a file, or opening a web page. You can also use an action to submit the form when the user completes the final field. To add an action, you choose the trigger (Mouse Down is a click, Mouse Up is releasing after a click, Mouse Enter is moving the pointer over the button, and Mouse Exit is moving the pointer away from the button) and then use the Add button to add the desired action. For example, you may want to use a "Submit" button so that the user can automatically submit (return) the document to you by email.

- **Signed Tab:** This tab determines what happens when the document is signed by a user. The default is "Nothing happens when signed," but you can choose other options to mark the document as read-only or to execute a script. (Figure 10-35)

Figure 10-35

- **Locked Button:** This choice appears on the bottom of each tab. If you check this box, the form field properties cannot be changed. Checking the box on one tab locks the options on all of the other tabs. If you need to make changes to the field properties, simply uncheck the box.

You can change the properties of multiple fields at one time by Ctrl-clicking or Cmd-clicking on the fields, right-clicking on one field, and choosing Properties. Note that depending on the properties of the fields you select (the type of field, etc.), all of the options will not be available.

Additional Options for Modifying Fields through Right-Clicking

You can modify the field's properties or add a new field by using the tools for each field type, but also by right-clicking on a field. Right-clicking provides quick options for accessing the Properties, Rename Field, Set as Required Field, or Add New Field options, as well as copying or deleting fields. There is also an option to Use Current Properties as New Defaults. If you modify properties for a specific type of form field such as a check box, and then choose the option to Use Current Properties as New Defaults, those properties will be saved as the defaults for any new fields of that type you insert in the form.

Figure 10-36

NOTE: Changing default properties will not change the settings for existing form fields, only new ones.

The Forms Pane

- The Forms pane allows you to navigate easily through the fields that are on the page and reorder them. It also provides additional tools that allow you to format the fields on the page. (Figure 10-36)
- Aligning and Centering Multiple Fields: [1] You can align a column of fields on a page

left, right, or vertically. You can align a row of fields on a page by the top, by the bottom, or horizontally. Additionally, you can center the fields vertically, horizontally, or both.

■ Adjusting Spacing between Form Fields: [2] You can use the Distribute command in the Forms pane to give a group of fields uniform spacing measuring from the centers of the fields. To distribute fields evenly between the topmost and bottommost fields, choose Distribute Vertically. To distribute fields evenly between the leftmost and rightmost fields, choose Distribute Horizontally.

■ Other tools are available to you when creating or modifying forms in Other Forms Tasks (the "More" section), located on the Forms pane above the Fields List. Some of the tools are only available when a field is selected; others are available at all times. Some of the more useful tools are discussed below. (Figure 10-37)

Figure 10-37

❖ **Duplicate across Pages:** When you have a field or fields selected, this tool allows you to duplicate the field(s) on all or selected pages. If you do not change the names of the copied fields, the new fields will be populated with the same data as in the original field. If the new fields are for different user data, they must be renamed once created.

❖ **Create Multiple Copies:** When you have a field or fields selected, this tool allows you to create copies of the field(s) any number of times you choose. If you do not change the names of the copied fields, the new fields will be populated with the same data as the original field. If the new fields are for different user data, they must be renamed once created.

❖ **Show Tab Numbers:** This tool allows you to change the order in which a user will be directed to fill a field. The fields will display the tab order number in the upper left corner. You can drag the fields in the Fields List panel to change the tab order.

❖ **Show Field Properties:** This tool is another method of showing the properties of selected fields.

❖ **Highlight Existing Fields:** This tool makes finding fillable fields easier for a user by causing the fields to appear with a colored background.

❖ **Import Data, Export Data, and Merge Data Files into Spreadsheet:** These tools are used when the form contains a Submit Form action that exported the form data into FDF, HTML, or XFDF format. This option is available to firms that desire to only export the data and not preserve the forms. Most firms will not use this option. For more information, go to https://helpx.adobe.com/acrobat/using/collecting-pdf-form-data.html.

❖ **Distribute and Track:** These tools allow you to distribute a form for completion and to track the return of forms; they are discussed more fully in the following two sections.

Distributing Forms

Once you have created a form, you can distribute it (email it) to others, who can complete and return it to you. To do so, open the PDF form you wish to distribute. Select Tools and Prepare Form. Click the Distribute button in the Forms pane. If you are prompted to save the form, click Save and save the form. You will be asked how you would like to distribute the form: by email or via your office's network server. In most cases, you will distribute forms by email. (Figure 10-38)

Figure 10-38

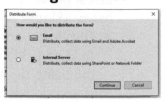

If you choose to distribute by email, you will be asked whether you want to send using Acrobat DC or to save a local copy and manually send later. The dialog box provides an area for you to type the email addresses of your recipients, the ability to customize the subject line, and a sample message that you can customize or leave as is. When you are ready, click Send.

In the Send Email dialog box, specify whether to use your default mail application such as Outlook or a webmail service like Gmail. If you use a webmail service, you will need to enter your account information when prompted, sign in to your webmail service, and then provide Acrobat permission to view and manage your mail.

NOTE: Some email applications will not automatically send messages from outside sources as a security measure. You may have to open your default email application to send the message.

You will see that Acrobat automatically created a PDF with the same name as your original and the suffix "_distributed," as well as a PDF with the suffix "_responses" in the same folder where your original form was saved.

Enabling Users to Fill Forms Out without Tracking (Reader Extended PDFs) (Figure 10-39)

Most of the time, you will be sending forms to clients or others without the need to track every form. For example, a client may contact you about preparing a will, living will, and power of attorney, and you have an office questionnaire that requests the information needed to begin preparing these documents. It is easier for you and the client to have the information in a typed form. Doing so eliminates

Figure 10-39

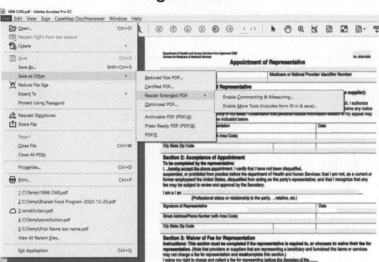

a lot of the need to ask for background information and prevents misspellings of names, etc.

Acrobat converts any form into a fillable PDF that does not require end users to have a paid version. In other words, all they need is the free Acrobat Reader or a similar product. To enable that feature, go to File>Save as Other>Reader Extended PDF. There are two types of Reader Extended PDFs, one that enables commenting and measuring and the other that can be filled and saved. If you want to allow users to fill and save the document, you will view the Enable Usage Rights in Adobe Acrobat Reader dialog. When you click Save Now on this dialog, users can save form data, digitally sign a PDF, and add comments. To prevent overwriting the original form, Acrobat will ask you to save the document either with a new name or in a different location from the original. Once you save the document, you cannot modify it.

Tracking Forms

By using Acrobat's forms Tracker, you can determine which recipients have responded, send the form to additional recipients, email all recipients, and view the responses for a form. (Figure 10-40)

You can manage the forms that you have distributed using the Tracker. You can also use the Tracker to view and edit the location of the response file. To open the Tracker, open the form you sent for distribution. Select Tools and Prepare Form. Click the Track button in the Forms pane. The Tracker opens and shows you reviews you have initiated for comment as well as forms you have distributed.

If you have sent more than one form for distribution, choose the one you wish to track. Here, you can see the location of the response file and change

Figure 10-40

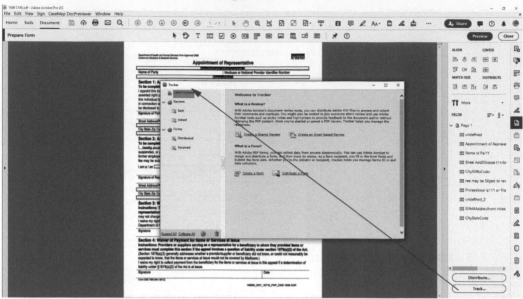

it by clicking Edit File Location, view all responses received by clicking View Responses, view the original form by clicking Open Original Form, send the form to additional recipients by clicking Add Recipients, email the recipients by clicking Email All Recipients, or email only those who have not yet responded by clicking Email Recipients Who Haven't Responded.

Collecting and Working with Form Data

■ As you receive responses to the forms you distributed, Acrobat creates a PDF portfolio for collecting the data as a file with the same name as your original form and the suffix "_responses." This file is saved in the same file location/folder as your original form.

When you open the responses file, the Welcome Page provides you with information on what you can do. The navigation panel on the left allows you to check for new responses, filter the responses based on some criteria, export the responses as a CSV file into a spreadsheet, add new responses, or archive the responses. When you are ready, click the Get Started button at the bottom of the Welcome Page.

■ **Update:** This function is not used in an email-based forms distribution system, which is the most common. In other distribution methods, you can update the responses file to include all recent responses by using the Add button.

- **Filter:** This function can be used to filter and view responses by Field Name. When you choose a field, the Tracker prompts you to add values to your filter such as "contains" or "does not contain," "begins with," etc. When you have entered each value, click Done.

- **Export:** To export user data from returned forms as a CSV file, click Export on the left navigation panel, click Export, and choose Export Selected. In the dialog box, specify the name and location of the file and click Save. You can then open the CSV file with Microsoft Excel or another spreadsheet program and convert the data into a fully functioning spreadsheet.

- **Archive:** This function allows you to archive all or some of the data from the original response file and save it to a new file in your selected location.

- **Add:** To add user data from returned forms, click Add on the left navigation panel, click Add File from the dialog box, and locate the returned form. Click Open. This form will now appear as part of the _responses portfolio.

- **Delete:** To delete a response from Tracker, highlight the response form on the list and click Delete on the left navigation panel.

- **Importing and Exporting Form Data as FDF or XML Files:** These tools are used when the form contains a Submit Form action that exported the form data into FDF, HTML, or XFDF format. This option is available to firms that desire to only export the data and not preserve the forms. Most firms will not use this option. For more information, go to https://helpx .adobe.com/acrobat/using/collecting-pdf-form-data.html.

Tracker Preferences

- You can modify your Tracker Preferences by choosing Edit>Preferences> Tracker in Windows or Adobe Acrobat>Preferences from the main menu on a Mac. Here you can specify how often to automatically check for new form data in a server-based data collection method, when to suspend the check, and whether to show notifications in your system tray or within Acrobat.

Filling Out PDF Forms

PDFs have two types of forms: PDFs with form fields and PDFs without form fields. You can convert the form into a fillable form and should do so if you will use the form again. If you are only using the form one time (for example, you are emailed a form to complete and you do not anticipate having to do so again), then you can use what was formerly known as the Typewriter tool, now known as Add Text, which is located by selecting Tools>Edit PDF. See "Adding Text in an Existing PDF (Formerly Known as the Typewriter Tool)" in Chapter 7.

Filling Out PDF Forms When You Must Use the Original Paper Document

There are times when you will need to fill in a form or other document and you must use the original paper form or document, not a copy that you generate and print on generic paper from your own printer. For example, if you need to create a corporate kit and have the original binder and pages, you need to fill in the information on the actual paper contained in the binder. In these instances, you do not need to use a typewriter.

First, you can scan the original paper document and create a PDF. After creating the PDF, you can either convert the document into a fillable form or manually add form fields. Fill out the form fields and then load the original paper document into your printer's paper tray and print the PDF using (1) the "Form Fields only" option in the Comments & Forms section, and (2) the "Actual size" option of the Page Sizing & Handling section of the Print dialog box.

NOTE: Before printing the final version of the document, you should print a test page on blank printer paper to ensure that the information you typed will be printed in the correct locations on the document. You can usually determine this by holding the typed document over the original form and viewing it in front of a light source. In addition, make sure you load the original documents correctly in your print trays (loaded so that page one pulls into the printer first, paper face up or face down, paper with top to the back of the tray or to the front).

Chapter 11

Reducing the Size of PDF Files

The size of a PDF file (how many megabytes it is) can vary dramatically depending on how it was created, such as by scanning, and the settings used to create it. Large files can create logistical issues because they take longer to open and may be too large to attach to an email (many email programs restrict the size of attachments that can be sent or received). Regardless of how the file was created, users can often reduce the size of the file.

Note: With greater frequency, courts, government agencies, and other entities require attorneys to file documents electronically. The following Acrobat features, while useful for a variety of purposes, outline how to reduce the size of a PDF file or, if the file cannot be reduced sufficiently, how to split the file into smaller ones.

How Big Is Your PDF File?

It helps to know how big a file is before trying to reduce its size. There are multiple ways to determine the size of a file. If you go to File>Properties of an open file and click on the Description tab, it will display the size of the file. (Figure 11-1) Alternatively, you can view the size of a file in Windows Explorer by either hovering your

Figure 11-1

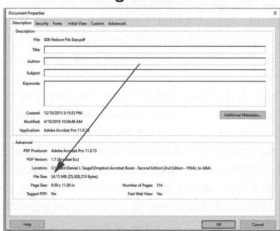

mouse over the file or viewing the file list in the Details view. Sizes of files vary and there is no formula to determine how big a file is or how small it can be reduced to.

Reducing File Size

PDF Optimizer—Reduce File Size Tool (Acrobat Professional only)

Figure 11-2

You can access the Reduce File Size feature from the File menu (to use on the currently open document) (Figure 11-2) or from the Optimize PDF toolbar. (Figure 11-3)

If you are only optimizing the current PDF, click File>Reduce File Size. Acrobat will ask you to specify where to save the reduced size file. You can select the current location (and overwrite the existing file) or another location. After you click Save, the process will begin. If your document has attachments, the tool will not process the attachments, which must be opened and optimized separately. Acrobat displays the Reducing PDF size progress bar and then saves the file, displaying its size before and after the reduction process. Generally, the file cannot be reduced more and, if you run the process again, Acrobat will advise you that the document is as small as possible. The length of the time for this process varies based upon the size of the file, the amount of graphics, etc.

Figure 11-3

Save as Reduced Size PDF

This method also allows users to specify a reduced size file's compatibility with prior Acrobat versions. Click on File>Save as Other>Reduced Size PDF. (Figure 11-4 and Figure 11-5) If your document has attachments, the tool will not process the attachments, which must be opened and optimized separately. A dialog appears asking which version of Acrobat you want to make your document compatible with. This is an important step because the later the version of Acrobat you make your document compatible with, the smaller the result is likely to be. Generally, most Acrobat users, including those using the free Reader, have a recent version. We therefore recommend making the document compatible with Version 10.0 and later. Click OK. Acrobat displays the Reducing PDF size progress bar and then saves the file but does not display its size before and after the reduction process, nor does it state whether the document is as small as possible.

The length of the time for this process varies based upon the size of the file, the amount of graphics, etc. Note that some settings might actually increase the file size.

Figure 11-4

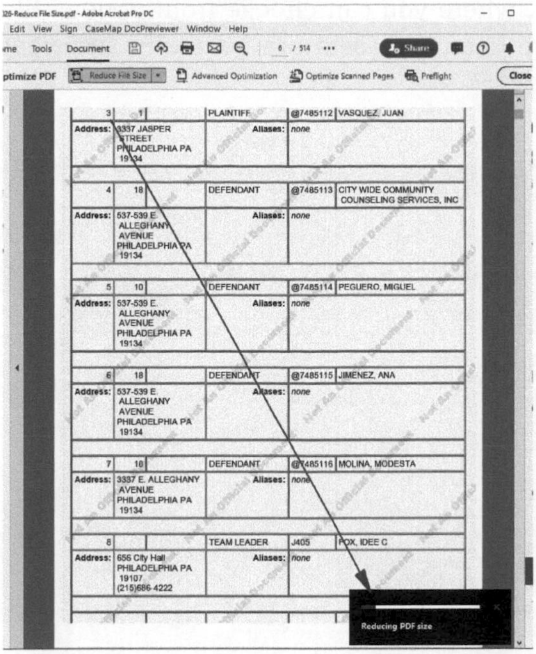

Figure 11-5

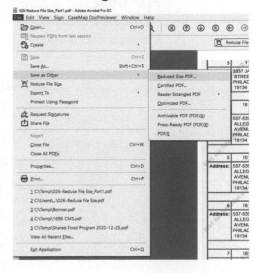

■ **Undocumented Solution:** Sometimes you will discover that Acrobat cannot reduce the size of a document further. If you still desire to reduce its size but not split the document, try printing the document using the Adobe PDF printer and saving the file with a new name. This solution often reduces the size of a file.

■ **The PDF Optimizer—Another Option That May Help When Reducing the Size of PDF Files:** Although these features are generally not necessary when reducing a file for e-filing or for attaching to email, they may be helpful if you are optimizing the PDF for printing or other uses.

❖ The PDF Optimizer

♦ Many factors affect a file's size and quality, especially when the file has many images. The Acrobat PDF Optimizer gives you additional control over a file's size and quality and more options than the Enhance Scanned PDF option that follows.

To access the PDF Optimizer, go to File>Save as Other>Optimized PDF (Figure 11-6) or Tools>Optimize

Figure 11-6

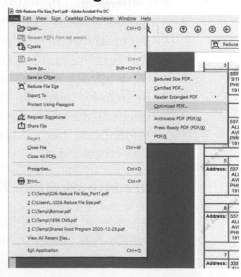

PDF>Advanced Optimization. (Figure 11-7) Acrobat will display the PDF Optimizer dialog box, where you can choose from various file compression methods. The default presets are generally sufficient for legal documents.

Figure 11-7

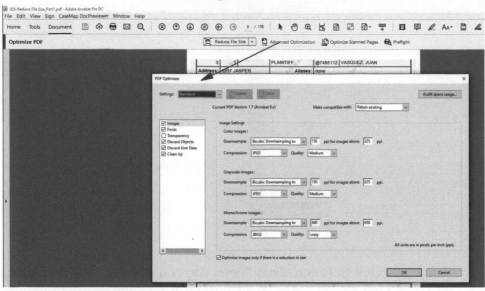

❖ The Enhanced Scanned PDF Option
  ◆ Scanned documents generally can be reduced in size. Acrobat includes the Enhance Scanned PDF option to assist. To access this tool, go to Tools>Optimize PDF>Optimize Scanned Pages and the Enhance Scanned PDF dialog will appear. (Figure 11-8) In the middle of the dialog is a sliding scale that allows you to specify whether the PDF should be a small size or high quality (larger). While the default settings are often sufficient, if a file is particularly large, you can move the slide closer to the Small Size option. You can also OCR the document while it is being optimized by selecting Recognize Text in the Text Recognition Option section.

  Note: If you choose to OCR your document, you can only select Searchable Image or Editable Text and Images, and not Searchable Image (Exact). Thus, you may choose to defer OCRing the document. Regardless, you should OCR all files using the Searchable Image (Exact) setting.

Splitting PDFs into Multiple Files

  ■ At times, you cannot reduce a file into a size small enough to electronically file or email. Or, you may need to limit the number of pages in your file

Figure 11-8

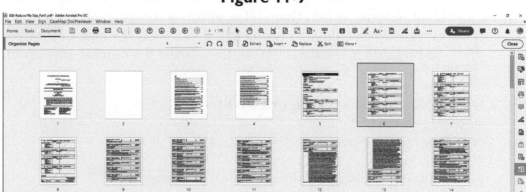

when sending it for binding and printing purposes. When that happens, you can split the file into smaller pieces and file, email, or bind it in smaller chunks. Acrobat includes a Split File tool to accomplish this.

❖ **Splitting One PDF File**

♦ Go to Tools>Organize Pages>Split. (Figure 11-9) Acrobat will display the Split toolbar, which offers the option to split the file by (1) the number of pages, (2) the file size, or (3) top-level bookmarks. Before splitting a file, you must determine the output criteria (pages, file size, or top-level bookmarks) as well as any Output Options. If you want the split document to be saved in a different folder from where the original was saved, click on Output Options and specify the location, selecting "A Folder on My Computer." You can also specify how

Figure 11-9

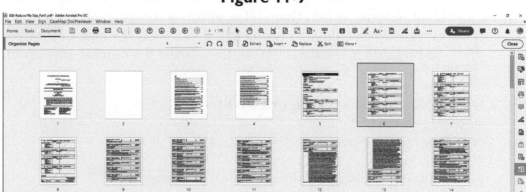

the output files will be named and prohibit Acrobat from overwriting any existing files.

If you are splitting the file for electronic filing or email, choose File Size from the menu and specify the maximum permissible file size. This value must be between 0.5 and 10, in 0.5 increments. Click Split and Acrobat will split the documents.

❖ Splitting Multiple PDF Files

♦ Acrobat can split multiple files at the same time, avoiding the need to perform the action repetitively. To do so, go to Tools>Organize Pages>Split. You must have at least one file open to use this feature. (Figure 11-10) Before splitting multiple files, you must determine the

Figure 11-10

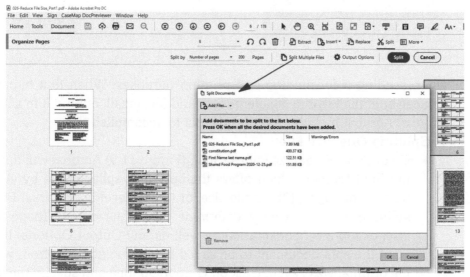

output criteria (pages, file size, or top-level bookmarks) as well as any Output Options. After making these choices, select Split Multiple Files. (Figure 11-11) This dialog permits users to Add Files, Add Folders, or Add Open Files, which is the same dialog box you access when OCRing documents. If you want the split documents to be saved in a different folder from where the original was saved,

Figure 11-11

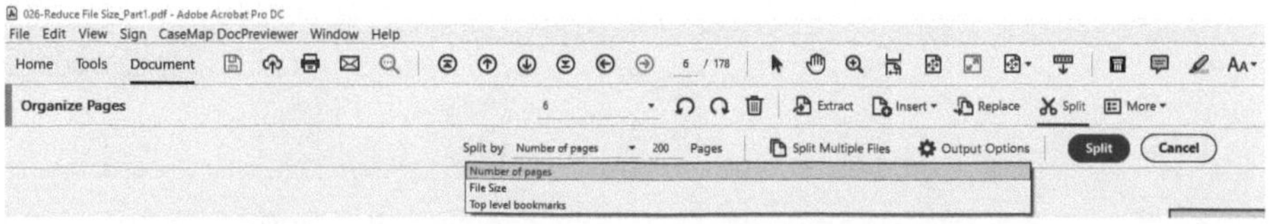

click on Output Options and specify the location, selecting "A Folder on My Computer." You can also specify how the output files will be named and prohibit Acrobat from overwriting any existing files.

If you are splitting the file for electronic filing or email, choose File Size from the menu and specify the maximum permissible file size. This value must be between 0.5 and 10, in 0.5 increments. Click Split and Acrobat will split the documents.

Chapter 12

Redacting Text
(Acrobat Professional Only)

Redaction is the process of permanently removing visible text and graphics from a document. Redaction, when used properly, prevents the inadvertent disclosure of privileged or otherwise confidential or sensitive information. In the past (and at times in the present), firms used a black marker to hide sensitive content, assuming it could not be viewed. This has proven to not always be true. Redaction ensures that the content being removed cannot be discovered by others.

Because law offices and other businesses may be required to redact (securely delete) private, confidential, or privileged information in order to comply with court or other legal requirements, Acrobat Professional includes a tool that simplifies this process.

Acrobat's Redaction tool can search for, mark, and permanently remove specific words, names, and common phrases, as well as telephone numbers, account numbers, and Social Security numbers; you can also search for common patterns. The way in which redactions are displayed is also customizable, ranging from a simple black or other colored box to overlay text that displays the bases for the redaction and/or its statutory or regulatory basis.

NOTE: The Find Text tool does not search secured (encrypted) PDFs.

How to Redact a Document Using the Redaction Toolset

- In order to redact specific text, your document must be OCRed or created from a text-based program such as Microsoft Word. If a document is not OCRed, you can only redact the region/area where the text appears, but you cannot search for and redact specific text.

❖ Go to Tools>Redact to display the Redact Text & Images toolset. (Figure 12-1)

Figure 12-1

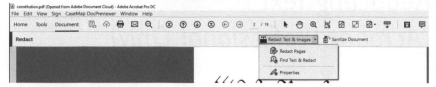

❖ Or, go to Edit>Redact Text & Images. (Figure 12-2)

■ If the Redaction toolset is open, highlight the text you want to redact and it will be marked immediately for redaction; when you hover your mouse over the text or region, it will display how the area will appear when redactions are applied. (Figure 12-3)

Figure 12-2   **Figure 12-3**

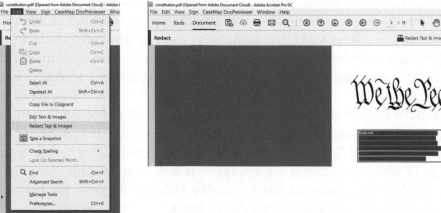

Or, if the redaction tools are not displayed, highlight the text, right-click, and select Redact. (Figure 12-4)

■ Alternatively, you can select Redact Text & Images>Redact Pages or select Redact Text & Images>Find Text & Redact.

❖ Select the text or image you intend to redact, right-click, and select Redact.

❖ You can also select any text or image (without using the Redact tool), right-click, and select Redact.

❖ In addition, you may drag your cursor to select a line or block of text. Repeat this process until all of the items you want to redact are marked.

Figure 12-4

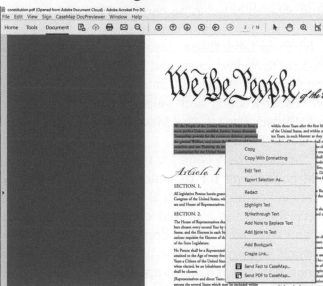

All proposed redactions will display as a preview of how they will appear when redacted when you hover your mouse over the redaction.

❖ If you want to change how the redaction appears, right-click on the redaction and select Properties. You can then change the redaction properties. (Figure 12-5) This is discussed in detail in "Changing the Appearance of Redaction Marks."

Figure 12-5

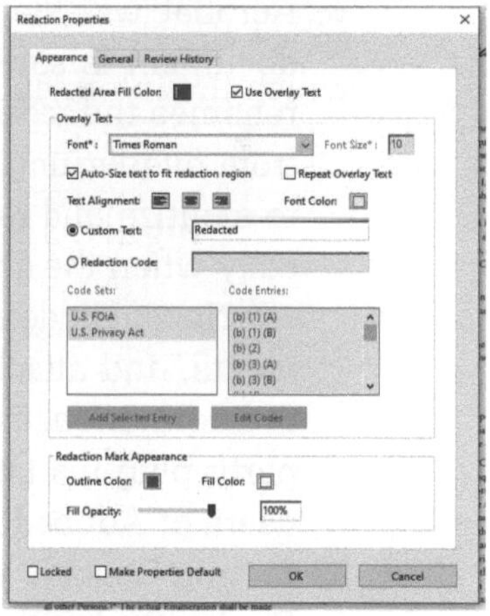

■ Once you have marked content for redaction, you can click "Apply" on the Redaction toolset. A dialog appears, stating that "This will permanently remove the redacted information. Once you save the document, you won't be able to retrieve the redacted information." It also explains and asks, "Your document might contain hidden data and metadata. Do you wish to remove them?" Then, click OK.

■ Acrobat will then ask you to save the redacted document. When the document is saved, the redactions are permanent. By default, Acrobat renames the redacted document with a _Redacted suffix to prevent you from overwriting the original/source document. If you allowed Acrobat to sanitize and remove hidden information, that will be done automatically when the document is saved.

NOTE: Hidden information may include hidden text, metadata, comments, and attachments, so be careful. This tool can remove a variety of information, including digital signatures, information added by third-party plug-ins (such as LexisNexis CaseMap), and features that allow users of Adobe Reader to review, sign, and fill PDF documents.

■ Redacting Complete Pages of Content

❖ Go to Tools>Redact and select Redact Text & Images>Redact Pages. The Mark Page Range dialog appears. (Figure 12-6)

Figure 12-6

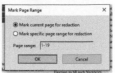

❖ Select "Mark current page for redaction" or "Mark specific page range for redaction." If you select a page range, you must provide it in the dialog box.

❖ To preview how the redacted content will appear, turn to one of the pages you selected for redaction and hover your mouse over the redaction, which will preview how it will look when redacted. If you want to change how the redaction appears, right-click on the redaction and select Properties. You can then change the redaction properties. This is discussed in detail in "Changing the Appearance of Redaction Marks."

❖ Once you have marked content for redaction, you can click "Apply" on the Redaction toolset. A dialog appears, stating that "This will permanently remove the redacted information. Once you save the document, you won't be able to retrieve the redacted information." It also explains and asks, "Your document might contain hidden data and metadata. Do you wish to remove them?" Then, click OK.

❖ Acrobat will then ask you to save the redacted document. When the document is saved, the redactions are permanent. By default, Acrobat renames the redacted document with a _Redacted suffix to prevent you from overwriting the original/source document. If you allowed Acrobat to sanitize and remove hidden information, that will be done automatically when the document is saved.

NOTE: Hidden information may include hidden text, metadata, comments, and attachments, so be careful. This tool can remove a variety of information, including digital signatures, information added by third-party plug-ins (such as LexisNexis CaseMap), and features that allow users of Adobe Reader to review, sign, and fill PDF documents.

■ Redacting Specific Words, Patterns, Etc.

❖ Go to Tools>Redact and select Redact Text & Images>Find Text & Redact. Acrobat warns you that it cannot search for images and line art and that you should "review your documents carefully to ensure that all sensitive information is properly marked for redaction." The Search dialog appears, which is virtually identical to the Advanced Search dialog. (Figure 12-7)

❖ The Search pane allows you to search in the current document or to search All PDF Documents in (1) My Documents, (2) Your Desktop, (3) Your PC, or (4) a location you specify by browsing for the folder using Windows Explorer (Windows). You can also search your Local Disks or your Documents or Desktop, or you can Browse for Location (Mac).

Figure 12-7

❖ The Search dialog also allows you to search for (1) a Single word or phrase, (2) Multiple words or phrases, or (3) Patterns.

   ◆ When you select Patterns, you can select from the following patterns: (1) Phone Numbers, (2) Credit Cards, (3) Social Security Numbers, (4) Email Addresses, or (5) Dates.

Figure 12-8

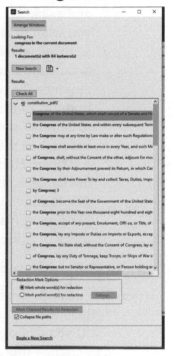

❖ After determining which document or location you will search, type the word or phrase you are looking for. This dialog allows users to search for whole words only. The search can also be case-sensitive. Click Search & Remove Text.

❖ The results will display below the dialog, with the search term appearing in bold typeface. These results differ from the basic search in a few key ways: (Figure 12-8)

   ◆ There is a check box to the left of each search result.

   ◆ There is a section toward the bottom of the Search pane entitled Redaction Mark Options.

   ▪ To mark whole words or partial words (characters) for redaction, select "Mark whole word(s) for redaction." To mark partial words, select "Mark partial word(s) for redaction." Next, specify the number and location of the characters for redaction. Character redaction is useful when searching for patterns such as credit card numbers and you want to leave part of the number (such as the last four digits) visible for identification purposes.

❖ You can then select individual results by checking the check boxes or using the Check All option to select all of the results for redaction.

❖ Next, click on Mark Checked Results for Redaction. Acrobat will mark all of the selected results. You can either close the Search box, click on

New Search, or click on Begin a New Search. Continue this process until all of the items you want to redact are marked.

❖ To preview how the redacted content will appear, go to a page with redactions and hover your mouse over the redaction, which will appear as a preview of how the document will look when redacted.

❖ If you want to change how the redaction appears, right-click on the redaction and select Properties. You can then change the redaction properties. This is discussed in detail in "Changing the Appearance of Redaction Marks."

❖ Once you have marked content for redaction, you can click "Apply" on the Redaction toolset. A dialog appears, stating that "This will permanently remove the redacted information. Once you save the document, you won't be able to retrieve the redacted information." It also explains and asks, "Your document might contain hidden data and metadata. Do you wish to remove them?" Then, click OK.

❖ Acrobat will then ask you to save the redacted document. When the document is saved, the redactions are permanent. By default, Acrobat renames the redacted document with a _Redacted suffix to prevent you from overwriting the original/source document. If you allowed Acrobat to sanitize and remove hidden information, that will be done automatically when the document is saved.

NOTE: Hidden information may include hidden text, metadata, comments, and attachments, so be careful. This tool can remove a variety of information, including digital signatures, information added by third-party plug-ins (such as LexisNexis CaseMap), and features that allow users of Adobe Reader to review, sign, and fill PDF documents.

Naming Redacted Files

■ By default, when you choose File>Save, Acrobat appends the suffix "_Redacted" to each file from which content is redacted.

If you do not want to automatically add this suffix to redacted files, you can change this setting by going to Edit>Preferences (Windows) or Acrobat Pro DC>Preferences (Mac) and going to the Documents category. In the Redaction section at the bottom of the window, you can select or deselect whether Acrobat will adjust a filename when saving applied redaction marks. If you choose this option, you can specify a custom suffix and/or prefix to apply to files with redacted information. (Figure 12-9)

Changing the Appearance of Redaction Marks

■ When you select an area or text or other items you mark for redaction, Acrobat places a thin box around the items. You can change the appearance of these areas, known as redaction marks, before you apply any redactions.

Figure 12-9

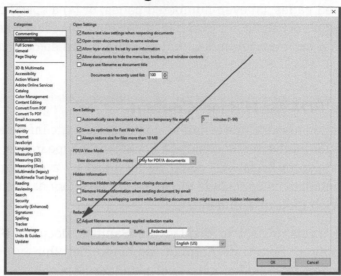

* For a specific redaction:
  * Before redacting your document, right-click on the redacted area of the document and select Properties. (Figure 12-10) You can also access the Properties from the toolset by selecting Properties on the Redact Text & Images dropdown.

Figure 12-10

  * Select the color of the redactions and whether they will contain overlay text such as "Redacted" or other text. Acrobat offers a list of standard overlays that refer to the U.S. Freedom of Information Act or the U.S. Privacy Act. You can also specify whether redactions are outlined (have a border) or have a fill color.
  * If you want to make these redaction properties the default for all future redactions, select the Make Properties Default box at the bottom of the Appearance section of the Redaction Properties dialog.

Repeating Redactions on Multiple Pages of a Document

■ After marking the area for redaction, but before applying the redaction, right-click on the area and select "Repeat mark across pages."

- Next, specify whether to apply the redaction to (1) all pages, (2) odd-numbered pages, (3) even-numbered pages, or (4) a specific page range.
- This feature is helpful, for example, if you want to redact a header or footer, such as a fax message mark, that appears in the same location on many pages.

Examining a PDF for Hidden Content

Hidden information may include sensitive content or private information as well as content that could inadvertently change a document's appearance, enable JavaScripts, or include form fields that could be modified by a subsequent user. For example, the metadata could include the name of the author and other information that you may wish to keep confidential.

- Choose Tools>Redact to display the Sanitize Document option. Select it. Acrobat explains that this process removes hidden data and metadata from the document so that sensitive information is not inadvertently passed along when you publish your PDF. If you want to preview the hidden information before removing it, you will have the option to "Click Here" to "selectively remove hidden information" when you click on Sanitize Document. (Figure 12-11)

    If you choose to review the hidden information, Acrobat will analyze the document and display the results in the Remove Hidden Information sidebar on the left of your document. You can then review and determine which hidden information to remove or preserve. Once you have made your selections, click Remove and Acrobat will remove those items.
- Save the document or documents, either with new names or by overwriting the original files. If you overwrite the original files, you cannot retrieve the redacted information. It is permanently deleted.

Figure 12-11

Creating Redaction Codes and Code Sets

- It can be very helpful to create and save redaction marks to use in future documents. That way, for example, if you are involved in ongoing litigation, or merely use the same conventions repeatedly, you can save your redaction properties and use them again without having to redefine or recreate them. For example, you may choose to simply "black out" the text, or you may want the word *redacted* to also appear where the text is blacked out. To do so, go to Tools>Redact Text & Images.

- Select Properties to view the dialog.
- Select Use Overlay Text to activate the Overlay Text section of the dialog.
- Select Redaction Code, then select Edit Codes. (Figure 12-12)

Figure 12-12

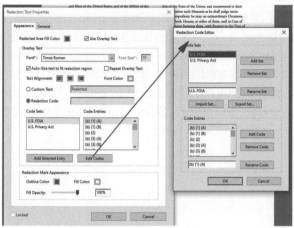

- Click Add Set or Add Code to add in any Code Sets or Code Entries, and then rename the item so it is easy to recognize. Click OK.
- When you return to the Redaction Tool Properties dialog, your new entries will appear.

Alternatively, instead of Codes, you can choose Custom Text; however, you cannot save the custom text for use in future documents.

NOTE: Using the Redaction Tool Properties dialog from the Redact toolbar does not change your default redaction properties. To change those properties, you must instead right-click on a redaction and select the Make Properties Default check box at the bottom of the dialog. This option does not appear in the dialog that opens when you select Properties from the Redact Text & Images dropdown menu.

Importing and Exporting Redaction Codes and Code Sets

Figure 12-13

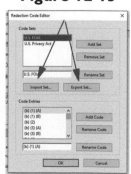

Transferring a set of redaction codes from one computer to another saves time and improves standardization. (Figure 12-13)

Exporting Redaction Codes and Code Sets

To export a redaction code set, open the Properties dialog by right-clicking either on an area to be redacted or on Properties in the Redact>Redact Text & Images dropdown menu.

Make certain that the Use Overlay Text box is checked. Select the Redaction Code button and select Edit Codes under the Code Entries list. Highlight the Code Set you want to export and select Export Set. Save the XML export file to a location on your computer. Send the exported file to the recipient.

Importing Redaction Codes and Code Sets

To import a redaction code set, open the Properties dialog by right-clicking either on an area to be redacted or on Properties in the Redact>Redact Text & Images dropdown menu. Make certain that the Use Overlay Text box is checked. Select the Redaction Code button and select Edit Codes under the Code Entries list. Select Import Set under the list of Code Sets and navigate to the XML file containing the Code Set you want to import. Select the Code Set and then OK. The Code Set will appear in your list of Code Sets.

Chapter 13

Bates Numbering (Acrobat Professional Only)

Bates numbering is the process of applying a unique number to documents, commonly used during the production of documents during discovery so that they can be easily identified. Unlike traditional page numbers that are inserted as footers, Bates numbers generally are multidigit items, which also contain unique alphanumeric prefixes and/or suffixes identifying the producing party and other information. Generally, parties agree upon and create a Bates numbering protocol for each case and apply the numbers to all electronic files produced during discovery. Because of security and other restrictions, you cannot use Bates numbering with protected or encrypted files, nor can you apply them to some forms.

Adding Bates Numbers

- Go to Tools>Edit PDF. Under the More dropdown on the toolset, select Bates Numbering. There are two options, Add or Remove. (Figure 13-1) Select Add to open the Bates Numbering dialog.

    NOTE: (1) This dialog works whether or not a document is open, and (2) Acrobat does not automatically detect existing Bates numbers when opening this dialog.

Figure 13-1

■ Using the Add Files dropdown menu, select the files you will be using. This menu allows you to add files (Ctrl+Shift+I for Windows and Cmd+Shift+I for Mac), add folders (all documents in the folders), or add other types of files. You do not need to merge the documents when applying Bates numbers. (Figure 13-2)

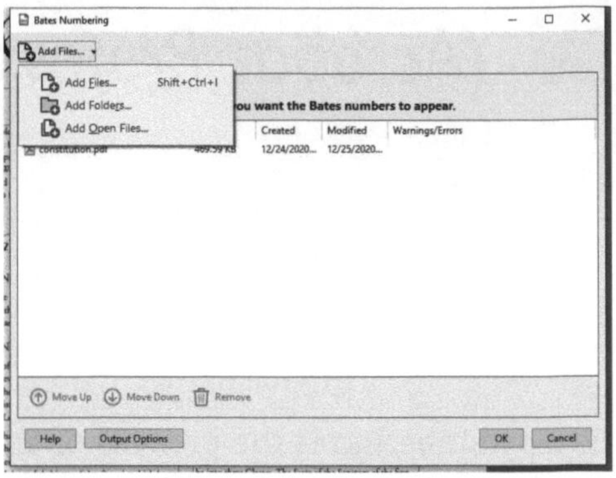

■ When designating documents for Bates numbering, you can add PDFs and any non-PDF files that can be converted to PDFs. The process converts non-PDF file types to PDFs and then adds Bates numbers to the resulting PDFs.

■ To change the order in which Bates numbers are assigned, highlight a file name and either drag it or click Move Up or Move Down.

■ You can sort the list by clicking on the name of a column. If you click again, the items will be sorted in reverse order.

   ❖ You may also use the Output Options button to specify whether the documents are stored in their original folder or a different folder you specify. You can also specify whether Acrobat maintains the original file names, overwrites the existing files, or adds a suffix or prefix to the file name. (Figure 13-3)

Figure 13-2

Figure 13-3

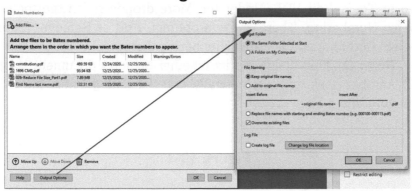

■ After you have added all of the files you want to Bates-number, click OK to open the Bates numbering dialog. The dialog, which is named Add Header and Footer, is identical to the Add Header and Footer dialog except that it has an Insert Bates Number button instead of the Insert Page Number button. (Figure 13-4)

Figure 13-4

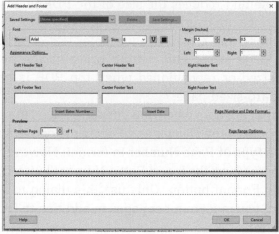

Note: When creating Bates numbers, you should enter information by completing the form from top to bottom, going line by line.

■ (Figure 13-5) If you are using a Saved Setting for Bates numbering, you would select it now. If not, proceed to the Font section to specify the font and size you want. These properties apply to any Bates number created with this specific dialog.

Figure 13-5

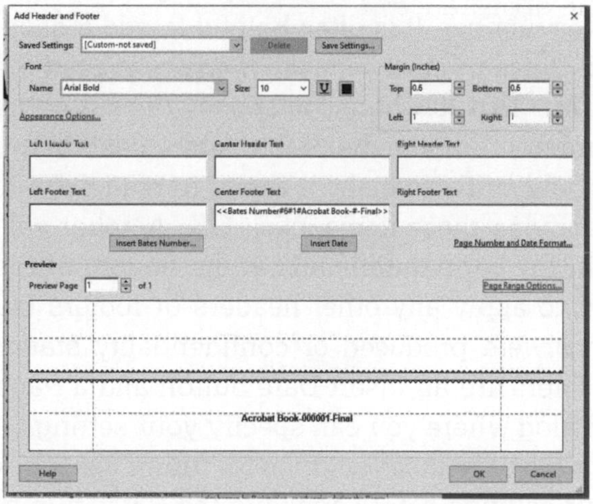

■ In the Margin section, determine whether the margins are acceptable. Note that the top and bottom margins are set at .5 inch because most documents have one-inch margins for the text.

■ Click on Appearance Options and adjust the following options as needed:

❖ Shrink document to avoid overwriting the document's text and graphics: This setting reduces the size of the PDF to ensure that any header or footer does not overlap existing content.

❖ Keep position and size of header/footer text constant when printing on different page sizes: This setting prevents the header or footer from being resized or repositioned when the PDF is printed on a large or nonstandard-sized page.

■ The dialog that appears when you click the Page Number and Date Format button differs from the Header and Footer dialog because it includes Bates Number as a type of Page Number to format. However, you should specify Bates numbers using the Insert Bates Number button, *NOT* the Page Number and Date Format button. Only use this dialog to number a page if, for some reason, you must number pages in addition to Bates-numbering them (a rare situation).

■ Next, place your cursor in the box for the location where you want to insert the Bates number: for example, Center Footer Text or Right Footer Text.

❖ Click on the Insert Bates Number button. You may now specify four items:

♦ **Number of Digits:** This is how many digits the Bates number will contain. This number must be between 3 and 15.

ı **Start Number:** This is the first Bates number for this batch of documents. If this is not the first group of documents being Bates-numbered in this case, your starting number should be the next number in the sequence of previously used Bates numbers.

ı **Prefix:** This is where you specify the prefix that precedes the Bates number. It is often helpful to add a dash between the prefix and Bates number to make it easier to read the information.

ı **Suffix:** This is where you specify the suffix that follows the Bates number. It is often helpful to add a dash between the Bates number and suffix to make it easier to read the information.

❖ After specifying these items, click OK. Acrobat will preview the Bates number in the page thumbnails at the bottom of the dialog box. If you also need to apply any other headers or footers (such as the date the documents were produced or confidentiality statements), you can do so now. There are an Insert Date button and a Page Number and Date Format dialog where you can specify your settings.

❖ If you want to save these settings for future use, click Save Settings and name your settings before applying the Bates numbers.

❖ Click OK and Acrobat will insert the Bates number on each specified document and advise you that Bates numbering has been successfully applied.

Removing Bates Numbers

- You can remove Bates numbers from an open document or multiple documents (regardless of whether or not they are open).
- Removing Bates Numbers from an Open File
  - ❖ Go to Tools>Edit PDF. Under the More dropdown on the toolset, select Bates Numbering. There are two options, Add or Remove.
  - ❖ Select Remove and Acrobat automatically removes existing Bates numbers in the document.
  - ❖ Click Save to save the document.
  - ❖ If Acrobat cannot detect Bates numbers, it will show a message.
- Removing Bates Numbers from Multiple Files
  - ❖ *Make sure you have no documents open.*
  - ❖ Go to Tools>Edit PDF. (Figure 13-6) Under the More dropdown on the toolset, select Bates Numbering. There are two options, Add or Remove. Select Remove.

Figure 13-6

- ❖ Using the Add Files dropdown menu, select the files you will be using. This menu allows you to add the files you want to remove the Bates numbers from, add folders (all documents in the folders), or add other types of files. You do not need to merge the documents when removing Bates numbers.
- ❖ You may also use the Output Options button to specify whether the documents are stored in their original folder or a different folder you specify. You can also specify whether Acrobat maintains the original file names, overwrites the existing files, or adds a suffix or prefix to the file names.
- ❖ When you click OK, Acrobat removes the Bates numbers from the documents. Click OK to finish.

Updating or Replacing Bates Numbers

- The only way to update or replace Bates numbers is to remove them and reapply them. This differs from headers and footers, which may be updated.

Chapter 14

Using Acrobat for Discovery, Document Production, and Other Matters

Portfolios

- A PDF Portfolio contains multiple files assembled into one PDF unit and can include various types of files. For example, you could assemble a Portfolio with PDFs and multimedia files, such as an accident recreation animation, and produce it to a mediator. Or, you could assemble a group of documents, emails, spreadsheets, and PowerPoint presentations and provide them to assist an expert in reviewing a case. If you were handling a zoning matter, you could include various plot plans, aerial photographs, and simulations of the final building design to assist a zoning hearing board in reviewing your client's application. In short, Portfolios allow lawyers to creatively prepare all types of matters and easily present the information in them to others, while retaining their original file types.

Deposition Summaries

Traditionally, lawyers have reviewed paper transcripts by using highlighters, writing notes on the pages of the transcripts, and/or creating separate notes about the testimony. While there are software programs that fully automate transcript reviews, Acrobat offers an alternative solution that enables lawyers to analyze testimony in a way that others can easily review.

- **Obtain the *Files* Electronically When Possible:** To improve your results, always obtain transcripts either as PDFs or in an electronic format, such as text (.txt or .ascii) or Word (.doc or .docx) formats that can be converted directly into a PDF. While scanning a document will work, it requires users to OCR the document and may not be as accurate as a document generated directly from another electronic file.

- **Organize Your Transcripts:** There are two common methods for organizing transcripts: placing them in one directory/folder or assembling them into a Portfolio. If you use a Portfolio, OCR the transcripts before assembling the Portfolio; this saves time and assures that all documents are searchable.

    Note: When converting a transcript that contains comments from a Word document, click on Preferences in the Create Adobe PDF section of the Acrobat tab, and select the Word tab. Check the box next to "Convert displayed comments to notes in Adobe PDF" to ensure that all comments will be included in the PDF. (Figure 14-1)

Figure 14-1

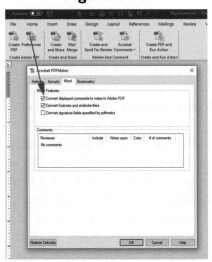

- **Use Comments:** As you review the transcript, insert your review notes as separate comments. Then you will be able to review the comments, search the comments, or print a summary of the comments.

    ❖ Consider also using special codes, such as DX for diagnosis or ACCF for accident facts. Thus, a note could state "DX: Dr. Jones diagnosed Plaintiff with a herniated disk at L4-L5," or "ACCF: Defendant disregarded the red light." When you search the document and prepare for further action in the case, you can narrow your results by searching for specific codes. (Figure 14-2) We recommend using codes with letter patterns that do not commonly appear in words. Then you can use the Advanced Search and limit your search to "Whole words only."

Figure 14-2

❖ After you view the search results, you can print the transcript as a PDF. To do so, select Print and select the Adobe PDF printer. (Figure 14-3) On the right side of the dialog, click on the Summarize Comments button and click Yes in response to the question whether you want to include the text of summarized comments in the document being printed. Next, name the document and click Print. The resulting PDF will display numbered notations where your comments were made and include a summary page at the end of the document.

Figure 14-3

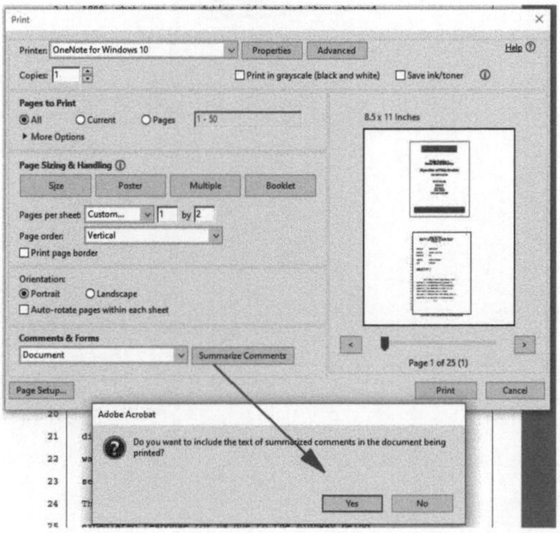

❖ Alternatively, you may save your results as a PDF or a CSV (Excel-compatible) file that summarizes all of your comments.

Discovery

Reviewing discovery is similar to reviewing transcripts, except that you should (1) OCR all of your documents, (2) verify that the OCR is accurate, and (3) use comments when the documents contain text or images that cannot be OCRed. After you have taken these additional steps, process the documents in the same manner as transcripts.

Using Portfolios for Discovery and Other Matters

Portfolios can facilitate advanced classification of documents. For example, you could compile documents, determine which are privileged, categorize documents, or perform actions for any other purpose. This method of analysis builds on the use of comments for discovery and depositions and can be used in almost any type of case.

■ Right-click on any thumbnail and select Portfolio Properties to view and select the data to display about each document, as well as the order in which the information will be shown. (Figure 14-4 and Figure 14-5)

Figure 14-4   **Figure 14-5**

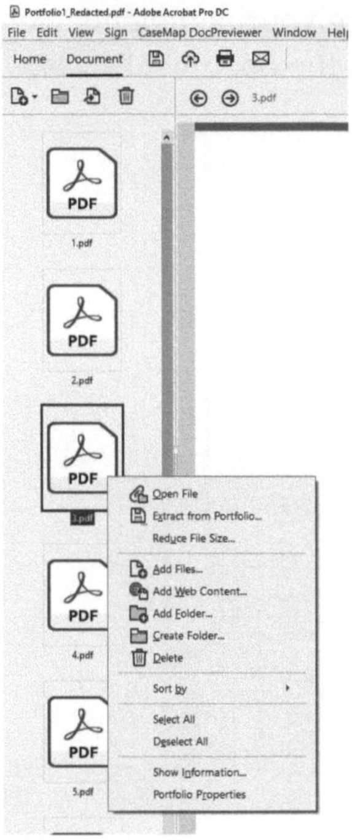

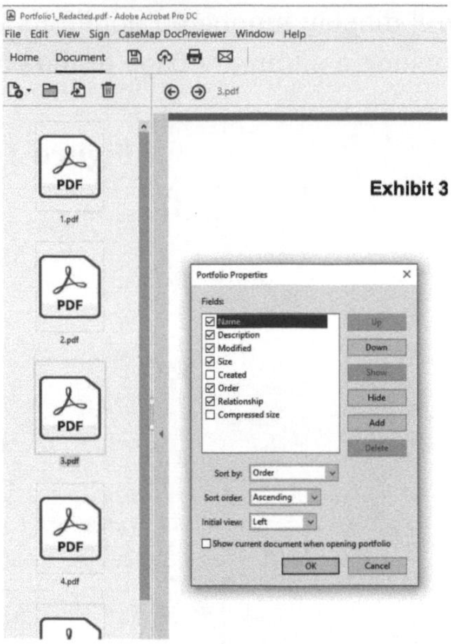

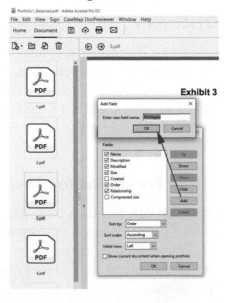

■ Next, while still viewing Portfolio Properties, click Add and create a new field, such as Privileged. Make sure there are checks in the boxes next to any fields you want to view, including the newly created ones. (Figure 14-6) Click OK when you are done.

■ Click on View>Portfolio and select Details. (Figure 14-7) The Portfolio will display all of your selected fields. (Figure 14-8) To edit the value in the field, such as adding Yes to the Privileged value, right-click on the file name, select Edit Value, and choose the item, such as Privileged. (Figure 14-9) Type in "yes" or whatever value you desire and click OK. (Figure 14-10)

Figure 14-6

Figure 14-7

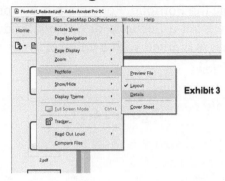

Figure 14-8

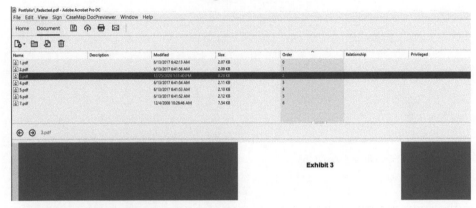

Figure 14-9

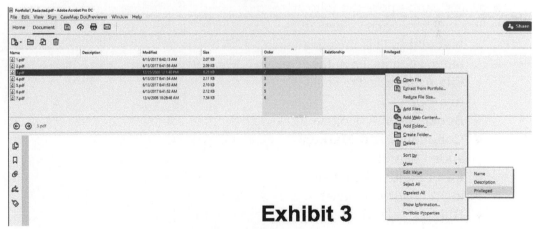

Figure 14-10

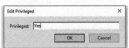

- You can then sort on any value or remove documents that do not have the desired value from the Portfolio. For example, by sorting on Privileged, you could then delete from a Portfolio of potentially discoverable documents any document that is marked with a value of "yes" in the field called Privileged. (Figure 14-11)

Figure 14-11

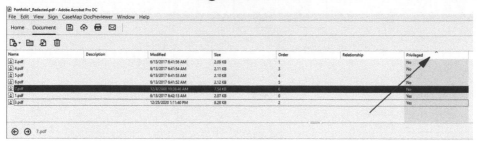

Chapter 15

Securing Your Documents

Adobe Acrobat is not a "security" product. Its primary purpose is to create a uniform appearance for every document, not to prevent unauthorized users from accessing documents, as Acrobat reminds users when they apply various security settings. In most cases, using Acrobat's security settings intelligently—that is, while using strong passwords, etc.—will suffice for most law offices. Strong, or complex, passwords have become critical to assuring the privacy of documents, and their use is consistent with a lawyer's obligation to preserve confidential client data and other sensitive information. Generally, a strong password will include a variety of symbols, numbers, and lower- and uppercase letters, and the longer the password, the more secure it is.

PDF users must remember, however, that PDF files are designed to allow document users to do something with the documents, including the most heavily secured documents, thus creating the possibility that the PDF will be compromised. In addition, there are many programs that can remove passwords from PDFs, although their success is based in large part upon the complexity of a given document's password. Thus, as with all other files and items, lawyers should act with reasonable care when securing and exchanging PDFs.

Viewing a PDF's Security Settings

If a PDF has security restrictions, it will show "(SECURED)" in the name of the file. In addition, Acrobat displays a Security Settings button in the Navigation pane on the left side of the document window. (Figure 15-1)

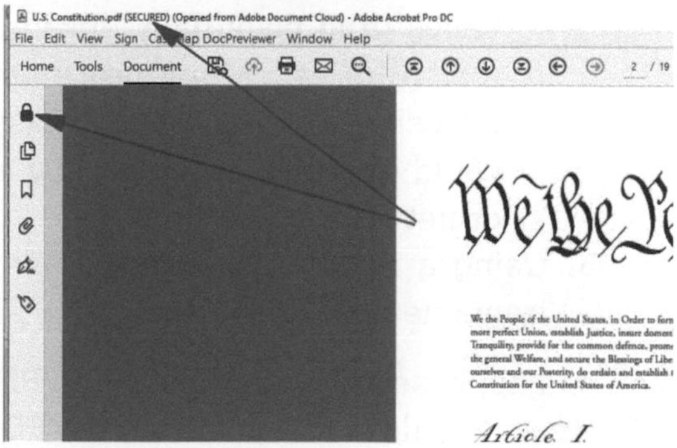

To view a document's security settings, go to File>Properties and select the Security tab. This will display the

Figure 15-1

document's current security settings. (Figure 15-2)

Figure 15-2

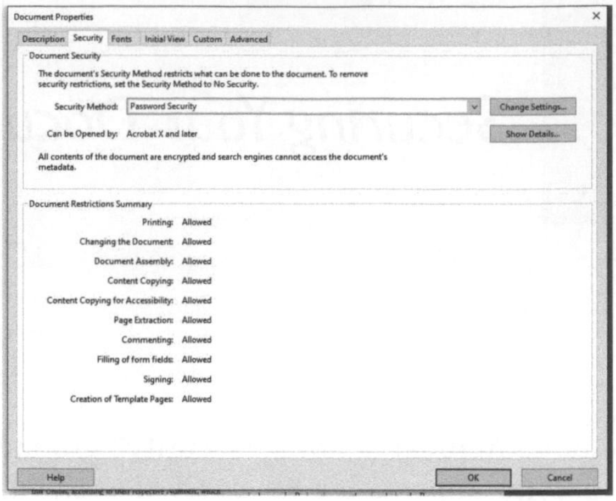

Adding Security Settings to a PDF

Five Ways to Restrict or Secure a PDF

1. Creating a password and specifying a PDF's security options to restrict opening, editing, and printing PDFs.
2. Encrypting a document so that only specific users may view it.
3. Saving a PDF as a certified document. When you certify a PDF, you add a certifying signature (which may be visible or invisible) that allows the author of the document to restrict changes to the document.
4. Using Enhanced Security restrictions:
   * **Enhanced Security:** Go to Edit>Preferences and select the Security (Enhanced) section, which includes specific predefined restrictions as well as a method to specify other "trusted locations" that are not subject to the restrictions. Using these settings, Acrobat users can block PDFs from what Adobe calls "dangerous actions" or "risky actions."

        In general, Enable Enhanced Security should be your default setting. Depending on the nature of your network, you may define additional trusted locations in this Preferences section.
   * **Protected View:** This is another Enhanced Security preference, which allows users to view PDFs in secure, read-only mode that will block most dangerous actions unless the user decides to "trust" the document. You can (1) turn off Protected View, (2) limit Protected View to "Files from potentially unsafe locations," or (3) enable Protected View for "All files." Many users turn off Protected View because it seems intrusive, but doing so increases the possibility that a virus or malware could cause damage not only to the document but also to the user's PC or network.
5. Using a Security Envelope: This feature protects a PDF when it is sent from one user to another.

You can apply security settings to any PDF when it is created and, generally, after it is created. Unless the creator of the PDF restricted the document's security settings, you can also apply security to a document created by another person.

To apply security settings, go to File>Properties and select the Security tab.

- Adding passwords:
  - ❖ You can add two kinds of passwords to protect your Adobe PDF documents: (1) a Document Open password, which allows only users who enter the correct password to open a document, and (2) a Permissions password, which allows only users who enter the correct password to perform other actions, such as printing or modifying the document.
  - ❖ To add a password, go to the Security tab of the Document Properties dialog. In the Security tab, change the Security Method from No Security to Password Security. (Figure 15-3) *Because most readers will not have access to Certificate Security or Adobe Experience Manager Document Security, this section will provide instructions for only Password Security.* Acrobat will display the Password Security—Settings dialog.
  - ❖ In the Document Open section, select the "Require a password to open the document" option *if you want to restrict who opens the PDF.* (Figure 15-4) Next, type a

Figure 15-3

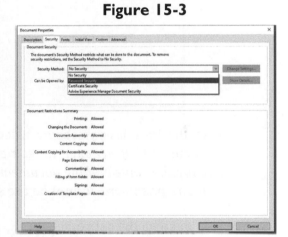

Figure 15-4

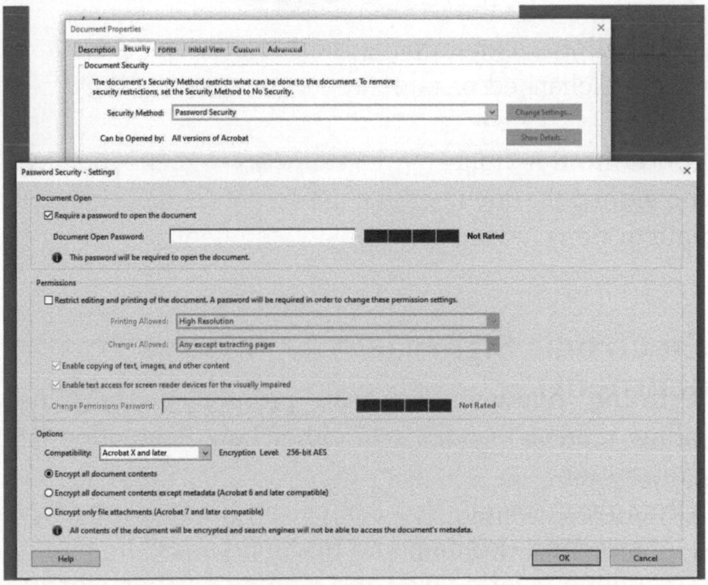

password. As you type the password, Acrobat will display its analysis of the strength of the password. (Figure 15-5) In general, a strong password contains at least 16 characters and includes uppercase and lowercase letters, numbers, and symbols.

Figure 15-5

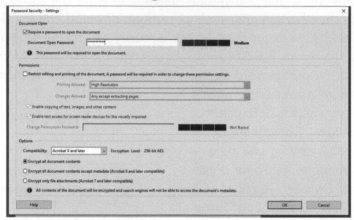

❖ In the Permission section, select "Restrict editing and printing of the document" *if you want to restrict whether a reader may print, modify, or copy the content of the document.* ***The open password and the permissions password cannot be the same.*** (Figure 15-6)

Figure 15-6

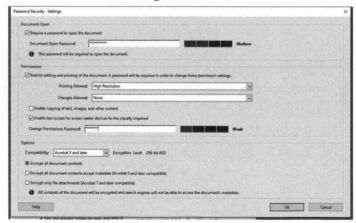

♦ **Printing Allowed:** You can prohibit printing the document or allow readers to print it in either Low Resolution (150 dpi) or High Resolution.
♦ **Changes Allowed:** You can permit the following types of changes:
  ▎ "Inserting, deleting, and rotating pages"
  ▎ "Filling in form fields and signing existing signature fields"

- ı "Commenting, filling in form fields, and signing existing signature fields"
- ı "Any [change] except extracting pages"
- ◆ **Two Other Self-Explanatory Settings in the Permissions Section**
    - ı "Enable copying of text, images, and other content": allows users to do so
    - ı "Enable text access for screen reader devices for the visually impaired"
- ◆ **Options Section:** In the Options section, you can make other changes that will enhance the security of the document.
    - ı Compatibility: This specifies the earliest (oldest) version of Acrobat that you will allow to open the document. Acrobat's default compatibility level is with Acrobat 7.0 or later. Adobe recommends setting the compatibility level to "Acrobat X and later" if recipients have Acrobat X or later because those versions have the strongest level of protection.
    - ı There are three encryption options, which only are relevant for documents stored on websites:
        - ı "Encrypt all document contents": prevents search engines from viewing the document and any attachments
        - ı "Encrypt all document contents except metadata": permits search engines to view the metadata (Document Properties) but prevents search engines from viewing the document and any attachments
        - ı "Encrypt only file attachments": only encrypts document attachments
- ■ When you have completed specifying all of the security settings, click OK.
- ■ If you added a document password, Acrobat will prompt you to reenter the password and advise you that the password will be required to open the document and that third-party products may not support the security settings. This applies only after you save the document. (Figure 15-7)

Figure 15-7

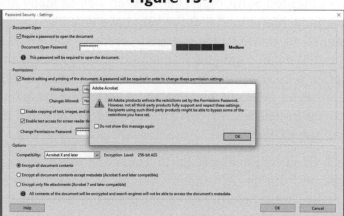

- If you added a permissions password, Acrobat will prompt you to reenter the password and advise you that the password will be required to change the document. (Figure 15-8)

Figure 15-8

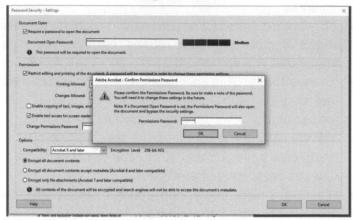

- Click OK to close the security tab. *You must save the document before the security settings will be applied.* (Figure 15-9)

Figure 15-9

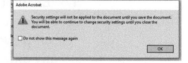

Using a Security Envelope

Acrobat permits users to create a Security Envelope, a secure container in which to send and receive files. Because Acrobat files may contain attachments in non-PDF format, a Security Envelope also provides a convenient way to include all of those files. An added benefit of using a Security Envelope is that a recipient can open the Security Envelope with the free Adobe Reader.

- **Security Envelopes Are a Great Solution for Ensuring Email Security (Undocumented Solution):** The ABA, as well as many state and local bar associations, has opined that lawyers have an ethical obligation to encrypt their email to prevent unauthorized persons from viewing sensitive and confidential email communications and attachments. Although Acrobat is not per se a secure product, if you use strong passwords, then a Security Envelope is an excellent way to comply with this ethical obligation because a Security Envelope may contain all types of files and does not have to include any PDFs.

To create a Security Envelope, go to Tools and select Protect. Select Create Security Envelope from the Advanced Options dropdown (Figure 15-10) on the toolset to view the Create Security Envelope dialog, which displays all of the steps in the process.

Figure 15-10

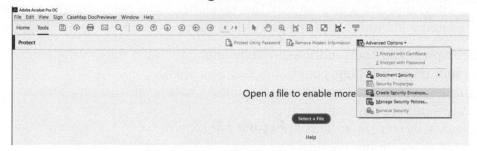

First, select the Files to Enclose by clicking the Add File to Send button and selecting the files (of any type) to include in the Security Envelope. By default, Acrobat includes any already-open documents in the list of files to include in the Security Envelope. You can use the Remove Selected Files button to remove any items you do not want to include. (Figure 15-11) Click Next.

Figure 15-11

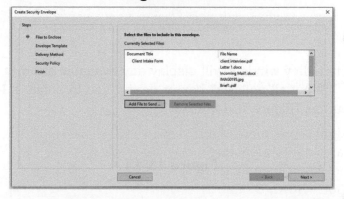

The envelope template window will display the available types of templates. There are generally three default options: (1) eEnvelope with Signature, (2) eEnvelope with Date Stamp, and (3) Interdepartment eEnvelope. Select the appropriate choice or browse to locate another template, if you have other templates. (Figure 15-12) Click Next.

Figure 15-12

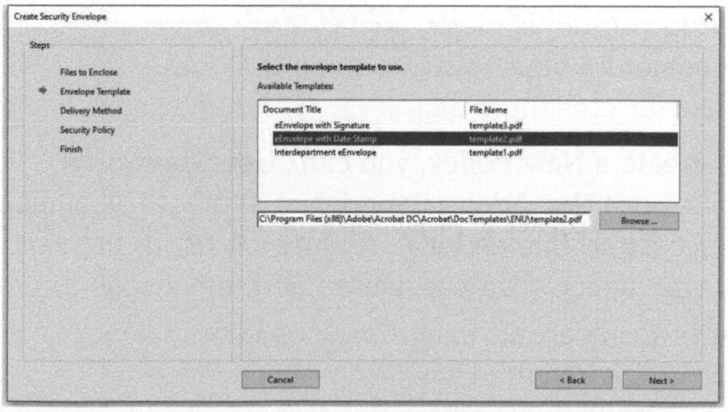

■ Depending on the template you choose, you can fill in various form fields to customize the appearance of the envelope. Some fields may be autopopulated with your username and a date stamp.

Select whether to "Send the envelope later" or "Send the envelope now" and click Next. (Figure 15-13)

Figure 15-13

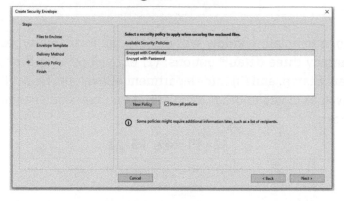

The security policy window will display any available security policies when you check the "Show all policies" box or permit you to create a New Policy by clicking that button. (Figure 15-14)

Figure 15-14

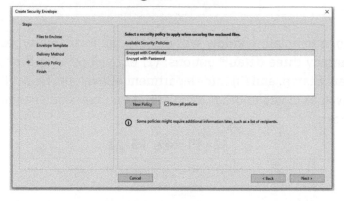

■ If you create a New Policy, you can "Use passwords," "Use public key certificates," or "Use Adobe Experience Manager Document Security" (if you have access to this service). (Figure 15-15) In the vast majority of cases, users will select "Use passwords" if they choose to create a New Policy. Click Next.

Figure 15-15

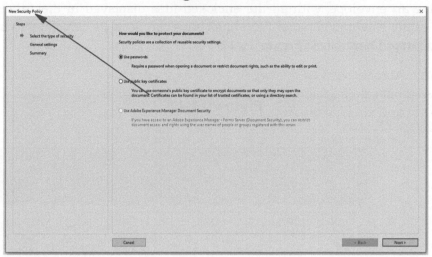

- When you create a New Policy, you will be able to save the policy setting as well as the passwords for the policy. Click Next.
- The Password Security—Settings dialog appears. This is the same dialog you use when changing security for a document by going to File>Properties. Create your settings and click OK.
- You will then see the Summary window of the New Security Policy dialog. Click Finish.

If you have previously created a security policy, or are using one of the Acrobat defaults, you will see the Password Security—Settings dialog. Complete the dialog by adding the appropriate security settings. Click OK to proceed to the next step.

- Next, Acrobat displays the "Finish" dialog, which lists the files to be included in the Security Envelope. Review the list and then click Finish. (Figure 15-16)

Figure 15-16

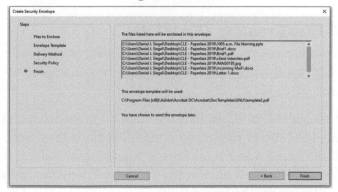

If you selected "Send envelope later," Acrobat displays the envelope, which looks like an envelope, with all the enclosed files displayed in the Attachments section of the Navigation panel. You must save the Security Envelope to use it as an email attachment later. (Figure 15-17)

Figure 15-17

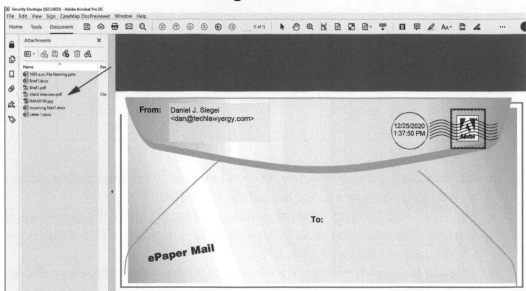

If you chose "Send envelope now," Acrobat will open your default email program with the Security Envelope as an attachment in a new email.

- When you send a Security Envelope, Acrobat copies your original files to the envelope and does not delete the source files.
- In addition, Acrobat applies security to the envelope, not the documents inside it. If you want to apply security to the individual files, you must do so before including them in the Security Envelope.

Certifying PDF Files/Creating Digital IDs

A certified document assures recipients that a document is authentic and has not been modified or tampered with. The following are two examples of when to use certified documents:

- You want recipients to know that the files originated from you and have not been accidentally or maliciously modified since they were published.
- You distribute forms that contain prepopulated information, and you want to prevent recipients from accidentally or maliciously modifying your form data when they return the forms to you.

The process by which Acrobat allows users to "certify" the contents of a PDF is very similar to the one used to create a digital signature. When a document is certified, users are still permitted to make approved types of changes to the document while preserving the certified status of the document. For example, you can certify a form to (1) ensure that all content is valid when a user receives the form and (2) be certain that a user completes the document as designed, without modifying any form fields. Users who try to modify a certified document, such as by removing or adding a form field, will invalidate the document.

- To certify a file, with a document open, go to File>Properties and select the Security tab to verify that there are no security settings or other restrictions in the document. Click Cancel.
- Next, click Tools and select the Certificates tool. (Figure 15-18) Click Certify (Visible Signature) or Certify (Invisible Signature) in the Certificates toolbar to display the Certificates dialog. If a PDF signature is invisible, no signature form field appears in the PDF document. If the signature is visible, the signature information appears to the user.

Figure 15-18

- ❖ If you choose Visible Signature, Acrobat will explain that you must drag your cursor to create a new signature field. In either case, you will see the Save as Certified Document dialog box. If you are creating a visible field, you will now be required to drag your cursor to the document location where you want to create a signature field. (Figure 15-19)

Figure 15-19

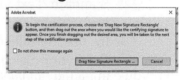

- Next, Acrobat displays the Save as Certified Document dialog that certifies that the document came from you. It also explains that you will need a digital ID to certify the document. (Figure 15-20)
- Next, you will either select the type of existing digital ID you have or create one. (Most users will create and store one on their computers and use it for their documents.)

Figure 15-20

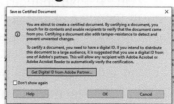

  - ❖ We will assume, in this section, that you do not already have a digital signature. If you select the "Configure New Digital

ID" option, Acrobat will display a window with three options: (1) Use a Signature Creation Device such as a smart card or token connected to your computer, (2) Use a Digital ID from a file stored on your computer, or (3) Create a new Digital ID. Because most users will create their own Digital IDs, you should select Create a new Digital ID.

❖ When you click Continue, Acrobat asks for the destination of the new Digital ID. You may either Save to File or Save to Windows Certificate Store. Most users will select Save to File; then click Continue. The next dialog, Create a self-signed Digital ID, asks you to fill in your Name, Organization Name, Email Address, and so on. (In general, the default 2048-bit RSA will suffice for Key Algorithm.) Complete the dialog and click Save.

❖ The next window, Save the self-signed Digital ID to a file, displays the default location for the Digital ID. You can store it in that location or browse to store it in another location on your computer. Next, type your password and retype the password in the Confirm the password dialog. Click Save to display the Certify Document dialog.

❖ If you already have a digital ID, or have completed the process of obtaining one, Acrobat will ask you to Sign with a Digital ID and continue. (Figure 15-21)

Figure 15-21

❖ If you chose a Visible Signature, Acrobat will then display your name and allow you to have the signature appear as Standard Text. You can also modify the signature's appearance by selecting Create, which allows users to use graphics and other custom features. In most cases, using Standard Text is sufficient. (Figure 15-22)

Figure 15-22

❖ In the Permitted Actions After Certifying dialog, you also specify what actions you will allow users to do:

  ♦ "No changes allowed": permits no changes.

  ♦ "Form fill-in and digital signatures": allows users to fill in form fields and digitally sign the document.

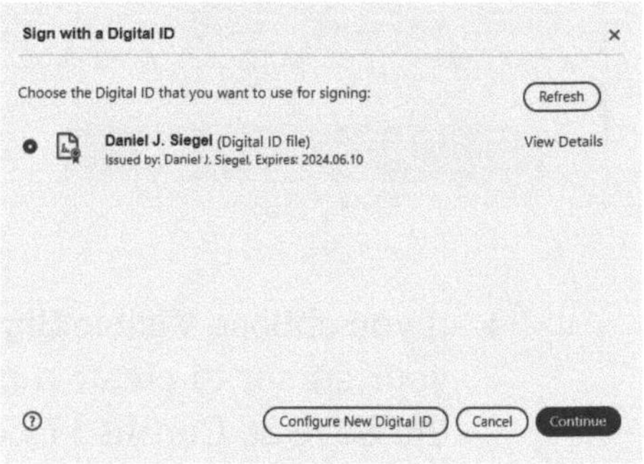

- ◆ "Annotations, form fill-in, and digital signatures": allows users to add annotations, fill in form fields, and digitally sign the document. (Figure 15-23)

Figure 15-23

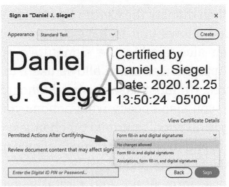

Next, you must review the document warnings and then click Sign. Next, save the file, which is now digitally signed. (Figure 15-24)

Figure 15-24

If you select an invisible signature, you will also see the Certify Document dialog, which allows you to specify what actions you will allow users to do:

- ◆ "No changes allowed": permits no changes.
- ◆ "Form fill-in and digital signatures": allows users to fill in form fields and digitally sign the document.
- ◆ "Annotations, form fill-in, and digital signatures": allows users to add annotations, fill in form fields, and digitally sign the document.
- ❖ In either case, whether you select a visible or invisible signature, you must then enter the password you had previously created in the "Enter certificate password and click the 'Sign' button" box. Then click Sign.
- ❖ Acrobat will then display the Explorer window so that you can select the location for and name the certified document. In general, you should create a new name for the document rather than merely saving over the original.

- If you have selected the "My existing digital ID from" option, you will select where Acrobat can locate the digital ID on your computer.
  - ❖ Acrobat will then allow you to locate the saved digital ID. After selecting the desired file, type the password into the dialog and select Next. Acrobat will then list possible digital IDs. Select the appropriate one and click Finish.
  - ❖ Acrobat will then display the Certify Document window, which displays your name and allows you to have the signature appear as Standard Text. You can also modify the signature's appearance by selecting Create New Appearance, which allows users to use graphics and other custom features. (In most cases, using Standard Text is sufficient.)
  - ❖ In this dialog, you also specify what actions you will allow users to do:
    - ◆ "No changes allowed": permits no changes.
    - ◆ "Form fill-in and digital signatures": allows users to fill in form fields and digitally sign the document.
    - ◆ "Annotations, form fill-in, and digital signatures": allows users to add annotations, fill in form fields, and digitally sign the document.
  - ❖ You must then enter the password you had previously created in the "Enter certificate password and click the 'Sign' button" box. Then click Sign.
  - ❖ Acrobat will then display the Explorer window so that you can select the location for and name the certified document. In general, you should create a new name for the document rather than merely saving over the original.
- If you have previously created a digital ID, Acrobat will display the Certify Document window.
  - ❖ The Certify Document window displays your name and allows you to have the signature appear as Standard Text. You can also modify the signature's appearance by selecting Create New Appearance, which will allow users to use graphics and other custom features. (In most cases, using Standard Text is sufficient.)
  - ❖ In this dialog, you also specify what actions you will allow users to do:
    - ◆ "No changes allowed": permits no changes.
    - ◆ "Form fill-in and digital signatures": allows users to fill in form fields and digitally sign the document.
    - ◆ "Annotations, form fill-in, and digital signatures": allows users to add annotations, fill in form fields, and digitally sign the document.
  - ❖ You must then enter the password you had previously created in the "Enter certificate password and click the 'Sign' button" box. Then click Sign.
  - ❖ Acrobat will then display the Explorer window so that you can select the location for and name the certified document. In general, you should create a new name for the document rather than merely saving over the original.

Removing Hidden Information

Acrobat allows users to remove hidden information using one of two processes: Sanitize Document, which is located in the Redact tool (Figure 15-25), or Remove Hidden Information, which is located in the Protect tool (Figure 15-26). Sanitize Document removes all hidden information but offers an option to selectively remove hidden information, which then opens the Remove Hidden Information panel within the Redact tool. (Figure 15-27 and Figure 15-28) When you select Sanitize Document and OK, Acrobat immediately begins the process but first provides the option to rename the file. The Remove Hidden Information option allows users to select the type of information to remove; that is, it provides the same

Figure 15-25

Figure 15-26

Figure 15-27   Figure 15-28

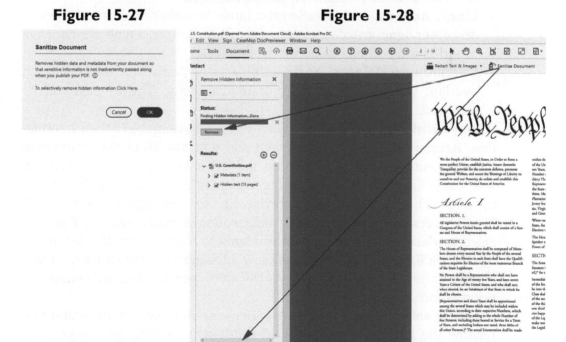

option that you are given when you select the Sanitize process but allows you to review information before removing it.

- Users can remove the following types of information from a PDF (assuming the information exists in the document):
  - ❖ **Metadata:** This includes information about the document and its contents, such as the author's name, keywords, and copyright information.
  - ❖ **File Attachments:** These are other files, not just PDFs, that are attached to a PDF.
  - ❖ **Bookmarks:** A bookmark takes a reader to specific pages in a PDF.
  - ❖ **Comments and Markups:** These are comments, etc., that have been added to a PDF.
  - ❖ **Form Fields:** Form fields are any fields that have been added to a document to allow a reader to add information.
  - ❖ **Hidden Text:** Hidden text includes items that are hidden or transparent (and therefore cannot be seen when viewing a PDF) or content that is the same color as the background color of the document.
  - ❖ **Hidden Layers:** When content is added to a PDF, it adds a layer (or overlay) to the file. Removing hidden layers deletes these items and flattens the document into one layer.
  - ❖ **Embedded Search Index:** An embedded index makes it easier to search a document, especially larger ones. This index can be removed.
  - ❖ **Deleted or Cropped Content:** Even after content has been "deleted" or pages "cropped," Acrobat often retains the items no longer visible to readers, and this information can be removed.
  - ❖ **Links, Actions, and JavaScripts:** Links to websites, email addresses, and other items are often created using JavaScripts, a type of interactive programming. These items can be removed.
  - ❖ **Overlapping Objects:** At times, objects or items in a document can overlap, whether intentionally or inadvertently. These items can be removed.
- **Remove Hidden Information:** When you select Remove Hidden Information, Acrobat analyzes the document and displays all of the information that you may remove in a pane on the left side of the screen. You can select specific portions of the results to display the information that will be removed. There is also a Show preview link for each type of result, which allows users to view the specific information Acrobat located. You may select or deselect the information you want to remove from the document. Next, click Remove to display a window advising you about all of the types of information Acrobat may remove. Click OK, and Acrobat will remove the information you have selected.

Next, select Save (or Save As). Because Acrobat suggests that you rename the document or store it in a different location so that you can access the original if necessary, it will display the Save As dialog. You can then view the Explorer window and specify where to store the file, as well as specify the name of the document. When you complete this dialog, the cleansed file is stored, and you cannot restore sanitized information.

- **Sanitize Document:** Sanitizing a document removes all of the items listed above, without providing the option to selectively remove only certain types of items. When you select Sanitize Document, Acrobat displays the Sanitize Document warning. If you click OK (rather than clicking Click Here to selectively remove information), Acrobat will display the Explorer window and ask where to store the file and what to name the document. After specifying this information, click OK and Acrobat processes the document. It is saved as part of the sanitizing process, and you cannot restore sanitized information.

Chapter 16

Adding Signatures, Initials, and Digital Signatures (Including the Fill & Sign Tool)

You can electronically sign or initial a document by placing a signature or initials on it, making it easier to email rather than mail or fax. There are two types of digital signatures, electronic signatures and digitally signed signatures.

An electronic signature (or initials) merely places a signature on a document but is no different from placing an image or watermark on a document. An electronically signed document can be changed by the user or recipient, and the signature can be removed in most cases with little difficulty.

A digitally signed document, on the other hand, contains added security that makes it more difficult to modify or remove the signature and is designed to assure the recipient (and any other persons or businesses that must rely upon the document) that it was signed and is legally binding. Thus, you may choose to place an electronic signature on a letter that you are sending digitally; you would use a digital signature on a contract or other legally binding document.

Advantages of Digital Signatures

Whenever possible, it is highly preferable to use a digital signature, which, unlike an electronic or nondigital signature, meets various legal requirements.

By using a digital signature, a user is in essence placing an electronic "seal" on the document. The recipient of the document containing a digital signature, therefore, knows that a known sender created the document and that the document was not modified after it was signed. In addition, although it is possible to change a digitally signed document (depending upon the settings used when the signature was applied), you are able to track any changes made after the digital signature was added, as well as remove any changes or revert the document back to its form before any changes were applied. Digital signatures can also contain additional information, such as the date and time when the document was signed, as well as why the document was signed.

- **Authenticity:** A digital signature helps to verify that the person who signs the document is who the person says he or she is.
- **Integrity:** A digital signature helps to verify that the content of a document has not been changed or tampered with after the document was digitally signed.
- **Nonrepudiation:** A digital signature helps to prove the identities of all parties who signed the document and reduces the possibility that a signer will repudiate or deny having signed the document.

Creating Electronic Signatures or Initials (Not a Digitally Signed Document)

Acrobat allows users to sign or initial a PDF document or form in a manner that displays the signer's name or initials. This function is different from digital signatures, which are secure. Nondigital signatures can still be useful, are commonly used, and can include other information, including the signer's company and title and the date. When saved, these signatures are part of a PDF.

You can customize Acrobat's default signature options by going to Edit>Preferences>Identity (Figure 16-1) or Edit>Preferences>Signatures (Windows) (Figure 16-2). You should customize these settings before creating a signature.

Figure 16-1

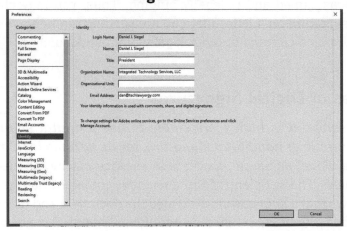

Figure 16-2

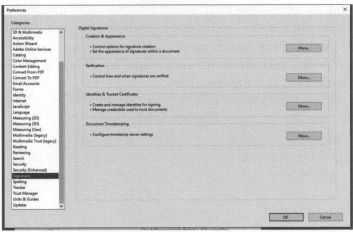

- When you select Identity, you can specify not only your name, but also the information that appears when creating digital signatures. This dialog also specifies the name that appears when creating comments or reviewing documents.
- When you select Signature, the dialog allows you to specify your preferences for signatures, including Creation & Appearance; Verification; Identities & Trusted Certificates; and Document Timestamping.

Next, create your signature or initials.

On Windows computers

Select Tools, and then select Fill & Sign. The toolbar allows you to Add text, Add X, Add checkmark, Add circle, Add line, Add dot, Change the color of your entry, Sign the document, or Request signatures. (Figure 16-3) If you are signing for yourself, (Figure 16-4) you can either Add Signature or Add Initials. Select the option that applies.

Figure 16-3

Figure 16-4

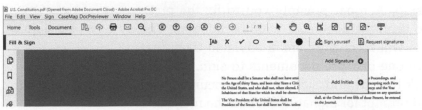

If you choose to add your signature, a dialog opens where you can type your name into the dialog box, draw your signature, or import a signature file. (Figure 16-5) You can also change the appearance of your signature. When you click on Apply, you are provided the opportunity to place the signature on the document and to also change the font, delete the signature, or add an X, checkmark, circle, line, or dot. (Figure 16-6 and Figure 16-7)

Figure 16-5

Figure 16-6   **Figure 16-7**

If you select "Request signatures," Acrobat displays the "Get documents signed fast with Adobe Sign" dialog, where you can fill in the email addresses of the signers and add a subject and message. (Figure 16-8) Acrobat will display the file or files to be signed, with an option to Add Files. There is also a warning that as part of this process, your file will be uploaded to Adobe Sign and that anyone with the link can view the file. If you select More Options, you are able to Password Protect the document and Set Reminder. When you click Next, or if you do not select More Options and instead Specify Where to Sign, Acrobat uploads the document and opens it so that you can place the signature box where you want it to appear. When you have completed that step, click Send, which appears at the bottom of the right panel. If signature fields are missing, Acrobat prompts you to fix the problem or to send the document without doing so. The recipients will receive an email advising them that they have one or more documents to sign. All they do is click Review and Sign, and the document will open and prompt for signature. When the recipients

Figure 16-8

sign the documents, they click the Click and Sign button, and both you and the recipient are notified that the document has been signed. You can then download the signed document to your computer.

On Mac computers

Select Tools, and then select Fill & Sign. In the Fill & Sign toolbar, Acrobat asks if you are going to Sign yourself or Request signatures. The colored dot at the beginning of the toolbar allows you to choose the color of the signature. If it is you signing the document, Acrobat asks if you want to Add Signature or Add Initials. Once you choose, a box opens for you to either Type, Draw, or insert Image. There is a dropdown that will allow you to Change style with limited font options. When you are finished, select Apply. You are returned to the document and you can place the signature or initials where you want it to appear. When the signature/initials box appears, you can also change the size or delete it.

If you choose to Request signatures, Acrobat displays the "Get documents signed fast with Adobe Sign" dialog, where you can fill in the email addresses of the signers and add a subject or message. Acrobat will display the file or files to be signed, with an option to Add Files. If you select More Options, you are able to Password Protect the document and Set Reminder. In this dialog, you also have the option to set individual passwords for each recipient by using the dropdown arrow to the right of his or her name. After you click Next, Acrobat uploads the document and opens it so that you can choose where the signature box should appear. When you have completed that step, click Send, which appears at the bottom of the right panel. If signature fields are missing, Acrobat prompts you to fix the problem or to send the document without doing so. The recipients will receive an email advising them that they have one or more documents to sign. All they do is click Review and Sign, and the document will open and prompt for signature. When the recipients sign the documents, they click the Click and Sign button, and both you and the recipient are notified that the document has been signed. You can then download the signed document to your computer.

Creating Digital (Digitally Signed) Signatures

This is essentially the same process used to certify a PDF and works on most documents and forms in the identical manner. To digitally sign a PDF document or form, go to Tools and select Certificates. On the Certificates toolbar, select Digitally Sign. (Figure 16-9) Next, you will be asked to click and drag to draw the area where your signature will appear.

Figure 16-9

If you are digitally signing a form with a previously created digital signature box, and the file does not have a signature box, you will see the Sign with a Digital ID dialog, which you can click on and Continue. (Figure 16-10) Acrobat will then display the Sign Document dialog, which allows you to select a previously created signature. If you have never created and stored a digital signature on your computer or if you select New ID from the Sign Document dialog, Acrobat

Figure 16-10

displays the Add Digital ID dialog. When you click Sign, Acrobat opens Explorer so you can rename the file and store it on your computer.

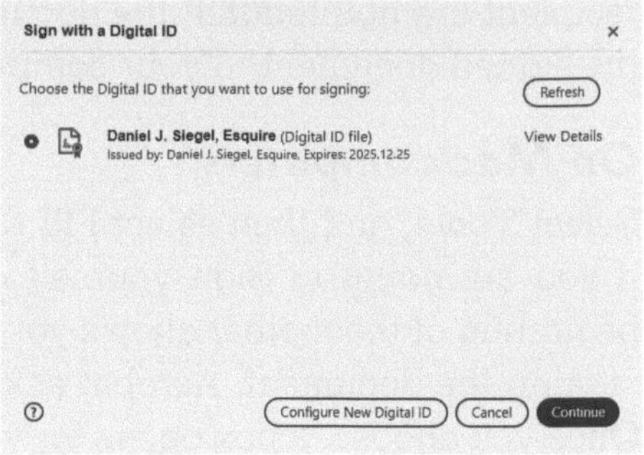

The process for creating a digital signature appears in Chapter 15.

Creating a Separate Copy of Your Actual Signature

One of the ways you can sign a document (either electronically or with a digital signature) is to insert an image of your actual signature onto the document (although this is not required for a digital signature to be valid). You can also capture a picture of your signature on a mobile device using the Adobe Acrobat Reader DC mobile app and save it in the Adobe Document Cloud so that it is synchronized and available for use across your desktop and other mobile devices. See Chapter 19 for further information.

There are many other ways to create a copy of your actual signature to use in Acrobat and other programs. You can simply search the Internet for "create a transparent signature stamp." We have also found the following two methods easy to use:

- Rick Borstein's Acrobat for Legal Professionals blog post: http://blogs .adobe.com/acrolaw/2007/02/creating_a_tran_1/
- Catherine Sanders Reach's YouTube video: https://www.youtube.com /watch?v=sBrfsVMN0GI (Courtesy of the Chicago Bar Association)

Validating Digital Signatures

By default, Acrobat verifies the validity of digital signatures. However, you should review Acrobat's default signature options by going to Edit>Preferences>Signatures (Windows) and clicking on More in the Verification section. (Figure 16-11)

Figure 16-11

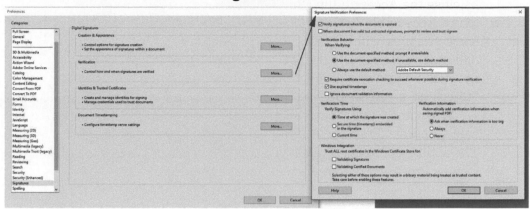

- To require Acrobat to validate all signatures in a PDF when you open a document, select Verify Signatures When the Document Is Opened. This should generally be your default setting.
- Generally, Acrobat's default settings are acceptable for most users. However, if you have more detailed needs, use Acrobat's Help function and search for "Validating digital signatures."

Chapter 17

Using Actions and Custom Commands (Acrobat Professional Only)

Actions, a feature available only in Acrobat DC Professional, allow users to automate repetitive tasks. If you think of one of the workflows in your cases (such as a list of the things you do to prepare for trial and the order in which you do them), Acrobat actions do the same type of thing with your PDFs. As a result, actions allow you to consistently handle your files. For example, you could create an action that OCRs files and then reduces their size.

Depending upon the action, you might be prompted to tell Acrobat what steps to take, while other actions can be performed once you specify which file, files, or folders to process. For example, if you include "Remove Hidden Information" in an action, Acrobat will require you to specify the information to remove. But if your action requires Acrobat to create bookmarks, that process can be performed automatically.

Acrobat Pro includes a limited number of actions, such as preparing documents for distribution or creating accessible PDFs, but most are not particularly focused on legal users. With a little practice, you will save time by creating and using actions.

Using Actions

All actions (whether created by Acrobat or by you) are available by going to Tools and selecting the Action Wizard. The Actions List on the right of the window displays all available actions.

When you select an action, Acrobat displays the steps in the action on the right of the window, as well as the files to be processed. You can select other files from this window. When you are ready to process the action, click Start. The Start button changes to a Stop button, which you can click on to stop the action at any time. If the process requires additional input, Acrobat will prompt you. When the action is done, the Start button will say "completed." Below the dialog is a "Full Report" link, which you can select to display a list of all tasks performed.

Creating an Action

You can create your own actions. Before doing so, you should write down all of the steps involved and determine what the best order should be for performing each task.

To open the Action Wizard, select Tools>Action Wizard to display the toolbar. (Figure 17-1) In the Action Wizard toolbar, click New Action to display the Create New Action dialog box. (Figure 17-2) The left pane of the dialog displays tools that you can include in the action (arranged by category). The right pane provides options for determining which files to process. You should always verify that an option is selected from the Add Files dropdown menu displayed below the Default Option menu. You can apply an action to an open file, prompt the user to select a file or folder, require the user to scan a document, or open a file stored in the cloud. Below that section is a list of the steps you have included with your action. You can use the buttons on the far right to design the action's appearance, including dividers, panels, and instructions.

Figure 17-1

Figure 17-2

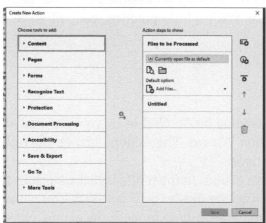

To add steps to an action, expand the category in the left pane (Note: Items in the categories do not correspond directly with the options in the Tools menus), (Figure 17-3) select the desired task, and click on the plus sign with the arrow in the middle of the dialog to add the step to the action. Many tasks include a Prompt User check box as well as a Specify Settings option to allow you to customize the process further. Continue adding tasks as needed. You can use the arrows on the right to rearrange the tasks (Move Up, Move Down, or Delete). Depending upon the selected task, Acrobat may prompt you for additional information.

Figure 17-3

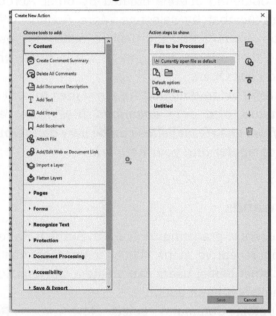

If you want to add a step that is not included on the dialog box, you may add instructions by clicking on the Add Instruction button on the right side of the dialog box. Generally, you should select the Pause check box for prompts such as these. It is also important to remember that you cannot access any tools while an action is running. Thus, if you need to access another tool, include a Go To step to permit the user to perform the desired task.

After you have added all of the steps to your action, including verifying that they are in the correct order and include all desired options, save the action by clicking the Save button. You will be prompted to name your action and to include a description of it. You should test every action after you create it. To do so, just go to Tools>Action Wizard, select the action, and press Start.

Managing Actions

You can edit (revise), rename, copy, or remove (delete) an action by selecting Manage Actions on the Action Wizard toolbar. You can also rearrange the order in which the actions appear on the list.

Obtaining Additional Actions

The Acrobat Actions Exchange (https://acrobatusers.com/actions-exchange) is a great website for obtaining actions created by other Acrobat users. You can access the site from Acrobat by selecting More Actions (Web) on the Action Wizard toolbar. After downloading the desired action to your computer, select Manage Actions and then Import. Navigate to the location where you saved the downloaded file, and click Open.

Warning: Be careful when downloading any files to your computer. Always run antivirus software, and only download files from reputable websites. Downloading files from unsafe websites can be very dangerous and could result in damage to your computer and your network.

Custom Commands

This feature allows users to preconfigure tasks in Acrobat Professional DC, saving time and eliminating repetitive steps. Thus, instead of creating custom water-marks, footers, and other items, users can create a Custom Command and add it to their toolbar or include it in an action.

Figure 17-4

To create a Custom Command, select New Custom Command from the Action Wizard. (Figure 17-4) Next, select the task from the options on the left of the dialog. You can also specify whether to display the command's options (e.g., the Add Watermarks dialog) or hide them because the options are always the same. Make sure to give the Custom Command a descriptive name so that you can use it in other parts of Acrobat. When you save the Custom Command, it will appear on the right-hand pane in the CUSTOM COMMANDS section (below the ACTIONS LIST section).

You can also add a Custom Command to your toolbar by opening a document and dragging the command onto the toolbar. Editing and managing Custom Com-mands is performed identically to how it is done with actions.

Sharing Actions and Custom Commands

It is easy to share (export or import) actions and Custom Commands.

Sharing/Exporting Actions and Custom Commands

You can share actions you create or edit with other users. To do so, open the Action Wizard. Next, select either Manage Actions (Figure 17-5) or Manage Custom Commands (Figure 17-6). Select the item you want to share, and click Export. Navigate to the location where you want to save the file, name the task, and click Save. Acrobat will save an action as a file with an .sequ extension; it will save Custom Commands as a file with an .xml extension. You can copy or attach the file to an email and share it with other users.

Figure 17-5   **Figure 17-6**

Sharing/Importing Actions and Custom Commands

You can use actions created by other users. To do so, open the Action Wizard. Next, select either Manage Actions or Manage Custom Commands. Click Import. Navigate to the location where the file you want is saved, and click Open. Actions will have an .sequ extension; Custom Commands will have an .xml extension. Acrobat adds the task to your list of actions or Custom Commands.

Sharing Actions and Custom Commands

It's easy to share (import or export) Actions and Custom Commands.

Sharing/Exporting Actions and Custom Commands

You can share actions you create or edit with other users. To do so, open the Action Wizard. Next, select either Manage Actions (Figure 17-5) or Manage Custom Commands (Figure 17-6). Select the item you want to share, and click Export. Navigate to the location where you want to save the file, name the task, and click Save. Action will save an action in a file with an .sean extension. It will save Custom Commands as a file with an .seal extension. You can copy or attach the files to email and share them with other users.

Figure 17-5

Figure 17-6

Sharing/Importing Actions and Custom Commands

You can use actions created by other users. To do so, open the Action Wizard. Next, select either Manage Actions or Manage Custom Commands. Click Import. Navigate to the location where the file you want is saved, and click Open. Actions will have an .sean extension. Custom Commands will have an .seal extension. Action adds the item to your list of Actions or Custom Commands.

Chapter 18

Working with Document Properties and Accessibility

Acrobat users can easily customize numerous document properties, ranging from the document's security levels to the look and feel of the PDF when another user views it. Using these options, users can modify or remove the metadata (information not visible on the PDF itself, but visible when viewing the document's Properties), add security to restrict how a user can modify or print a PDF, and add or enhance a PDF's accessibility. Adding security allows attorneys to address any ethical concerns they might have about transmission of documents and, if necessary, to prevent unauthorized persons from viewing, modifying, or printing the document.

Viewing and Setting Document Properties and Metadata

Users can modify many document properties and security settings. To do so, go to File>Properties (Ctrl+D for Windows or Cmd+D for Mac) to display the Document Properties data and dialog. This box has six tabs. Generally, you will not use the Custom and Advanced tabs, which are not discussed further.

- **Description Tab:** (Figure 18-1) The tab has numerous fields and two sections. You are able to modify some of the Description section settings but cannot change any Advanced properties.
  - ❖ **Description Section**
    - ◆ **File:** This section displays the name of the file (the actual file name, e.g., Interrogatories.pdf).
    - ◆ **Title:** Unlike the file name, this is the descriptive name you give to the document, such as Answers to Plaintiff's Interrogatories, and you can display this information instead of the file name by changing the Show setting on the Initial View tab (see later point entitled "Initial View Tab").
    - ◆ **Author:** You can specify the name or names of the authors, or you could use an organization, etc.

Figure 18-1

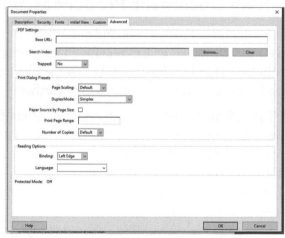

+ **Subject:** You can specify the subject of the document.
+ **Keywords:** You can include keywords about the contents of the documents. This is important if you are loading the document onto a website and want search engines to be able to review the document and point others to it.
❖ **Advanced Tab:** (Figure 18-2) This section provides information about the document's basic properties.

Figure 18-2

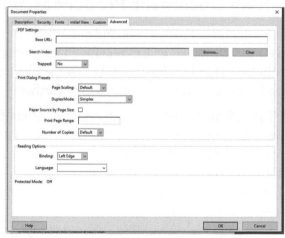

+ **PDF Producer:** This explains what type of software the document was created from, such as Microsoft Office Word 2007.
+ **PDF Version:** This lists the lowest/oldest version of Acrobat that may view the document, such as Acrobat 7.x.
+ **Location:** This specifies the location where the file is stored on your computer or network.

- ◆ **File Size:** This section specifies the file size (e.g., 1.85 MB) and is very helpful when you must limit the size of a document (such as for use as an email attachment or an electronically filed document). When you know this information, it is far easier to know if you must reduce the file size or split the document into smaller subdocuments, or possibly both.
- ◆ **Page Size:** This is the size of the paper the document is intended to be printed on.
- ◆ **Tagged PDF:** A Tagged PDF file contains metadata that describes the document's structure and the order of different elements in the document, such as images, titles, and text blocks. When a PDF is tagged, it is easier to extract text or graphics from the file. Accessibility standards may require PDF files to be tagged.
- ◆ **Number of Pages:** This is the total number of pages in the document, regardless of numbering.
- ◆ **Fast Web View:** A PDF formatted for Fast Web View allows a web server storing the document to download it one page at a time. With Fast Web View, a web server will send only the requested page, rather than the entire PDF, to the reader. This setting is helpful for larger documents that would take a long time to download.
  - ı Saving a PDF for Fast Web View requires that you change your Preferences.
    - ı To do so, go to Edit>Preferences (Windows) or Acrobat Pro DC>Preferences (Mac) and select the Documents category.
    - ı In the Save Settings section, check the box for "Save As optimizes for Fast Web" and click OK.
  - ı This setting will remain until you change it, although there is generally no need to uncheck the setting.
- ■ **Security Tab: (**Figure 18-3) This tab displays a document's current security settings and is where you can change many of a document's security settings. Modifying these settings is discussed in Chapter 15.

Figure 18-3

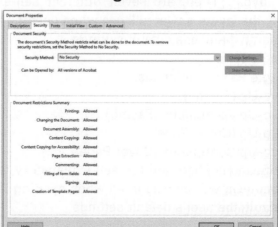

- **Fonts Tab:** This tab displays the fonts used in the document.
- **Initial View Tab: (**Figure 18-4) This tab provides different ways to display a document when it opens. Initial view is important, for example, when sharing a document with those not familiar with Acrobat features because it forces the document open in a certain way to help the user understand the utility of the document and enhance its value. *These settings are document-specific and cannot be applied globally to all documents.*
  - ❖ Layout and Magnification

Figure 18-4

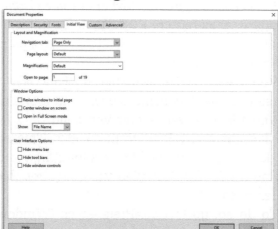

- ◆ Navigation tab: There are five different self-explanatory ways to specify how a document displays when it opens:
  - ▮ Page Only
  - ▮ Bookmarks Panel and Page
  - ▮ Pages Panel and Page
  - ▮ Attachments Panel and Page
  - ▮ Layers Panel and Page
- ◆ Page layout: There are seven different self-explanatory ways to specify the layout a user will see when opening a document:
  - ▮ Default: the user's default settings
  - ▮ Single Page
  - ▮ Single Page Continuous
  - ▮ Two-Up (Facing)
  - ▮ Two-Up Continuous (Facing)
  - ▮ Two-Up (Cover Page)
  - ▮ Two-Up Continuous (Cover Page)
- ◆ Magnification: There are ten self-explanatory ways to specify how the document will be magnified when opening it:
  - ▮ Default: the user's default settings

- Actual Size
- Fit Page
- Fit Width
- Fit Height
- Fit Visible
- 25%
- 50%
- 75%
- 100% (magnification levels go to 6400%)
  - ♦ Open to Page: opens to the specified page in the document
- ❖ Window Options
  - ♦ Resize window to initial page
  - ♦ Center window on screen
  - ♦ Open in Full Screen mode
  - ♦ Show: You can choose to display either the File Name (Document. pdf) or Document Title (the information displayed on the Title line of the Description tab).
- ❖ User Interface Options
  - ♦ Hide menu bar
  - ♦ Hide toolbars
  - ♦ Hide window controls
- ❖ **Custom Tab:** Not frequently used, this tab allows users to add custom properties and information about the file.

Accessibility of PDF Documents

The accessibility and flexibility of a PDF file determine how easily vision- and motion-impaired users can view and use the file. Although making documents accessible is not strictly necessary for most lawyers, it is good practice. As law offices are becoming more paperless and thus more digital, it is imperative that the content be accessible to all audiences, including those with disabilities. Additionally, Section 508 of the Rehabilitation Act requires federal agencies to make their electronic information accessible. If you work with the federal government, you likely are required to meet the Section 508 standards. The American Bar Association, through its Commission on Disability Rights, offers resources to help you better understand the concept of accessibility and how you can implement it in your firm.

Adobe PDF files support three levels of structure: tagged, structured, and unstructured. Tagged PDFs have the most structure. The more structure a file has, the more easily the file can be used in terms of accessibility. Examples of how you can build structure into your PDF are by adding bookmarks and alternate text for graphics. When you create a PDF from Microsoft Office or many other applications, the PDF is tagged automatically.

Checking for Accessibility

■ **Accessibility Tool (Acrobat Professional Only):** Checking for accessibility can be done with Acrobat's Accessibility tool. Once you have a PDF open, from the main toolbar, choose Tools and select the Accessibility tool. Choose Accessibility Check from the right-hand pane. The Accessibility Checker Options dialog box opens. (Figure 18-5) You should accept the defaults (to create the report, check all pages, and have all check boxes selected) and click Start Checking. Acrobat quickly checks the document for accessibility issues and displays the results of the check in the Navigation pane.

Figure 18-5

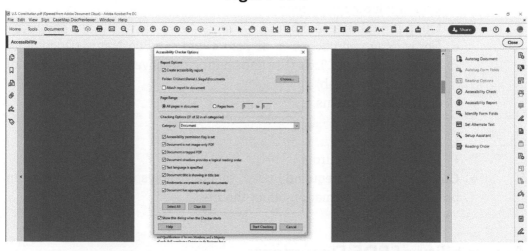

If your document has accessibility issues, these issues will display in categories. Each item in the category will have a status:

❖ **Passed:** The item is accessible and no action is needed.

❖ **Skipped:** This option was not selected in the Accessibility Checker Options dialog box and was not checked.

❖ **Needs Manual Check:** The Full Check feature could not check the item automatically, and it needs to be reviewed manually.

❖ **Failed:** The item is not accessible and needs action.

■ Right-clicking on issues provides the following options:

❖ **Fix:** This option provides you with a dialog box so that you can correct the issue.

❖ **Skip Rule:** This option allows you to disregard the issue and ignore it in future accessibility checks.

❖ **Explain:** This option provides more details about an issue in the online Help.

❖ **Check Again:** This option reruns the checker on all issues after you have made modifications.

* ❖ **Show Report:** This option displays a report of issues with tips on how to fix them.
* ❖ **Options:** This option opens the Accessibility Checker Options dialog box.
* ■ **Other Methods of Checking Accessibility (Standard and Professional):** In addition to the Accessibility Checker, Acrobat provides other methods for checking accessibility, such as the Reflow View and the Read Out Loud options.
  * ❖ **Reflow View:** To check the readability of your PDF, you can use the Reflow View. This view temporarily converts your PDF to a single column the width of the document pane so that it is easier to read on a mobile device or magnified on a monitor. NOTE: *You cannot reflow forms, comments, digital signatures, or headers and footers (including page numbers).* To use the Reflow View, choose View>Zoom>Reflow from the main menu. The document will display in Reflow View, where you can see where there may be issues that need to be resolved. If your document does not display well in Reflow View, you can use the Reading Order tool to resolve reflow issues. This tool is discussed in "Other Options in the Accessibility Tool." To return to the traditional view, choose View>Zoom>Reflow again.
  * ❖ **Read Out Loud:** This option will read the text of your PDF, including the text in comments and alternate text for images, using system-installed voices on a user's device or computer. Content is read in the order it appears in the PDF's tagged structure. If a document is untagged, the reading order is inferred.

    You must first activate Read Out Loud before use. From the main menu, choose View>Read Out Loud>Activate Read Out Loud. To deactivate it, choose View>Read Out Loud>Deactivate Read Out Loud.

    To use Read Out Loud, choose View>Read Out Loud>Read This Page Only, *or* Read to End of Document. To interrupt or stop the reading, choose View>Read Out Loud>Pause *or* Stop.

    To read form fields, you must first activate the option in your Preferences. From the main menu, choose Edit>Preferences, and in the Reading category, check the box for "Read form fields." Click OK. In a PDF form, tab to the first form field. You can enter text or make selections and then tab through the fields in the PDF. Acrobat will read the state of the selected check boxes and radio buttons.

    By listening to the order in which your PDF is read, you can determine where you may need to retag your document.

Adding Accessibility

- **Accessibility Tool (Acrobat Professional Only)**
  - ❖ You can change a PDF's accessibility with the Accessibility tool. Once you have a PDF open, from the main toolbar, choose Tools and select the Accessibility tool. Choose Accessibility Check from the right-hand pane. The Accessibility Checker Options dialog box opens. You should accept the defaults (to create the report, check all pages, and have all check boxes selected) and click Start Checking. Acrobat quickly checks the document for accessibility issues and displays the results of the check in the Navigation pane.

    If your document has accessibility issues, these issues will display in categories. Each item in the category will have a status:
    - ♦ **Passed:** The item is accessible and no action is needed.
    - ♦ **Skipped:** This option was not selected in the Accessibility Checker Options dialog box and was not checked.
    - ♦ **Needs Manual Check:** The Full Check feature could not check the item automatically, and it needs to be reviewed manually.
    - ♦ **Failed:** The item is not accessible and needs action.
  - ❖ Right-clicking on issues provides the following options:
    - ♦ **Fix:** This option provides you with a dialog box so that you can correct the issue.
    - ♦ **Skip Rule:** This option allows you to disregard the issue and ignore it in future accessibility checks.
    - ♦ **Explain:** This option provides more details about an issue in the online Help.
    - ♦ **Check Again:** This option reruns the checker on all issues after you have made modifications.
    - ♦ **Show Report:** This option displays a report of issues with tips on how to fix them.
    - ♦ **Options:** This option opens the Accessibility Checker Options dialog box.
  - ❖ Once you have fixed the necessary issues, you can save the PDF and close the Accessibility Checker panel and the tool.
- **Make Accessible Action:** This action allows you to automatically set and correct issues with document properties, tab order, tags, alternate text, and other accessibility features all at once. You can access this action by first using the Accessibility tool and running a Full Check, as described in "Checking for Accessibility."

  When the Full Check runs, choose Tools from the main toolbar and select Actions. From the Actions List, choose Make Accessible. Click Start. The action will run and guide you through the three sections where it finds issues: Prepare, Set Language & Tags, and Run Accessibility Check.

❖ **Prepare:** In this section, you will add document titles, open options, OCR the text, detect form fields, and set tab order.

❖ **Set Language & Tags:** In this section, you will set the reading language, autotag the document, and set alternate text for images.

❖ **Run Accessibility Check:** This section runs the Full Check in the Accessibility Checker. You do this by selecting Start Checking in the Accessibility Checker Options dialog box. The action will display Completed when done. If you made changes in the various dialog boxes that appeared while running the action, you will see that your accessibility issues have been resolved other than those that require a manual check.

■ When you have resolved all of the manual issues, if any, you should save the document and can close the Make Accessible action and the Accessibility Checker.

Other Options in the Accessibility Tool

There are options in the Accessibility tool in addition to Full Check, some of which may be more than most users need, but we will briefly explain them below:

■ **Autotag Document:** This option automatically detects existing tags and reports results.

■ **Autotag Form Fields and Identify Form Fields:** These options will add form fields, detect existing ones, and provide some options for modifying the field properties.

■ **Reading Options:** This option allows you to set the reading order as tagged, left to right, top to bottom, etc.

■ **Accessibility Report:** This option allows you to open the accessibility report generated when running a Full Check.

■ **Identify Form Fields:** This option allows you to identify form fields.

■ **Set Alternate Text:** This option allows you to review and set alternate text for figures.

■ **Setup Assistant:** This option allows you to set options for how the PDF interacts with assistive technology.

■ **Reading Order:** This is a complex tool that allows you to "Touch Up" the Reading Order of a document by drawing rectangles around text and choosing how to read that text, for example, as text, as a figure, as a form field, as a header, etc.

Accessibility and Security

Adding security such as passwords that prohibit copying, printing, extracting, or editing text can affect a document's accessibility. Although document security is an important issue, you should be aware that setting such restrictions on a document could interfere with a screen reader's ability to read the document.

When you add a password to a document in File>Properties>Security to restrict editing of the document by choosing "None" in Changes Allowed, the option to "Enable text access for screen reader devices for the visually impaired" is by default selected, and we recommend that you do not uncheck the box.

Accessibility and Preferences

As a user who needs accessibility accommodations, you can set various accessibility options for how PDFs are viewed on your own computer in Preferences by selecting Edit>Preferences>Accessibility (Windows) or Acrobat Pro DC>Preferences>Accessibility (Mac). (Figure 18-6)

Figure 18-6

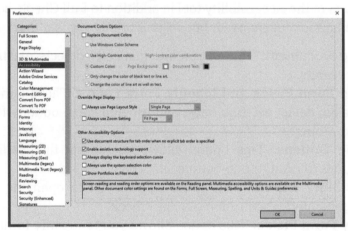

Chapter 19

Using the Acrobat DC Mobile Reader Apps

At the time this book was released, Adobe was offering three different free apps for both iPhones/iPads/iOS and Android devices: (1) Adobe Acrobat Reader, (2) Adobe Scan, and (3) Adobe Fill & Sign. These are excellent apps that can improve the ability to work remotely and are versatile—they do more than merely display PDFs. In general, the Android and Apple apps have similar features, although Adobe does change the features at times and it is, therefore, best to review the apps' features when you download them and when they are updated.

Adobe Reader App (Figure 19-1 Figure 19-2 Figure 19-3 Figure 19-4)

This app has an interface similar to the desktop program's. Because of its excellent design, it is easy to use on a mobile device. Among the app's features are:

- Viewing PDFs
- Annotating and commenting on PDFs
- Sharing and accessing shared PDFs
- Storing files in the Adobe Document Cloud or in other file-sharing apps such as Dropbox or Google Drive
- Printing PDFs directly from your device
- Creating PDFs from JPG format
- Accessing recently viewed files (if you have a licensed Adobe Acrobat account)
- Creating PDFs (at a cost if you do not have an appropriate license) from document formats such as Microsoft Word, reducing file size, and adding passwords to PDFs

Figure 19-1

Figure 19-2

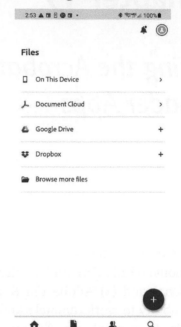

Figure 19-3

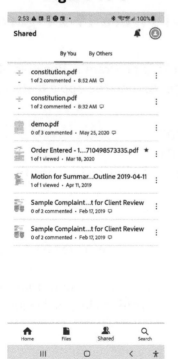

Figure 19-4

Adobe Scan App (Figure 19-5)

Considered one of the best scanning mobile apps, Adobe Scan is a must-have for lawyers and other professionals who need to capture documents while on the go. The app allows you to scan just about anything, including whiteboards, forms, documents, and business cards, and store the items in the Adobe Document Cloud or share or email them.

Figure 19-5

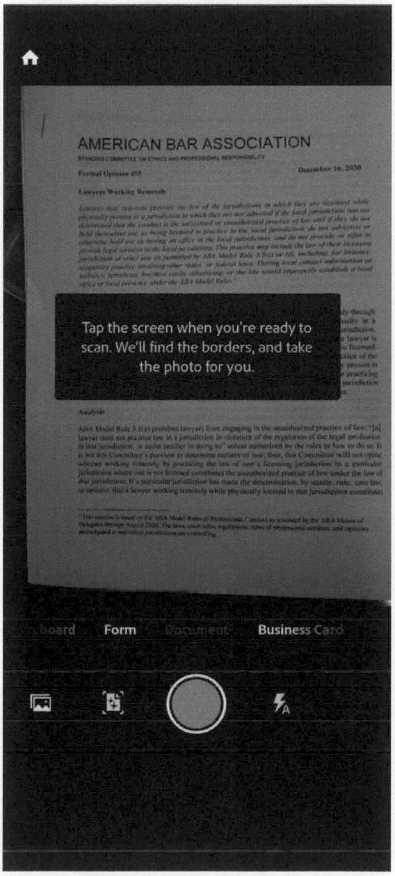

Adobe Fill & Sign App (Figure 19-6)

With this app, you can fill in and sign PDFs and then send them from any mobile device. The app also allows users to automatically fill form fields with its form filler tools.

Figure 19-6

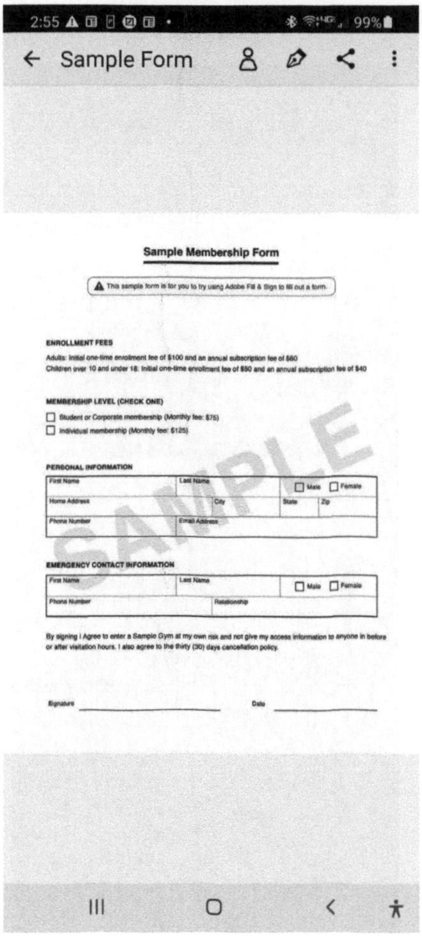

Appendix A

Liquid Mode, Resources, Add-Ons, and Scripts

Liquid Mode

In late 2020, Adobe introduced "Liquid Mode," which it describes as "a revolutionary mobile reading experience powered by Adobe Sensei, Adobe's artificial intelligence (AI) and machine learning technology. Liquid Mode enhances your PDF layout and adds features on-the-fly to help you easily read documents on your phone and tablet. Its AI technology evolves and improves the Liquid Mode experience as it learns over time."[1]

Simply described, Liquid Mode is intended to mimic how text and images appear on web pages. To use Liquid Mode, open a file in an Acrobat mobile app and tap on the "lmodeicon." Liquid mode will work on iOS version 12 and later, and Android devices with version 5.0 and later, with 1 GB of RAM. While Liquid Mode does not work on all documents and images, Adobe plans to increase its functionality.

Resources, Add-Ons, and Scripts

Warning: Be careful when downloading any files to your computer. Always run antivirus software, and only download files from reputable websites. Downloading files from unsafe websites can be very dangerous and could result in damage to your computer and your network.

Web Resources for Acrobat
The following websites offer excellent resources for Acrobat users.

---

1. https://www.adobe.com/devnet-docs/acrobat/android/en/lmode.html

- **Acrobat Tutorials:** https://helpx.adobe.com/acrobat/tutorials.html.
- **Acrobat DC Help:** https://helpx.adobe.com/pdf/acrobat_reference.pdf; download a complete Help reference.
- **Acrolaw:** Acrobat for Legal Professionals Blog: http://blogs.adobe.com /acrolaw/. This site is Rick Borstein's excellent resource for legal professionals. Although the blog has not been updated in a few years, it still contains a wealth of information of interest to legal professionals and Acrobat users generally.
- **Acrobatusers.com:** https://acrobatusers.com/. Also known as the Acrobat Library, this site offers a wealth of information about Acrobat and numerous ways to get more out of the program.
- **IT Tools:** https://acrobat.adobe.com/us/en/resources/it-tools.html. Primarily for IT administrators, this toolkit enables firms to customize and deploy Acrobat in a variety of ways.

Accessibility Resources

- **Adobe Acrobat Accessibility Training Resources:** www.adobe.com /accessibility/products/acrobat/training.html. This guide details the accessibility features of Acrobat.
- **Adobe Accessibility Resource Center:** www.adobe.com/accessibility. html. This site provides information and resources for end users with disabilities.
- **Adobe Acrobat Accessibility Resources:** www.adobe.com/accessibility/ resources.html.

Add-Ons and Scripts

Often called scripts, add-ons, or automation tools, these small files, which are available from third-party websites, help to automate certain tasks in Acrobat, while others create shortcuts that should have been included in the program. After you download the files from the websites, you copy them into the program's JavaScript folder. Acrobat creates this program in different locations, but in many computers it is found at C:\Program Files (x86)\Adobe\Acrobat 2015\Acrobat \Javascripts.

Some of the most useful Acrobat tools are available only as third-party add-ons. The following websites offer some helpful add-ons:

- **http://www.pdfscripting.com** (free add-ons at http://www.pdfscripting .com/public/Free_Acrobat_Automation_Tools.cfm). Among the free tools available at this site are:
  - ❖ Close All Docs Menu Item: This tool adds a menu item to the Acrobat File menu that closes all open documents.
  - ❖ Find Required Fields (in forms).

❖ Menu/Toolbar Item Report: This tool lists the Language Independent Menu Item and toolbar button names in a menu format and generates a PDF report on request.

❖ New Document Tool: This toolbar button creates a new, blank, one-page PDF of a specified size.

❖ Resize Pages Tool.

❖ Flatten Page Content Tool: This toolbar button flattens interactive elements, such as form fields, into the page content.

■ **https://acrobatusers.com/tool-sets-exchange:** This page links to many helpful scripts and other items.

■ **http://blogs.adobe.com/acrolaw/2009/05/add-dynamic-exhibit-stamps -in-acrobat-using-a-free-stamp-set/:** This provides a script for creating an Exhibit Stamp.

■ **https://www.utd.uscourts.gov/pdf-exhibit-stamps:** This web page from the U.S. District Court for the District of Utah links to a PDF file that you copy to your Acrobat installation folder, which creates excellent, easy-to-use exhibit stamps for deposition, trial and other transcript exhibits.

■ **https://acrobatusers.com/tutorials/dynamic_stamp_secrets/#:** This web page explains how to create dynamic PDF stamps, and is credited as the basis for the Exhibit stamp created above.

Appendix B

Creating a Document or File Naming Protocol

A File Naming Protocol is a firmwide guideline requiring all staff to name saved files in a consistent manner, thus making it easier for users to identify, locate, and sort documents. We have used the following suggested File Naming Protocol for more than a decade; it was also featured in the ABA book *Paperless in One Hour for Lawyers*.

- Before implementing a File Naming Protocol, it is important to have a directory structure and substructure in order for files to be located in the appropriate directories rather than willy-nilly or in one large directory. Thus, many firms have separate directories for client files and firm business files, with each client file divided into subdirectories.
  - ❖ **Suggested Directory/Folder Names**
    - ◆ COR: Correspondence, Letters, Faxes, and Email
    - ◆ EXP: Expenses and Bills
    - ◆ MED: Medical Records
    - ◆ MEM: Memoranda, Notes, Research, Interview Records, Fee Agreements, HIPAA Authorizations, etc.
    - ◆ PLD: Pleadings and Discovery (some firms use a DISC directory for discovery)
    - ◆ TRL: Trial and Pre-Trial-Related Documents
  - ❖ **Placing Dates on File Names**
    - ◆ The most effective way to determine when a document was created is to place the date on which it was created in the name/description of the document. Doing so makes searching for documents easier and eliminates the need to examine the file's properties.

      When naming files, dates should always be entered YEAR-MONTH-DATE (YYYY-MM-DD) (e.g., 2006-12-25) so that similarly named documents will sort alphabetically in date order. If dates are listed in any other manner, they will not sort chronologically properly.

❖ **Suggested File Naming Protocol**
  ◆ A File Naming Protocol should reflect how your office operates and, when possible, use universally understood naming conventions. These examples are intended as a starting point and should be adapted to each firm's specific needs.
    ı **Correspondence**
      ı Letters from the Firm
        ◆ Ltr to Name Date Subject
        ◆ E.g., Ltr to Atty Scott 2005-01-25 With Doc Requests
      ı Letters to the Firm
        ◆ Ltr from Name Date Subject
        ◆ E.g., Ltr from Atty Scott 2005-01-25 With Doc Requests
    ı **Faxes**
      ı Fax to Name Date Subject
      ı Fax from Name Date Subject
    ı **Email**
      ı Email to Name Date Subject
      ı Email from Name Date Subject
    ı **Memoranda**
      ı Memo to Name Date Subject
      ı E.g., Memo to JDF 2001-05-25 re Expert Witness
    ı **Pleadings and Discovery:** Documents in this directory should be named based on the type of document/filing—or the response to the document/filing—and the date created/filed, such as:
      ı Complaint—Answer of Party Filed Date
      ı Complaint (Amended)—Filed Date
      ı Complaint Filed Date
      ı Complaint—Answer of Party to New Matter of Party Filed Date
      ı Interrogatories (Set XX) of Party 2005-01-10
      ı Interrogatories (Set XX) of Party—Answer of Party Date
      ı Motion to/for Subject 2005-01-10
      ı Motion to/for Subject—Answer of Party Filed Date
      ı Order Subject of Order Date
      ı Request for Admissions (Set XX) of Party Date
      ı Request for Production (Set XX) of Party Date
      ı *Other pleadings should be similarly named. Generally, do not name documents starting with "Plaintiff's," for example, because of the large number of documents that will be named that way.*
    ı **Trial Documents:** This directory should contain only pretrial documents and documents intended to be used at trial, including transcripts, depositions, and CaseMap summaries, such as:
      ı Deposition Witness Name Date
      ı Expert Witness Report of Witness Name for Party Date

- Proposed Jury Interrogatories of Party Date
- Proposed Points for Charge of Party Date
- Transcript Description/Subject Date
- **Medical Records:** Name documents based on the provider's name, with dates of treatment or other identifying information, such as:
  - Lankenau Hospital Records, Date(s) In-Patient Hospitalization
  - Lankenau Hospital Records, Various Emergency Room Visits
  - William Smith, M.D., Treatment Records 2005–2006
  - John James, D.O., Office Notes 2005-01-23 to 2006-02-02

Appendix C

Keyboard Shortcuts (for Windows and Mac)

The following list of keyboard shortcuts can make using Acrobat easier (reprinted from https://helpx.adobe.com/acrobat/using/keyboard-shortcuts.html).

Keyboard Shortcuts for Selecting Tools

To enable single-key shortcuts, open the Preferences dialog box (Edit>Preferences), and under General, select the Use Single-Key Accelerators to Access Tools option.

Tool	Windows Action	Mac OS Action
Hand tool	H	H
Temporarily select Hand tool	Spacebar	Spacebar
Select tool	V	V
Marquee Zoom tool	Z	Z
Cycle through zoom tools: Marquee Zoom, Dynamic Zoom, Loupe	Shift+Z	Shift+Z
Temporarily select Dynamic Zoom tool (when Marquee Zoom tool is selected)	Shift	Shift
Temporarily zoom out (when Marquee Zoom tool is selected)	Ctrl	Option
Temporarily select Zoom In tool	Ctrl+spacebar	Spacebar+Command
Select Object tool	R	R
Edit Object tool	O	O

Tool	Windows Action	Mac OS Action
Enter/Exit Forms editing	A	A
Crop tool	C	C
Link tool	L	L
Text Field tool	F	F
Cycle through tools in forms authoring mode: Text Field, Check Box, Radio Button, List Box, Dropdown Box, Button, Digital Signature, Barcode	Shift+F	Shift+F
3D tool	M	M
Cycle through Multimedia tools: 3D object, SWF, Sound, Video	Shift+M	Shift+M
Edit Document Text tool	T	T
Redaction	Shift+Y	Shift+Y
Cycle through Touch Up tools: Touch Up Text, Touch Up Reading Order, Touch Up Object	Shift+T	Shift+T
JavaScript Debugger	Ctrl+J	Command+J
Insert Blank Pages tool	Ctrl+Shift+T	Command+Shift+T
Insert Files	Ctrl+Shift+I	Command+Shift+I
Delete pages	Ctrl+Shift+D	Command+Shift+D
Touch Up Reading Order tool (or if already selected, return focus to dialog box)	Ctrl+Shift+U	Command+Shift+U

Keyboard Shortcuts for Working with Comments

To enable single-key shortcuts, open the Preferences dialog box (Edit>Preferences), and under General, select the Use Single-Key Accelerators to Access Tools option.

Result	Windows Action	Mac OS Action
Sticky Note tool	S	S
Text Edits tool	E	E
Stamp tool	K	K
Current highlighting tool	U	U
Cycle through highlighting tools: Highlighter, Underline Text, Cross Out Text	Shift+U	Shift+U
Current drawing markup tool	D	D
Cycle through drawing markup tools: Cloud, Arrow, Line, Rectangle, Oval, Polygon Line, Polygon, Pencil tool, Eraser tool	Shift+D	Shift+D
Cloud tool	Q	Q
Text Box tool	X	X
Current Stamp or Attach tool	J	J
Cycle through Stamp, Attach File, Record Audio Comment	Shift+J	Shift+J
Move focus to next comment or form field	Tab	Tab
Move focus to previous comment or form field	Shift+Tab	Shift+Tab
Add a checkmark in the Comments List for the selected comment	Shift+K	Shift+K
Open pop-up note (or text field in Comments List) for comment that has focus	Enter	Return
Reply to the comment, in the Comments List, that has focus	R	R
Closes pop-up (or text field in Comments List) for comment that has focus	Esc	Esc

Keyboard Shortcuts for Navigating a PDF

Result	Windows Action	Mac OS Action
Previous screen	Page Up or Shift+Enter	Page Up or Shift+Return
Next screen	Page Down or Enter	Page Down or Return
First page	Home or Ctrl+Shift+Page Up or Ctrl+Shift+Up Arrow	Home or Command+Shift+Up Arrow
Last page	End or Ctrl+Shift+Page Down or Ctrl+Shift+Down Arrow	End or Command+Shift+Down Arrow
Previous page	Left Arrow or Ctrl+Page Up	Left Arrow or Command+Page Up
Next page	Right Arrow or Ctrl+Page Down	Right Arrow or Command+Page Down
Go to page	Ctrl+Shift+N	Ctrl+Shift+N
Previous open document		Command+F6
Next open document		Command+Shift+F6
Scroll up	Up Arrow	Up Arrow
Scroll down	Down Arrow	Down Arrow
Scroll (when Hand tool is selected)	Spacebar	Spacebar
Zoom in	Ctrl+equal sign	Command+equal sign
Zoom out	Ctrl+hyphen	Command+hyphen

Keyboard Shortcuts for Working with Forms

To enable single-key shortcuts, open the Preferences dialog box (Edit>Preferences), and under General, select the Use Single-Key Accelerators to Access Tools option.

Result	Windows Action	Mac OS Action
Toggle between editing and previewing your form	P	P
Toggle Guides On / Off	G	G
Align selected fields left	L	L

Result	Windows Action	Mac OS Action
Align selected fields right	R	R
Align selected fields top	T	T
Align selected fields bottom	B	B
Align selected fields horizontal	H	H
Align selected fields vertical	V	V
Center fields horizontally	Shift+H	Shift+H
Center fields vertically	Shift+V	Shift+V
Highlight fields	Shift+L	Shift+L
Show Tab Order	Shift+N	Shift+N
Document JavaScripts	Shift+D	Shift+D

Keyboard Shortcuts for Working with PDF Portfolios

These keys are available in the files list of the Details pane.

Result	Windows Action	Mac OS Action
Move focus to the next or previous row when in the body of the file list on the left	Up Arrow or Down Arrow	Up Arrow or Down Arrow
If pressed in the body of the file list, navigate one level up from within a folder	Backspace	Delete
Press the Go Back button in a folder if focus is on the button	Enter or Spacebar	Enter or Spacebar
If pressed when focus is on a row in the file list representing a subfolder, navigate to a subfolder, or open an attachment in Preview mode	Enter	Enter
If in the body of the file list, move to the first or last row	Home or End	Home or End
If in the body of the file list, move to the next or last set of rows to fit the screen	Page Down or Page Up	Page Down or Page Up

Result	Windows Action	Mac OS Action
Select or deselect all files	Ctrl+A or Ctrl+Shift+A	Command+A or Command+Shift+A
If in the body of the file list, extend the selection by adding the next row above or below the selected row	Shift+Up Arrow or Shift+Down Arrow	Shift+Up Arrow or Shift+Down Arrow
Change whether the row with focus is in the selection	Ctrl+Spacebar	Command+Spacebar
Move focus up or down one row without changing the selection	Ctrl+Up Arrow or Ctrl+Down Arrow	Command+Up Arrow or Command+Down Arrow

Keyboard Shortcuts for Navigating Task Panes

Result	Windows Action	Mac OS Action
Move focus to the next item among Document pane, Task panes, Message bar, and Navigation bar	F6	F6
Move focus to the previous item among Document pane, Task panes, Message bar, and Navigation bar	Shift+F6	Shift+F6
Move focus to the next panel in the Task pane	Ctrl+Tab	Option +Tab
Move focus to the previous panel in the Task pane	Ctrl+Shift+Tab	Command+Shift+Tab
Navigate to the next panel and panel control within an open Task pane	Tab	Tab
Navigate to the previous panel and panel control within an open Task pane	Shift+Tab	Shift+Tab
Navigate to the next command button within a panel	Down Arrow	Down Arrow
Navigate to the previous command button within a panel	Up Arrow	Up Arrow

Result	Windows Action	Mac OS Action
Expand or collapse panel in focus (press F6 to move focus to Tools pane, then tab to desired panel)	Spacebar or Enter	Spacebar or Enter
Open or close the Task pane	Shift+F4	Shift+F4
Close the pane that lists the tasks of an action	Ctrl+Shift+F4	Ctrl+Shift+F4
Open the menu and move the focus to the first menu option when focus is on a command with a submenu or submenu element with a flyout	Spacebar or Enter	Spacebar or Enter
Move the focus back to the parent command button with a submenu or submenu element with a flyout	Esc	Esc
Run the command in focus	Spacebar or Enter	Spacebar or Enter
Navigate to the next item in the active panel in the Create New Action, Edit Action, Create Custom Tool, or the Edit Custom Tool dialog boxes	Tab	Tab
Navigate to the previous item in the active panel in the Create New Action, Edit Action, Create Custom Tool, or the Edit Custom Tool dialog boxes	Shift+Tab	Shift+Tab

Keyboard Shortcuts for General Navigating

Result	Windows Action	Mac OS Action
Move focus to menus	F10	Control+F2
Move focus to toolbar in browser and application (In application, sets focus to the first button in the top bar—Home)	Shift+F8	Shift+F8
Navigate through the other controls in the top bar—Home, Tools, Document	Right/Left Arrow or Tab/Shift Tab	Right/Left Arrow or Tab/Shift Tab

Result	Windows Action	Mac OS Action
Select a highlighted control in the top bar	Enter or Spacebar	Return or Spacebar
Move to next open document tab (when multiple documents are open in same window)	Ctrl+Tab	Control+Tab
Move to previous open document tab (when multiple documents are open in same window)	Ctrl+Shift+Tab	Control+Shift+Tab
Move to next open document window (when focus is on document pane)	Ctrl+F6	Command+F6
Move to previous open document window (when focus is on document pane)	Ctrl+Shift+F6	Command+Shift+F6
Close current document	Ctrl+F4	Command+F4
Close all open documents	Not available	Command+Option+W
Move focus to next comment, link, or form field in the document pane	Tab	Tab
Move focus to document pane	F5	F5
Move focus to previous comment, link, or form field in the document pane	Shift+Tab	Shift+Tab
Activate selected tool, item (such as a movie clip or bookmark), or command	Spacebar or Enter	Spacebar or Return
Open context menu	Shift+F10	Control+click
Close context menu	F10	Esc
Return to Hand tool or Select tool	Esc	Esc
Move focus to next tab in a tabbed dialog box	Ctrl+Tab	Not available
Move to previous search result and highlight it in the document	Shift+F3 or Ctrl+Shift+G	Shift+Command+G
Find in document	Ctrl+F	Command+F

Result	Windows Action	Mac OS Action
Move to next search result and highlight it in the document	F3 or Ctrl+G	Command+G
Search previous document (with Search results displaying multiple files)	Alt+Shift+Left Arrow	Command+Shift+Left Arrow
Search next document (with Search results displaying multiple files)	Alt+Shift+Right Arrow	Command+Shift+Right Arrow
Select text (with Select tool selected)	Shift+arrow keys	Shift+arrow keys
Select next word or deselect previous word (with Select tool selected)	Ctrl+Shift+Right Arrow or Left Arrow	Not available
Increase or decrease the value of a slider	Right Arrow or Left Arrow	Control+Option+Right Arrow or Left Arrow

Keyboard Shortcuts for Working with Navigation Panels

Result	Windows Action	Mac OS Action
Open and move focus to navigation pane	Ctrl+Shift+F5	Command+Shift+F5
Move focus among the document, message bar, and navigation panels	F6	F6
Move focus to previous pane or panel	Shift+F6	Shift+F6
Move among the elements of the active navigation panel	Tab	Tab
Move to previous or next navigation panel and make it active (when focus is on the panel button)	Up Arrow or Down Arrow	Up Arrow or Down Arrow
Move to next navigation panel and make it active (when focus is anywhere in the navigation pane)	Ctrl+Tab	Not available
Select or deselect a file in file list (open/close Context pane with file selection)	Space	Space

Result	Windows Action	Mac OS Action
Select or deselect a To Do card (open/close Context pane with To Do card selection)	Space	Space
Open selected file in file list	Enter	Enter
Open selected To Do card	Enter	Enter
Move focus to the next/previous file row in file list for selecting single file row	Arrow keys	Arrow keys
Extend the selection by adding the next row above or below the selected row	Shift+Arrow keys	Shift+Arrow keys
Move focus up or down one row without changing the selection	Ctrl+Arrow keys	Command+Arrow keys
Expand the current bookmark (focus on Bookmarks panel)	Right Arrow or Shift+plus sign	Right Arrow or Shift+plus sign
Collapse the current bookmark (focus on Bookmarks panel)	Left Arrow or minus sign	Left Arrow or minus sign
Expand all bookmarks	Shift+*	Shift+*
Collapse selected bookmark	Forward Slash (/)	Forward Slash (/)
Move focus to next item in a navigation panel	Down Arrow	Down Arrow
Move focus to previous item in a navigation panel	Up Arrow	Up Arrow

Keyboard Shortcuts for Navigating the Help Window

Result	Windows Action	Mac OS Action
Open Help window	F1	F1 or Command+?
Close Help window	Ctrl+W or Alt+F4	Command+W
Move back to previously opened topic	Alt+Left Arrow	Command+Left Arrow
Move forward to next topic	Alt+Right Arrow	Command+Right Arrow

Result	Windows Action	Mac OS Action
Move to next pane	Ctrl+Tab	See Help for your default browser
Move to previous pane	Ctrl+Shift+Tab	See Help for your default browser
Move focus to the next link within a pane	Tab	Not available
Move focus to the previous link within a pane	Shift+Tab	Not available
Activate highlighted link	Enter	Not available
Print Help topic	Ctrl+P	Command+P

Keyboard Shortcuts for Accessibility

Result	Windows Action	Mac OS Action
Change reading settings for the current document	Ctrl+Shift+5	Command+Shift+5
Reflow a tagged PDF, and return to unreflowed view	Ctrl+4	Command+4
Activate and deactivate Read Out Loud	Ctrl+Shift+Y	Command+Shift+Y
Read only the current page out loud	Ctrl+Shift+V	Command+Shift+V
Read out loud from the current page to the end of the document	Ctrl+Shift+B	Command+Shift+B
Pause reading out loud	Ctrl+Shift+C	Command+Shift+C
Stop reading out loud	Ctrl+Shift+E	Command+Shift+E

Compare Acrobat Professional Features with Acrobat Standard Features

(Reprinted in part from https://acrobat.adobe.com/us/en/acrobat/pricing.html)

Feature	In Acrobat Professional	In Acrobat Standard
Create PDFs and export to Word, Excel, or PowerPoint	✔	✔
Edit text and images right in your PDF	✔	✔
Easily create, fill, sign, and send forms	✔	✔
Share PDFs for viewing, reviewing, signing, and track activity	✔	✔
Open PDFs are protected by Microsoft Information Protection solutions, including Azure Information Protection and Microsoft 365.	✔	✔
Compare two versions of a PDF to review all differences	✔	✘
Turn scanned documents into editable, searchable PDFs	✔	✘
Take advantage of advanced mobile editing features	✔	✘
Validate and fix PDFs for ISO and accessibility standards	✔	✘
View, interact, and comment on PDF content from your computer, mobile device, or web browser	✔	✔
Store, manage, and share files online with instant access to files across devices	✔	✔
Track activity across desktop, mobile, and web for documents sent for viewing, reviewing, and signatures	✔	✔
Access, edit, and store files in your Box, Dropbox, Google Drive, and Microsoft OneDrive accounts	✔	✔

Feature	In Acrobat Professional	In Acrobat Standard
Be more productive on the latest Windows touch-enabled devices including Surface Pro	✔	✔
Take advantage of MacBook Pro Touch bar support	✔	✗
Compare two versions of a PDF to review all differences	✔	✗
Measure the distance, area, and perimeter of objects in PDFs	✔	✗
Convert documents and images to PDF files	✔	✔
Create PDFs from any application that prints	✔	✔
Create, protect, and send PDFs in Microsoft 365 apps for Windows	✔	✔
Combine multiple documents and file types into one PDF	✔	✔
Convert web pages to interactive PDFs, complete with links	✔	✔
Prevent others from copying or editing information in PDFs	✔	✔
Create a password-protected PDF	✔	✔
Recognize text in scans, and then preview and correct suspect errors with a side-by-side view	✔	✔
Automatically fix photos of documents to remove backgrounds and adjust perspective	✔	✔
Turn Adobe Photoshop (PSD), Illustrator (AI), or InDesign (INDD) files into PDFs from your desktop or mobile device	✔	✔
Create and export PDFs on your mobile device	✔	✔

Feature	In Acrobat Professional	In Acrobat Standard
Turn scanned paper documents into instantly searchable PDFs with fonts that match the original	✔	✘
Use one-click creation of rich PDFs and other Acrobat features within Microsoft 365 2016 for Mac	✔	✘
Prepare PDFs consistently with guided actions	✔	✘
Convert and validate PDFs for compliance with standards such as PDF/A and PDF/X	✔	✘
Create technical PDFs in Microsoft Project, Visio, or Autodesk AutoCAD	✔	✘
Create and validate PDFs to meet accessibility standards for people with disabilities	✔	✘
Edit PDF text and images with full-page paragraph reflow	✔	✔
Turn PDFs into editable Microsoft Word, Excel, or PowerPoint files	✔	✔
Convert PDFs to JPG, TIFF, or PNG image formats	✔	✔
Insert, delete, and organize pages in a PDF	✔	✔
Add bookmarks, headers, numbering, and watermarks	✔	✔
Permanently remove hidden sensitive information in PDFs	✔	✔
Redact to permanently remove sensitive visible information in PDFs	✔	✘
Add audio, video, and interactive objects to PDFs	✔	✘
Add Bates numbering to legal documents	✔	✘

Feature	In Acrobat Professional	In Acrobat Standard
Add or edit text and images on your tablet and mobile phone	✔	✗
Reorder, delete, or rotate PDF pages on your iOS or Android tablet	✔	✗
Share links of PDFs for viewing, reviewing, and signing	✔	✔
Get real-time status and activity notifications for documents sent for viewing, comments, or signature	✔	✔
Collect group feedback in one PDF file online with no reviewer login required	✔	✔
Add comments to PDFs with a full suite of commenting tools including text editing, highlighter, and sticky notes	✔	✔
Collect legally binding e-signatures from others and track responses in real time	✔	✔
Work with certificate signatures	✔	✔
Fill, sign, and send forms faster using data from your autofill collection on your computer or mobile device	✔	✔
Turn paper or Word docs into fillable PDF forms	✔	✔
Choose comments and export to Word	✔	✔
Mark PDFs with stamps, such as "approved" or "draft"	✔	✔
Enhance PDF forms by adding interactivity with JavaScript	✔	✔
Automatically optimize PDFs to reduce file size and customize settings	✔	✔
Preflight and prepare files for high-end print production	✔	✔

Appendix D

Acrobat Compatibility with Microsoft Office Products

Older versions of Acrobat are not fully compatible with newer versions of Microsoft Office, especially Microsoft Outlook. Generally speaking, the latest version of Outlook requires users to have the latest version of Acrobat. The following table lists which versions of Acrobat are fully compatible with which versions of Office.

Third-party version / Acrobat version (ship date)	Acrobat DC (April 2015)	Acrobat 2017 (June 2017)	Acrobat 2020 (June 2020)
MS Office (Word/Excel/PPT)			
Office 2010 or earlier	✗	✗	✗
Office 2013 (Office 15) 32 bit and 64 bit	✔	✔	✔
Office 2016 (Office 16) 32 bit and 64 bit	✔ (October 2015)	✔	✔
Office 2019 (Office 16) 32 bit and 64 bit	✔ (December 2018)	✔	✔
MS Outlook			
Outlook 2010 or earlier	✗	✗	✗
Office 2013 (Office 15) 32 bit and 64 bit	✔	✔	✔
Office 2016 (Office 16) 32 bit and 64 bit	✔ (October 2015)	✔	✔
Office 2019 (Office 16) 32 bit and 64 bit	✔ (December 2018)	✔	✔

Third-party version / Acrobat version (ship date)	Acrobat DC (April 2015)	Acrobat 2017 (June 2017)	Acrobat 2020 (June 2020)
Mac Office			
Office 2011 or earlier	✘	✘	✘
Office 2016	✔ (PDFMaker for Word)[†]	✔ (PDFMaker for Word)[†]	✔ (PDFMaker for Word)[†]
Office 2019	✔ (PDFMaker for PowerPoint, Word, and Excel)[‡]	✔ (PDFMaker for PowerPoint and Word)[‡]	✔ (PDFMaker for PowerPoint and Word)[‡]
Office 365	✔ (PDFMaker for PowerPoint, Word, and Excel)[‡]	✔ (PDFMaker for PowerPoint and Word)[‡]	✔ (PDFMaker for PowerPoint and Word)[‡]

[†]PDFMaker for Word 2016 (32-bit, version 15.22 or later)

[‡]PDFMaker for PowerPoint, Word, and Excel Office 2019 and Office 365 (64-bit, version 16.35 or later).

Versions marked with parentheses and a version number require the installation of the correct Acrobat update to work with PDFMaker.

Reprinted from https://helpx.adobe.com/acrobat/kb/compatible-web-browsers-pdfmaker-applications.html

Index